ENLIGHTENMENT, RIGHTS AND REVOLUTION SERIES

WOMEN'S RIGHTS AND THE RIGHTS OF MAN

£ 2·99

ENLIGHTENMENT, RIGHTS AND REVOLUTION SERIES

WOMEN'S RIGHTS AND THE RIGHTS OF MAN

A J Arnaud and E Kingdom

Series Editors: Zenon Bankowski, Neil MacCormick

ABERDEEN UNIVERSITY PRESS
Member of Maxwell Macmillan Pergamon Publishing Corporation

First Published 1990
Aberdeen University Press
© Aberdeen University Press for the collected works 1990

British Library Cataloguing in Publication Data

Women's rights and the rights of man—(Enlightenment, rights and revolution series).
1. Women. Rights
I. Arnaud, A-J   II. Kingdom, E   III. Series
323.34

ISBN 0 08 040923 7

Typeset and printed by AUP Glasgow/Aberdeen—a member of BPCC Ltd.

General Editors' Foreword

The Fourteenth World Congress of the International Association for Philosophy of Law and Social Philosophy (President: Professor Alice Erh-Soon Tay, University of Sydney, Australia) was held in August 1989. It was organised in Edinburgh, Scotland, in August 1989 on behalf of the UK Association for Legal and Social Philosophy (President: Professor Tom Campbell, University of Glasgow). There were over five hundred participants from some forty countries. It focused prophetically on the theme 'Enlightenment, Rights and Revolution'.

The sessions of the Congress produced a considerable number of papers discussing various aspects of the history of ideas and the theory of rights and of revolutions. Following on the volume of papers produced for the Congress's plenary sessions (*Enlightenment, Rights and Revolution*), it was decided to produce, under our general editorship, a series of volumes of selected papers from the Congress dealing in thematic form with some of the most pressing issues in legal and social philosophy and the history of ideas to emerge from the Congress. The present volume is the second of this series.

The Editorial Advisory Committee for these volumes comprises all those who presided over Plenary or Group Sessions of the Congress. Its Members are:

Aulis Aarnio, Helsinki; Ake Frändberg, Uppsala; Letizia Gianformaggio, Siena; Elena Gourko, Minsk; Eugene Kamenka, Canberra; Mikail Karlsson, Reykjavik; Roberta Kevelson, Reading, Pa; Jacques Lenoble, Louvain-la-Neuve; Adam Łopatka, Warsaw; Nicolás López Calera, Granada; Alan Milne, Durham; Karl Mollnau, Berlin (E); Enrico Pattaro, Bologna; Hubert Rottleuthner, Berlin (W); Roger Shiner, Edmonton; Ton-Kak Suh, Seoul; Raymond Wacks, Hong Kong; Ota Weinberger, Graz; Elizabeth Wolgast, Hayward, Cal.; Mitsukuni Yasaki, Seijo; Marek Zirk-Sadowski, Łódz.

All of them gave us, immediately after the Congress, their impressions of papers presented in the various sessions, some indeed giving extremely thorough appraisals and comments. This was of great value, both to the general editors of the series and to the individual editors of particular volumes.

We record our warm gratitude to them all, and to other colleagues who helped in the editorial process. Anne Bankowska was an extremely thorough assistant editor. Sheila Macmillan as Congress Secretary, and Elizabeth Mackenzie, who succeeded her as our secretary in the Centre for Criminology and the Social and Philosophical Study of Law, both gave very great help. The series editors (and their helpers) acted with an unfailing promptness and efficiency and kept to a demanding schedule which enabled us to achieve the ambition of having all the texts ready for publication within a year of the Congress itself.

Finally we record particularly warm thanks to Colin Maclean, who has recently retired from his post as Managing Director of Aberdeen University Press. From the earliest stages of Congress planning and preparation he gave us wise advice and kind support. Without his enthusiasm and shrewdness, it would have been impossible to get so much of the proceedings of the Congress so speedily into print.

Zenon Bankowski
Neil MacCormick
General Editors
Edinburgh
July 1990

The Volumes in the present series are:

1 *Enlightenment, Rights and Revolution*, edited by Neil MacCormick and Zenon Bankowski
2 *Women's Rights and the Rights of Man*, edited by André-Jean Arnaud and Elizabeth Kingdom
3 *Revolutions in Law and Legal Thought*, edited by Zenon Bankowski
4 *Issues of Self-Determination*, edited by William Twining
5 *Shaping Revolution*, edited by Elspeth Attwooll
6 *Revolution and Enlightenment in Europe*, edited by Timothy O'Hagan
7 *Law and Enlightenment in Britain*, edited by Tom Campbell

A further two volumes of Congress Proceedings, on themes concerning human rights, are being published as *Beihefte* of the *Archiv für Rechts- und Sozialphilosophie* for 1990 under the editorship of Werner Maihofer and Gerhard Sprenger.

Contents

List of Contributors

ANDRE-JEAN ARNAUD, Professeur, Directeur de Recherche au CNRS, Directeur Scientific, Institut International de Sociologie Juridique d'Oñati (Spain)

NICOLE ARNAUD-DUC, Centre National de la Recherche Scientifique (France)

GINERVA CONTI ODORISIO, Professoressa, Libera Università Internationazionale degli Studi Sociali, Rome (Italy)

DAVID E COOPER, Professor, Department of Philosophy, Northern Michigan University (USA)

LETIZIA GIANFORMAGGIO, Professoressa Dipartimento de Studi politici e Storia giuridico-politica, Siena (Italy)

LESLIE GOLDSTEIN, Professor, Department of Political Science, University of Delaware (USA)

JUDITH GRBICH, Department of Legal Studies, La Trobe University, Bundoora (Australia)

RITA MAE KELLY, Professor of Public Affairs, Arizona State University (USA)

ELIZABETH KINGDOM, Department of Sociology, Social Policy, and Social Work Studies, University of Liverpool (UK)

J RALPH LINDGREN, Professor, Department of Philosophy, Lehigh University, Bethlehem (USA)

RICHARD B PARKER, Professor of Law, Hiroshima Shudo University (Japan)

JUHANI PIETARINEN, Professor, Department of Philosophy, University of Turku (Finland)

PATRICIA WARD SCALTSAS, University of Edinburgh and Open University (UK)

FANNY TABAK, Professor of Political Science and Director, Women's Studies Centre, Ponteficia Universidade Catolica de Rio de Janeiro (Brazil)

SYBIL WOLFRAM, Sub-Faculty of Philosophy, University of Oxford (UK)

Editors' Preface

Women's Rights and the Rights of Man: the Enlightenment and its Consequences

The inclusion in the Fourteenth World Congress of a Working Group entitled 'Women's Rights and the Rights of Man' is neither controversial nor insignificant. It is not controversial, because few academic institutions or practices in the humanities and in the social sciences have remained quite immune to critiques deriving from women's movements. Indeed, whether out of satisfaction or cynicism, it could be said that these days conference organisers would have to be very sure of their intellectual and political ground to defend a conference which formally or informally allowed neither time nor place for the discussion of women's issues.

On the other hand, as Virginia Held points out in her contribution to the volume of the plenary papers of the Congress (Held, 1989, p 214), it is only since the 1970s that a feminist contribution to such a conference would be invited. Given the usual speed of academic change, then, it may well be that the appearance of such a contribution is still controversial for some academics. And, of course, there has been considerable debate among feminist academics about whether women's issues are best dealt with in the mainstream of academic structures and practices, or in specially demarcated spheres within those structures and practices, or outside them altogether. Judith Grbich's contribution to this volume rehearses some of these issues in the context of women's studies scholarship within the law.

In the short term, there seems no reconciling two feminist politics. The first is pursued by feminist academics who want their analyses incorporated into mainstream academic spheres, because they suspect that women's issues are marginalised by consigning them to separate arenas of discussion. The second is pursued by feminist academics who see the demarcation of special academic spheres as a key intellectual and organisational condition of the development of a sophisticated and practicable feminist politics.

So long as there is no immediate prospect of reconciling those two feminist politics, the title of this Working Group is apt. This is because it recognises the tension between rights as they feature under the convenient aegis of the phrase 'rights of man' and rights as they feature in the phrase 'women's rights'. The title recognises that women's rights are not automatically protected either by the proclamation or by the implementation of the rights of man.

Recognition of the discrepancy between women's rights and the rights of man informs every contribution to the present collection and constitutes its philosophical theme. Both to elucidate and to problematise this theme in this Introduction, we offer, first, some philosophical and, then, some economic, social, and political analyses. The impetus for these analyses is the identification of a major paradox of the Enlightenment.

The paradox of the Enlightenment

For jurisprudence and legal philosophy, the Enlightenment constitutes a major paradox. On the one hand, the Enlightenment made possible the theoretical promotion of subjective rights. By 'subjective rights', we mean the equal/identical and absolute rights of every subject. These rights could be described as philosophical rights. On the other hand, the economic, social and political framework which made the Enlightenment possible was one which could not support the full and objective development of those rights.

The paradox first appears as the transition from the concept of natural reason to the concept of what is naturally grounded in reason. Letizia Gianformaggio's analysis of key pages from Diderot's *The Refutation of Helvetius* reveals him to be caught in that transition. She exposes his ambivalence on the matter of the natural equality of the sexes. A fascinating example is Diderot's vacillation between the thesis that women should be educated, since they are the intellectual equals of men, and his belief that their devoutness is less reasoned.

Whatever the contradictions of Diderot's position, however, it exhibits a view of women which constituted a break with the classical natural law tradition. For the objective observation of the inferiority of women in all animal societies, there is substituted a subjective vision. Henceforth, it will be the natural light of reason that will govern relations between individuals.

This natural light of reason has a positive or progressive aspect, and a negative or reactionary aspect. Its positive aspect is that, for the Enlightenment philosophers, the natural light of reason is engraved on the heart of the human being, occasioning the presentiment that all are born possessed of free and equal rights. This philosophy is distinguished by the attempt to establish universal moral truths. Inevitably, the attempt took a variety of forms, several of which are addressed and evaluated in this volume.

First, David E Cooper notes the deficiencies, identified by contemporary feminist psychological research, of the Lockean individualist conception of rights for a characterisation of human rights. He then proposes that these can be met by greater emphasis on another Enlightenment doctrine, a universalised Scottish moralist conception of rights. Next, Leslie Goldstein assesses the work of two Enlightenment feminists, Fanny Wright and Harriet Martineau. She depicts them as examples of the two alternative Enlightenment traditions shaping American political history. She argues that they exemplify, respectively, the classical virtuous republic tradition and the tradition of liberal individualism. Indeed, it is from this twin expression of Enlightenment philosophy in the theory of law that there developed, in the following century, the feminist struggles for the equal enjoyment of rights. So, Nicole Arnaud-Duc identifies the aftermath of the 1789 Declaration of the Rights of Man and of Citizen as the grim precursor of the weak juridical status of women on the eve of the First World War.

Even so, it is curious that the world-wide repercussions of the Declaration of the Rights of Man and of Citizen should have been so great—like a slap in the face for the monarchies surrounding France—when the Declaration of the Rights of Woman and of Citizen, published by Olympe de Gouges in 1791, had no such impact. On the basis of Elizabeth Kingdom's analysis, we can draw conclusions about the dangers, at all times, of the formal separation of women from men in the political arena. It seems obvious that the real presence of both genders is essential if the political victories of either gender are to be substantive. At one level of politics, of course, individual consciousness is neither feminine nor masculine. For, in the event that liberty and equality are achieved *via* gender struggle, the achievement would not be *attributed to* gender struggle. Gender struggle is not an item on the political agenda of the social progress of humanity.

The negative or reactionary aspect of the natural law vision of the 'modern' age concerns the transition from the concept of what is grounded in reason to the concept of what is reasonable. Pertinent to this transition are the contributions from Juhani Pietarinen and Ginevra Conti Odorisio. Whilst defending both Hobbes and Locke against the criticism, Pietarinen points to the inconsistency of adopting both the principle of equality and the principle of patriarchy. The latter principle is here expressed in the recognition of the father as the most 'sensible' choice for the securing of authority in the family. Similarly, Conti Odorisio analyses the theory of natural rights to follow the evolution of women's position. She argues that its construction of sexual difference belies its character as innovatory and revolutionary within the historical and ideological framework. She describes the attempt to establish a positive law—in the sense of law posited by the legislator—more in conformity with the subjective rights discovered before the birth of the state, that is, in nature. She observes that this attempt was to be balanced by the official and willing recognition of the difference between people, with nature providing no denial of the inequality of the sexes.

These contributions bring us to a consideration of the economic, social, and political conditions of the pre-revolutionary period. At the time of the Enlightenment, the debate is no longer whether girls should receive an education but what its content should be. So, Patricia Ward Scaltsas argues that the works of Wollstonecraft and Taylor Mill represent the resolution of the eighteenth-century tension between functionalist grounds for the education of women and the liberal/perfectionist principles of self-fulfilment as the ultimate justification of women's education.

At the same time, however, economic conditions imposed a redefinition of the roles which confirmed the traditional distribution. Whilst the husband had to be able to devote himself entirely to his task, the wife had to maintain the house. This was to provide the husband with the equilibrium he needed to sustain competition. Next came the man's right to regulate the line of succession, the line of succession which was to guarantee the manangement of patrimony. This meant the right to regulate the mode of reproduction, to regulate the act of reproduction itself, and to regulate its product, the offspring. In contrast, women saw the establishment of legal limits with respect to their right to regulate their private life. Before long, it is from the state itself that there emanate limitations as to everyone's right to manage their private life. The gains and losses of the use of the right to privacy as the grounds of reproductive freedom are evaluated by J Ralph Lindgren. He argues that the historically-inspired movements for equality of opportunity were unfortunately seduced by the attractions of the right to privacy, ironically a right which has assisted in the patriarchalist confinement of women to the domestic sphere.

In political terms, whilst the Enlightenment developed within a monarchical framework, it could lead only to a democratic form of government. Now, the traditional model of the family thrives in a monarchical framework. But in discussing the identification of the husband as the person constituted by the marriage of the husband and the wife, Sybil Wolfram charts the decline of the doctrine of this unity. For it is with difficulty that the traditional model of the family adapts to the principles of democracy. Will there be two 'masters' at the head of the family cell? Will they be genuinely equal? Is there not a risk of confusing the sexes? Of course, the Enlightenment philosopher's anxiety is not at the loss—by the man, the husband, the father—of his historically privileged position. Rather, the anxiety is at a redefinition of the individual, a redefinition of relations between individuals, and in consequence a redefinition of the institutions within which these relations are inscribed. Accordingly, André-Jean Arnaud interrogates revolutionary and post-revolutionary constitutions to show that the submission of women to men in civil law can be seen as the vestige of a political view of democracy as impossible to achieve in large nations.

Politics and the consequences of 'modernism'

What, then, are the implications of the above anlysis of the rights of women in the Enlightenment epoch? What objectives might the philosophy of law set for men and women engaged in women's studies? And what are the relations between thought, philosophical analysis, reality and action?

With respect to women's rights, the modern age led to the exacerbation of the differences between men and women. That was how, with a view to ensuring the future of democracy, it was thought possible to exorcise the fear of the sexes being confused in the mass of equal people. Consequently, effective struggle for equal rights of men and women had to be sited, in the first place, in the political instance. And it was accompanied by action at the social level, and eventually at the juridical level, action for a change in the ideology, in the mental habits, that had been forged over past centuries.

We consider this theme under two headings: first, the struggle against the political-philosophical roots of the symbolism of woman as object; secondly, the daily struggle against the ideology, the mental habit, of the sexual division of tasks and of personal conduct.

In the same way that Napoleon had imposed the wearing of the cassock on the priests, so that everyone could easily recognise the members of his new body of functionaries, so the bourgeoisie of the nineteenth century wasted no time in imposing on women certain forms of apparel. These were clothes to impede movements judged improper for those described as persons 'of the sex' (as if men had none!) and white clothes for young women 'ascending to the altar', that is, marrying. This entire symbolism of the porcelain-woman found its canonisation in the establishment of the modern codes which, with the aid of dress, rapidly inured ideologies, mental habits, to the idea of woman as object.

But because this way of approaching femininity is grounded in political life, the transformation of these ideologies, these mental habits, can be achieved only if the struggle takes place at the political level. The inauguration of a process of unclenching the juridical differentiation of the sexes will begin, Arnaud proposes, with the search for a response which can meet the claim that democracy is inadequate to people's daily reality.

Several avenues are open to post-modern analysis of the rights of women. Richard B Parker explores one. He resumes the theme of the alleged inadequacies of traditional liberalism for the goals of women. He argues that the difference between male and female should be seen as similar to a profound difference of religious belief and that, therefore, modern liberalism can accommodate feminism. Other critical authors, under-represented in our immediate discussions, have taken different routes. For immediate purposes, however, we would stress the importance of developing explicitly political responses, particularly in resistance to orthodox opinions and stereotypes.

None of the above arguments implies that we should abandon everyday action at the social and economic level. We have seen that whilst the Enlightenment period questioned neither whether women had a soul, nor—with certain exceptions—whether they should have an education, it did pose the question of what the content of their education should be. It was agreed that women should of course learn how to sustain their social position, that is, to stay in their place. Later, but only much later, the problem would be displaced. Once girls had access to instruction on an equal footing with boys, it becomes a question of the professions to which girls might aspire.

Even today, women's access to the labour market is far from being as easy as men's, and there still exist constitutional restrictions against women which are not compatible with their role as wives and mothers. In this connection, Rita Mae Kelly gives an overview of the legal and political status of women in the USA in the context of professional careers and public roles. She traces the development of the struggle for equal access, opportunity and pay in the labour market, and she concludes with a number of policy proposals for overcoming persisting obstacles.

Just as it would be absurd to deny the existence of these obstacles, so it would be absurd to claim that the struggle is not at this stage a political one. But irrespective of one's position in political philosophy, it would be indefensible not to struggle for equal outcomes in day-to-day matters. Fanny Tabak tackles this issue. She pays special attention to the political and economic obstacles to the implementation of equal rights in Third World countries. She stresses the importance of sociological enquiry into the specific reasons why women do not enjoy equal rights. In this way, her contribution resumes the general theme of the Working Group—the discrepancy between women's rights and human rights, or the rights of man.

To return to the wider theme of the Congress, however, we note that in their Editors' Preface, Neil MacCormick and Zenon Bankowski correctly identify Edinburgh as one of the best homes of the Enlightenment (Mac-Cormick and Bankowski, 1989, p xi). We would add that it was the peculiar mark of the Scottish Enlightenment that it combined new forms of historical and jurisprudential analysis with political economy, to further its under-standing of the progress of society. We applaud that emphasis on the political, and it is in tribute to that great intellectual project that we offer this modest volume of papers, with its diversity of intellectual analysis—the historical, the jurisprudential, and the political-economic—and with its commitment to the analysis of the social progress, albeit too slow, of women's rights.

Clearly, this volume cannot exhaust the theme of the rights of women. We would like to thank the conference organisers, Neil MacCormick and Zenon Bankowski, for their invitation both to hold the Working Group in the Fourteenth World Congress and to publish this volume. One outcome is that there will be annual meetings of the participants in the Working Group to develop the work included in the present volume. The next meeting will be under the auspices of the Research Committee on Sociology of Law of the International Sociological Association, in its founding institution, the Oñati International Institute for the Sociology of Law. We therefore present these concluding remarks as a new point of interrogation, namely, the relations between philosophy and sociology of law. These relations both in turn and jointly, invite research on the demands for equal treatment for women and men which are made in the relations between law and society.

BIBLIOGRAPHY

Virginia Held, 'Liberty and equality from a feminist perspective', in MacCormick and Bankowski, eds (Aberdeen, 1989).

Neil MacCormick and Zenon Bankowski, eds, *Enlightenment, Rights and Revolution: Essays in Legal and Social Philosophy* (Aberdeen University Press, 1989).

CHAPTER 1

Women in the Boudoir, Women at the Pools: 1804, The History of a Confinement

André-Jean Arnaud

Abstract

Women's vote appears as an ambiguous question. Although tied to the principles of human rights according to 'modern' thinking, it was the object of a conspiracy of silence, albeit unofficially, on the part of all the revolutionary and post-revolutionary constitutions. The pretext can be found in a comparison between those texts and the legal definition of private life in the Code Napoléon. The pretext is to be found in the substantive reference in the Code to female nature and to the necessities of everyday life. Even today, as we enter the post-modern age, this area remains ambiguous because of the permanence of modern thinking in political life.

L'un des apports à la fois le plus fructueux et le plus paradoxal du siècle des Lumières, consista sans doute dans l'élaboration du concept de démocratie. L'un des apports majeurs de la Révolution française consista indubitablement dans la mise en oeuvre de ce concept. Mais cette mise en oeuvre elle-même, pour fructueuse qu'elle fut, n'en apparaît pas moins, à l'observateur post-moderne, comme empreinte d'une certaine ambiguïté. Cela se manifesta clairement dans un matière comme celle des droits des femmes face aux droits de l'homme tels qu'ils furent proclamés en ces temps-là.

   La démocratie, en effet, gouvernement du peuple par le peuple, requiert par essence l'égalité des individus. L'égalité absolue, qui s'exprime dans la démocratie directe, fait fi de toute différence, qu'elle tienne à la naissance, à la fortune ou au sexe. Bien des conséquences radicales s'ensuivent, qui apparaissent comme autant de dangers. On a souvent relevé la paralysie qui naîtrait d'une part de l'application des mécanismes de démocratie directe à des nations complexes, et d'autre part de l'admission d'individus incompétents aux organes, sinon de décision et de gestion, du moins de choix des décideurs et des gestionnaires. Il convient aussi de reconnaître les suites qu'entraîne la fusion des différences, c'est-à-dire l'unification des rôles civiques sans égard aux genres, dans la distribution des rôles sociaux en général, et dans les relations du Droit privé en particulier.

Sur ces deux points, les années 1789–1804 ont apporté, malgré la diversité des circonstances politiques, une réponse quasi-uniforme, mêlant non sans ambiguïté les questions touchant à la représentation à celles qui concernaient les droits civiques des femmes. Cette ambiguïté, que nous autres, à l'aube du post-modernisme, nous devons de lever, tient à la conception 'moderne' de la cité. Et c'est pourquoi, bien que la critique que j'ai entreprise du Code Napoléon, daté maintenant de vingt ans, je me prêterai volontiers à l'exercise requis des participants à cet atelier sur les droits de la femme dans la Révolution française. Le recours à l'histoire sera pris non comme un moyen de dénoncer encore ce qui l'a déjà été depuis plusieurs lustres, mais comme une occasion de décortiquer les racines d'un mal dont les séquelles actuelles nous empêchent trop de repenser et l'usage de la démocratie, et la place des genres, dans une société au seuil d'un processus alternatif de déjuridicisation et de rejuridicisation.

Notre démonstration s'appuiera sur les textes contemporains du Code civil concernant le mécanisme des élections aux assemblés détentrices du pouvoir—considéré comme souverain—de légiférer. Et notre question sera formulée à partir des conclusions qu'on avait, sur le point précis de la situation de la femme, tirés de notre analyse structurale de *Code Napoléon* (Arnaud, 1973). Ce dernier avait, on le sait, consacré la figure de la femme au foyer. S'agit-il d'une image privée construite pour la commodité des relations interindividuelles: une famille, un chef, un seul gestionnaire, un seul responsable? Ou bien y a-t-il homothétie entre cette figure privée et la conception politique des années post-révolutionnaires? Autrement dit, la femme, en tant que citoyenne, appartient-elle à la même classe d'équivalence que l'homme?

Reportons-nous à des textes contemporains du *Code Napoléon*:[1] on commencera par un décret du 17 janvier 1806 qui contient les dispositions réglementaires pour l'exécution des actes des constitutions de l'Empire des 22 frimaire an 8, 16 thermidor an 10 et 28 floréal an 12, en ce qui concerne particulièrement la formation des registres civiques, préalable indispensable à la convocation et à la tenue des assemblées cantonales. A première vue, pas de distinction entre l'homme et la femme. En ce qui concerne les intéressés, en effet, le texte les désigne sous des formules pouvant s'appliquer grammaticalement à l'un et l'autre genre: 'tout Français', 'ceux qui ...', 'les membres du ...', 'les personnes désignées', 'chacun des citoyens'.

Mieux: le texte distingue ouvertement le 'domicile politique' du 'domicile civil'. On pourrait en conclure que le foyer 'civil' où se trouve cantonnée la femme, pourrait bien ne pas la lier pour les actes de sa vie de citoyenne, et notamment les élections. En réalité, la doute naît à la lecture des conditions imposées pour l'inscription sur le registre civique: résider pendant un an dans un Commune de l'arrondissement. Comment une épouse pourrait-elle le faire en dehors du foyer conjugal et sans le déserter? Ou encore avoir été appelé à des fonctions qui exigent un domicile politique dans un arrondissement: la femme fonctionnaire du Gouvernement constitue une hypothèse d'école.

Alors les expressions antérieures prennent un sens tout différent: 'tout Français' ne veut pas dire 'toute Française'; 'ceux qui' n'est pas 'celles qui'; 'les membres' visés sont ceux du Sénat, du conseil d'Etat, du corps législatif, du Tribunat, de la cour de cassation, de la légion d'Honneur, tous corps dont sont exclues les femmes; 'chacun des citoyens', enfin, n'est pas un pluriel global comprenant 'chacune des citoyennes'.

A vrai dire, la femme pourrait au moins avoir droit de cité dans la cir-conscription du domicile fixé par son mari. Les constitutions auxquelles renvoie le décret du 17/1/1806 pourraient à ce sujet rassurer le lecteur. Celle du 22 frimaire an 8 (13 décembre 1799) instituant le Consultat, commence par un titre sur ''l'exercice des droits de cité'. L'art.2 de ce titre Ier dit que 'tout homme né et résidant en France ... est citoyen français'. 'Tout homme' pourrait s'entendre au sens de la *Déclaration des droits de l'homme*, au sens d''individu'. Et les articles suivants laissent planer la doute: 'pour exercer les doits de cité d'un arrondissement communal, il faut y avoir acquis domicile par une année de résidence ...' (art.6); 'Les citoyens de chaque arrondissement communal désignant par leurs suffrages ceux d'entre eux qu'ils croient les plus propres à gérer les affaires publiques ...' (art.7).

De même, le sénatus-consulte du 16 thermidor an 10 (4 août 1802) instaur-ant le Consulat à vie, précise que 'l'arrondissement de canton se compose de tous les citoyens domiciliés dans le canton ... inscrits sur la liste communale d'arrondissement ... et qui y jouissent des droits de citoyen' (art.4); que 'les collèges électoraux d'arrondissement ont un membre par 500 habitants' (art.18) et ceux de département, 'un membre par 1000 habitants' (art.19). Quant à la qualité de citoyen, le texte renvoie pour cela à la constitution précédente.

Quand on arrive au sénatus-consulte organique du 28 floréal an 12 (18 mai 1804), 'confiant' le gouvernement 'de la république' à un empereur, on n'y trouve plus, pour commencer, de précisions sur le droit de cité ou les élections, mais sur l'hérédité de la dignité impériale, sur la famille impériale et sur les grandes dignités de l'Empire. Ici, il n'est plus question que de 'mâles' et d''exclusion perpétuelle des femmes et de leur descendance' (leitmotiv, art.3, 5, 6, 7, 18, 30). Lorsqu'on arrive à la matière des élections, on ne parle plus que des collèges électoraux, non des citoyens et de leurs droits. Il apparaît tout à fait clair au lecteur que la question n'est pas de savoir si la femme y joue un rôle.

A-t-elle jamais été considérée de ce point de vue? En d'autres termes, si, jusqu'à présent, dans les textes contemporains du Code civil, nous n'avons recontré qu'une classe de citoyens, n'est-ce pas, plutôt qu'une reconnaissance de l'inclusion de la femme dans cette classe, tout simplement un aveu que la femme n'a jamais été prise en considération dans les affaires de la cité?

Pourquoi, sinon, un député à la Convention aurait-il plaidé pour l'égalité de l'homme et de la femme et pour le suffrage direct comme étant le mode le plus démocratique (Guyomar, 1793)? L'époque révolutionnaire avait pourtant agité ces idées: les femmes doivent-elles exercer les droits politiques? Les femmes doivent-elles se réunir en association politique? A la première question, le député Amar, au nom du Comité de Sûreté générale, répondait que 'l'opinion universelle repousse cette idée' (Amar, 1793); à la seconde, il répond également: 'non, parce qu'elles seraient obligées d'y sacrifier des soins plus importants auxquels la nature les appelle'. D'ajouter: 'les fonctions privées auxquelles sont destinées les femmes par la nature même, tiennent à l'ordre général de la société'. Et conclure: 'il n'est pas possible que les femmes exercent les droits politiques'. Le député Charlier a beau lui rétorquer: 'A moins que vous ne contestiez que les femmes font partie du genre humain, pouvez-vous leur ôter le droit commun à tout être pensant?', un autre député, Bazibe, trouvera le moyen de détourner le sujet et de contenter tout le monde: 'Il est donc uniquement question de savoir si les *Sociétés de femmes* sont dangereuses. L'expérience a prouvé, ces jours passés, combien elles sont funestes à la tranquillité publique: cela posé, qu'on ne me parle plus de principes' (Amar, 1793).

Il était pourtant bien question de principes. En 1790, Condorcet avait démonté, dans un article 'Sur l'admission des femmes au droit de cité', tous les prétendus arguments contre ce principe. On y lit notamment, en ce qui concerne la relation entre le domaine civil et le domaine public de la vie des individus, qu''on ne peut alléguer la dépendance où les femmes sont de leurs maris, puis qu'il serait possible de détruire en même temps cette tyrannie de la loi civile, et que jamais une injustice ne peut être un motif légitime d'en commettre un autre' (Condorcet, 1790, p 8).

Il n'est donc pas exagéré de remonter à la Constitution du 3 septembre 1791 pour comprendre un texte de 1806. Non point pour y retrouver ce qui apparaîtrait comme des poncifs: que la déclaration des 'droits de l'homme' évoque d'une manière générale les 'individus' (art.3), la 'volonté générale' des 'citoyens', déclarés 'également admissibles à toutes dignités, places et emplois publics, selon leur capacité, et sans autre distinction que celle de leur vertus et de leurs talents' (art.6). Ce qui nous intéresse plutôt, ici, est la définition que donne la constitution, du citoyen français, et la fonction assignée à cette qualité.

S'agissant de la qualité, elle s'acquiert sans que soit établie une distinction entre les personnes. Il suffit d'être né en France d'un père français ou, à défaut, de satisfaire à des exigences de résidence, voire de serment civique. Une fois acquise la qualité de citoyen, point de classes d'individus disposant de pouvoirs différents. 'Les citoyens français ... forment les *communes*' (titre II, art.8) et ont, à ce titre, 'le droit d'élire à temps, et suivant les formes déterminées par la loi ...' (T.II, art. 9). Voilà bien qui change tout: quelles sont donc les formes déterminées par la loi?

La réponse se trouve dans la lecture du texte consacré aux modalités de la représentation: le pouvoir législatif est *délégué* à une assemblée (T.III, art.2–3). Malgré une évocation du 'peuple', qui 'élit librement' ses représentants (T.III, art.3), la démocratie ne sera point directe. Comment s'organise le mode de représentation? Sur 745 députés, 247 sont attachés au territoire (3 députés par département, un seul pour Paris), 249 à la population active, 249 à la contribution directe.

En ce qui concerne la *population active*, les citoyens 'actifs' se réunissent en assemblées primaires. Sont citoyens 'actifs' les Français âgés de 25 ans, domiciliés dans leur ville ou leur canton depuis un temps fixé par la loi, payant une certaine contribution directe, n'étant pas dans un état de domesticité, chacun étant 'inscrit, dans la municipalité de son domicile, au rôle des gardes nationales' (T.III, ch.1er, sect.2, art.2) et ayant prêté le serment civique. A-t-on jamais vu une femme inscrite au rôle des gardes nationales?

A partir de là, tout s'enchaîne: le texte a beau parler plus loin, en termes non discriminatoires, eu égard aux genres, du rôle des assemblées primaires, des conditions de l'électeur et des conditions d'éligibilité, plusieurs classes d'acteurs se trouvent instaurées. Certaines ont expresses: à côté des citoyens actifs, il y a ceux qui ne le sont pas, comme les serviteurs à gages ou ceux qui ne paient pas une contribution directe au moins égale à la valeur de trois journées de travail; et, parmi les citoyens actifs, même, il y a ceux qui ne sont pas propriétaires ou usufruitiers ou locataires d'un bien supérieur au montant fixé par la loi. D'autres sont tacites: ne sont pas citoyens actifs les citoyennes, puisqu'elles ne sont pas inscrites au rôle des gardes nationales. Il suffisait d'une toute petite phrase dans le long texte d'une constitution de la République pour écarter des urnes, sans avoir l'air d'y toucher, plus de la moitié de la population de la France, celle-là même dont le Code civil allait, par ailleurs, faire des mineures soumises au mari.

La constitution du 24 juin 1793 ne retient pas cette phrase. L'article 29 de la *Déclaration des droits de l'homme et du citoyen* qui le précède reprend même, en l'amplifiant, la formule selon laquelle 'chaque citoyen a un droit égal de concourir à la formation de la loi et à la nomination de ses mandataires ou de ses agents'. Mais dans l'acte constitutionnel, après qu'il soit affirmé que 'le peuple français est distribué, pour l'exercice de sa souveraineté, en assemblées primaires de cantons' (art.2), lorsqu'il s'agit de savoir qui est admis à l'exercice des droits de citoyen français, une distinction des genres est opérée. 'Tout homme né et domicilié en France, âgé de 21 ans accomplis' (art.4, al.1), cela pourrait s'entendre de tout individu. Mais, s'agissant de l'étranger (al.2), il est précisé qu'il peut devenir citoyen français s'il 'épouse une Française'; la réciproque n'est pas prévue. Donc une étrangère ne peut être admise à l'exercice des droits de citoyen français. La terme 'homme' de l'alinéa 1, mis sur un pied d'égalité avec l'étranger' de l'alinéa 2, concerne donc le 'mâle'.

Quand l'article 7 déclare que 'le peuple souverain est l'universalité des citoyens français', cela s'entend donc des citoyens, non des citoyennes.

Comment expliquer cette distinction en classes d'individus? Par une mise en rapport avec ce qui se passe dans le *Code Napoléon*, et en partant de l'hypothèse, point trop audacieuse, que les conceptions motivantes du législateur privé et du constituant relèvant d'une même structure mentale, on peut comprendre aisément cette dernière.

Les constituants, on le sait, étaient épris du désir d'instaurer, en France, une monarchie constitutionnelle. Or, d'une part, la famille représente, à l'état atomique, une monarchie; et la forme du gouvernement monarchique s'apparente à la gestion d'une grande famille. Constitutionnelle, elle n'en est que meilleure, puisqu'elle assure la participation des familles au gouvernement de la cité. Cela s'entend de deux manières. Premièrement, participation des familles ne signifie pas participation de toutes les familles. Le vrai 'joueur' (celui du Code Civil) est celui qui peut effectuer des 'mises', parce qu'il est propriétaire. Les familles qui participeront au grand 'jeu' de la cité seront celles des propriétaires. Par ailleurs, les familles participeront au gouvernement en tant que familles, non en fonction des individus qui la composent. Simplification majeure du système de la représentation, le mari représente 'naturellement' son épouse. C'est ainsi que les classes d'individus reconnues dans le Droit privé constituent un préalable nécessaire au fonctionnement d'une monarchie constitutionnelle: il y a homothétie entre la structure de la société civile et celle de la société publique.

Les juristes de 1789 à 1804 rêvaient depuis longtemps, en France, d'une monarchie constitutionnelle. Or, la soummission de la femme peut apparaître, dans le droit privé, comme un résidu d'une conception politique selon laquelle la démocratie directe est interdite—par les complications pratiques qu'elle entraîne—aux grandes nations. Car si le fait que les individus sont libres et égaux en droits implique que le groupe soit géré par le principe de démocratie, du moins cette démocratie, pour être viable, ne peut tolérer que tous s'expriment à un titre véritablement égal.

On va donc imaginer une pyramide, c'est-à-dire une structure d'ordre, celle-là même qu'on retrouve dans le *Code Napoléon*. L'élu, du seul fait de son élection, n'appartient plus à la classe d'équivalence de ses électeurs. Autrement dit, la structure d'ordre passe par l'écrasement, à chaque étage, d'une multitude par un seul qui se retrouve, avec les autres élus, dans une nouvelle classe d'équivalence, et ainsi de suite jusqu'au sommet de l'Etat.

Tenir certains 'égaux' en tutelle permet, à la base, c'est-à-dire là où se trouve le plus grand nombre, d'épargner un premier choix. En élisant son mari comme 'son' maître, l'épouse rejoint un foyer, une famille. Elle renonce, avec toute la dignité du qualificatif d''épouse', aux droits dont elle pouvait jouir comme célibataire. Que la constitution ne reconnaisse pas à la femme le droit de voter, fût apparu comme un scandale si cette même femme avait joui de l'égalité de droits dans un domaine aussi important que la vie de droit privé. Mais l'homothétie qu'on relève entre la conception politique des hommes de 1804 et leur image privée de la femme, fait que le rejet de la femme du corps électoral pouvait n'apparaître que comme un aspect particulier, dans le champ politique, de la tutelle exercée 'naturellement' sur la femme de par un choix qu'elle-même effectuait en se mariant. Quant à celle qui ne se mariait pas, elle méritait d'être sanctionnée pour le fait de négliger—ou de ne pas se montrer capable—d'accéder au rang d'épouse. N'ayant pas su élire un mari dans sa vie privée, elle n'eût point été capable d'élire un député dans la vie politique.

La règle du jeu dans la paix bourgoise est 'une'. Celle qu'on a vue à l'oeuvre dans le *Code Napoléon* n'est qu'une application de la règle du jeu politique à une partie donnée, où sont mis en jeu des rapports privés.

Malgré l'accès tardif des femmes au droit de vote, l'ambiguïté n'a pas cessé: elle n'a fait que changer de nature. Les hommes politiques savent que les femmes ont le pouvoir de les plébisciter, et certains en usent volontiers. Ce n'est pas là-dessus que je voudrais conclure.

Au nombre des leçons que l'acteur social peut tirer à l'aube du post-modernisme, de ces épisodes révolutionnaires et post-révolutionnaires, j'en vois une qui déborde ces temps et prend un valeur anthropologique. Nous avons problématisé la question des droits des femmes à partir du concept de démocratie. Nous avons vu comment les constituants se sont acharné à écarter à la fois le principe d'une démocratie directe et l'accès des femmes aux urnes. Sur ce point précis, une chercheuse française a émis cette idée que l'idée de démocratie, en tant qu'elle requiert l'égalité parfaite, toucherait en connotation un niveau de notre intellect qui refuse l'égalité des genres, laquelle supposerait jusqu'à l'exclusion de toute rivalité entre l'homme et la femme, partant la généralisation de l'amitié et l'insupportable dissolution du lien amoureux dans le lien amical (Fraisse, 1989). Ce qui est vrai, au fond de tout cela, c'est que la définition d'une société—ce qu'on nomme parfois lien social—passe nécessairement par une prise de parti sur la question du lien sexuel. Du moins dans les termes classiques—c'est à dire 'modernes'—où continue d'être posé le débat.

Mais on peut se demander si le combat des genres, qui continue à faire rage dans les boudoirs et dans la rue, est réellement inhérent au principe de démocratie. Si, comme le note bien un observateur spécialisé 'le forum républicain a changé de lieu' (Duhamel, 1989, p 6), passant progressivement des bancs des Assemblées au petit écran, est-il sensé de continuer à poser le problème de la mise en oeuvre des institutions démocratiques dans les termes traditionnels de la représentation? Réinventer une culture de participation exigera non seulement le véritable 'aggiornamento' institutionnel dont parle l'auteur, mais aussi celui de notre manière—autant à vous, femmes, qu'à nous, hommes—d'aborder la coexistence des genres dans la societé.

NOTES

1 On sait que le Code civil, promulgé le 30 ventôse an xii (21 mars 1804), est le résultat aménagé du projet de l'an VIII. On trouvera le texte de ce dernier dans Fenet 1827. Les textes constitutionelles cités ci-après sont extraits de Sirey à partir de 1791.

REFERENCES

Amar, *Rapport, Moniteur*, XVIII (30 octobre 1793), pp 299–300.

André-Jean Arnaud, *Essai d'Analyse Structurale du Code Civil Français: la Règle du Jeu dans la Paix Bourgeoise* (Paris, 1973).

Alain Duhamel, 'La sclérose des institutions', *Le Monde* (29–30 octobre 1989).

Condorcet, 'Sur l'admission des femmes au droit de cité', *Journal de la Société de 1789*, V (3 juillet 1790).

Fenet, *Receuil Complet des Travaux Préparatoires du Code Civil* (Paris, 1827).

Geneviève Fraisse, *Au Colloque La Famille, la Loi, l'Etat (Beaubourg 1988–89)* (Paris, 1989).

Pierre Guyomar, *Le Partisan de l'Egalité Politique entre les Individus, un Problème très Important de l'Egalité en droits et de l'inequalité en fait* (Paris, 1793).

Jean-Baptiste Sirey, *Receuil Général des Lois et Arrêts, en Matière Civil, Criminelle, Commerciale et de Droit Public* (Paris, from 1791).

CHAPTER 2

Women Entrapped: from Public Non-existence to Private Protection

Nicole Arnaud-Duc

Abstract

In which domain, on the eve of the First World War, might women be indebted to the 1789 Declaration of the Rights of Man? The days following the Revolution were some of the darkest times in the history of women. What was the outcome of the legislative work, of the jurisprudence of the tribunals, and of women's struggles in the domains of public and private rights? Was woman a legal subject, a citizen? In short, what were the rights of women in the nineteenth century in the country of the Code Napoleon?

> Que faire des femmes? Vieille réponse de l'histoire: les mettre au singulier ... .
> E G Sledziewski, *Révolutions du sujet*, Paris, Méridiens Klincksieck, 1989, p 79.

La condition juridique de la femme reflète l'idée qu'une société se fait de l'ordre, qu'elle énonce et protège par son droit. En 1789, en France, la contestation de l'ordre régnant passe par le bouleversement de la famille, entendue comme la première organisation fondatrice de toute société. La femme sera souvent perçue comme un enjeu symbolique mais pendant la Révolution et son prolongement bourgeois du dix-neuvième siècle, l'image que les projets et les textes législatifs dessinent d'elle n'est pas la même que celle des hommes, devenus des êtres raisonnables, libres d'exercer leur volonté, autonomes dans la cité.

Plusieurs directions de recherche sont envisageables. Comment pour les juristes, aborder le problème des droits de la femme, en contrepoint du discours philosophique? Une double question se pose: en pratique, quels droits publics et privés étaient reconnus? Il s'agira surtout, ici, de tracer quelques voies de recherche sans prétendre aller au fond d'un processus d'identification des sexes, toujours en question.[1]

Nature et fonction de la femme

A la fin du dix-huitième siècle, il importe de savoir ce qui fonde la différence entre homme et femme à l'intérieur de l'espèce humaine et, par suite, de fixer leur place respective dans l'espace social. Si personne ne nie cette différence évidente, la définition des rôles reconnus à chacun des sexes varie suivant que l'on attribue cette dissemblance la *nature* et/ou à la *fonction*, interrogations ravivées par les réflexions révolutionnaires sur le'égalité sociale. Sur quels critères doivent se fonder les différences de traitement, de droits? Quelles sont les conséquences des attributs physiques et dans quelle mesure rendent-ils les femmes impropres à l'exercice de certains droits et à la disposition de la liberté individuelle? Dans un moment de rupture, le risque est de les écraser sous les pesanteurs d'une *nature* dont les révolutionnaires s'émancipent au nom de la raison qui ne serait reconnue qu'aux hommes. L'ordre ancien avait-il posé le problème du statut de la femme? En réalité, c'est l'Eglise qui peut apporter une réponse, puisque la femme n'existe que par sa fonction maternelle et que sa condition est ainsi régie essentiellement par le sacrement du mariage. Quant au droit au sens strict, il se préoccupe essentiellement des biens, échangés à travers la personne de l'épouse. En effet, une fois admise son infériorité naturelle, ce qui ne gêne en rien le droit inégalitaire d'une société fondée sur les privilèges, on ne rencontre qu'une disparité de pratiques, que l'on peut regrouper suivant la division classique entre pays de coutumes et pays de droit écrit. Le pouvoir royal, quand il légifère dans ce domaine, ne fait qu'accorder ou refuser certaines exceptions au principe de l'incapacité. Au moment des discussions concernant les régimes matrimoniaux, dans les travaux préparatoires du Code civil de 1804, on évoqua la *capacité* des épouses mariées sous le régime dotal dans les pays de droit écrit, concernant leurs biens extra-dotaux. S'il est exact que, notamment en Provence, tel était bien le principe, il ne s'appliquait en réalité qu'à un petit nombre de femmes fortunées qui ne laissaient pas à leur mari la gestion de leur patrimoine propre. Les affirmations des juristes sudistes visaient plus à exalter leur particularisme qu'à défendre la liberté des femmes.

Le droit issu de la Révolution va, au contraire, énoncer la capacité juridique des femmes, et, du même élan, le réduire en matière civile et la nier en matière politique, en s'appuyant sur la *nature* qui commande les mœurs et distribue les rôles. C'est pour cela qu'il est vain, par exemple, de comparer le statut de la femme issue de la Révolution avec celui qu'elle avait pendant l'Ancien Régime, en citant les droits d'élection à certaines assemblées, qu'elles tenaient de leur status exceptionnel de propriétaires, issue du droit féodal. Il est peu pertinent aussi de déduire de la liste des incapacités d'exercice visant les femmes du dix-neuvième siècle, qu'elles n'avaient pas été vues comme des sujets de droit par les législateurs des assemblées révolutionnaires. Même si cela ne se traduit pas dans les faits, la Révolution a posé, pour la première fois, le problème du rôle de la femme dans la cité. Et la société en demeurera ébranlée: la réaction anti-féministe a été à la mesure de l'aspect bouleversant de la question. Car le discours sur la nature féminine conservera la même formulation tout au long du dix-neuvième siècle, renforçant le partage et les exclusions: à l'homme le pouvoir (politique, religieux, militaire), à la femme, le savoir pratique. Portalis exaltait au moment de la rédaction du Code civil,

> ce tact fin et délicat qui remplit chez elles l'office d'un sixième sens, et qui ne se conserve ou ne se perfectionne que par l'exercice de toutes les vertus, enfin, cette modestie touchante ... qu'elles ne peuvent perdre sans devenir plus vicieuses que nous.

C'est donc dans leur 'vocation naturelle' qu'elles doivent 'chercher le principe des devoirs plus austères qui leur sont imposés pour leur plus grand avantage et au profit de la société' (Fenet, IX, p 181). Tout est dit. De l'éternelle malade de Michelet à l'hystérique de Charcot, on peut dire que plus grande est la demande des femmes, surtout quand elle se manifeste au grand jour par la voix de quelques unes, plus est vaste la part des fantasmes masculins sur la *fragilité* féminine, si peu vérifiée parmi les travailleuses, doublement brimées par leur patron et leur mari (Livi, 1984; Moreau, 1982). Du domaine fantasmatique resort aussi le très grand succès fait aux thèses de Bachofen et de Morgan sur le matriarcat, œuvres qui, en définitive, mettent en valeur le pouvoir masculin instaurateur de l'ordre.

Si on leur refuse l'égalité des droits, on leur confère par contre une fonction qu'exaltent les discours faisant l'éloge du féminin/maternel, reconnaissant aux femmes une mission civilisatrice qui doit s'exercer dans l'éducation des petits enfants, l'assistance, la charité, la compassion. La plupart des femmes souscrivent d'ailleurs à ce schéma qui les assure d'une différence qu'elles revendiquent, puisque toute leur éducation les prépare à cet emploi. Si elles constituent un enjeu entre l'Eglise et l'Etat, les hommes leur prêtent volontiers une influence occulte de muse, de 'compagne d'un homme de génie qui exalte son inspiration et conserve sa mémoire'[2] (Michaud, 1985; Perrot, 1980; Agulhon, 1979). La notion même de *patriarcat* apparaît d'ailleurs au dix-neuvième siècle, comme mode de transmission patrilinéaire des biens mais aussi comme système de domination de la femme. En dehors des arguments moraux fondés sur les mœurs, de savants juristes invoquèrent aussi de pseudo-anatomiques interdits s'appliquant aux femmes, en s'appuyant sur les multiples avis de non moins savants médecins (Knibiehler, Fouquet, 1983). Toute cette littérature avait pour but de cantonner la femme dans la sphère du privé, pour obéir à la *loi naturelle*, tenir compte de la *nature féminine*, de la mission maternelle réduisant la femme à un utérus qui fait d'elle une infirme et borne son utilité à l'époque où elle peut être reproductrice.

A la fin du siècle, à la veille de la Première Guerre mondiale, des hommes politiques, des députés radicaux, minoritaires à la Chambre des Députés, protestèrent contre cet usage restrictif du genre masculin, 'qui n'a jamais sauvé une femme de l'application des lois',[3] du paiement de l'impôt ou de l'échafaud, comme le rappela, en son temps, Olympe de Gouges. L'opinion demeura longtemps fidèle à cette image rassurante de la femme faible, peu raisonnable et si peu attirante dès qu'elle a passé sa prime jeunesse, quand, dès quarante ans, 'plus fatiguée que l'homme et vieillissant plus rapidement que lui (elle) éprouve le besoin de se reposer' ... et donc ne peut voter, comme le proposait une féministe.[4] En raison des préjugés des juristes et des politiciens, l'histoire de l'émancipation juridique des femmes françaises doit se lire en filigrane du discours normatif masculin, au travers du modèle idéologique dominant. Dans ce domaine apparaît bien l'aspect récupérateur du droit, attentif aux faiblesses du système juridique, toujours prêt à le 'replâtrer' pour l'empêcher de s'écrouler sous la pression sociale, qui provoque des ruptures dans l'ordre public. Si des lois, des arrêts ne suffisent pas à changer à eux seuls les mentalités, la promulgation d'un texte hostile aux femmes peut par contre amener une régression de leur condition. Par des voies détournées, l'équilibre tendra cependant à se rétablir, souvent basé sur les ressources qu'offre la 'sororité': on en veut pour preuve la législation édictée en 1920 en France contre l'avortement et la contraception.

Exclue de l'activité juridique, la femme le sera de la culture et du politique. Et si des droits sont acquis, il ne faut pas s'imaginer qu'en seront pour autant réglés tous les conflits qui échappent à la sphère du juridique. L'histoire de la condition juridique féminine révèle particulièrement bien à quel point la production juridique n'est consécration ponctuelle des idées dominantes, à la fois statique par son formalisme et dynamique par les forces qui la sous-tendent: des vécus, des imaginaires, en contrepoint du droit posé. Fixant la norme (et par là le *normal*) d'une société, le droit a aussi un rôle symbolique. Même si le droit napoléonien ressort plus de l'autoritarisme que du volon-tarisme de l'individu, il entend cependant masquer le vraie nature de son pouvoir. Et si la femme n'existe dans la Code civil que par rapport à l'homme, père, mari, enfant, le discours philosophique, moral, juridique affirme qu'elle *adhère* à ce statut d'être relatif et dépendant, parce qu'elle est consciente des bornes que lui impose sa nature.

L'impossible citoyenne

a)   Le droit de vote

La conquête des droits publics a souvent été perçue comme la partie immergée de l'iceberg' revendicatif des femmes. Sans doute parce que ce type de revendications, surtout dans les pays anglo-saxons, mobilisa la presse et l'opinion publique, permit aux femmes de s'associer et de manifester pub-liquement et parfois violemment, leur irritations. Les droits publics com-prennent l'exercice du droit de vote et le pouvoir de remplir des fonctions publiques. La Révolution opérera une mutation historique incontestable, en reconnaissant à la femme le statut de sujet de droit civil. Ce principe ne sera pas remis en cause, même si l'application en est dramatiquement restreinte dès le 'retour de l'ordre' et que la politique lui est interdit.

La *Déclaration des droits de l'homme et du citoyen* assure aux femmes la liberté, la propriété, la sûreté, la résistance à l'oppression, c'est-à-dire la liberté d'opinion et l'intégrité de leur personne et de leurs biens. Mais dès le 27 août 1789, la Constituante rappellera les principes de la prétendue loi salique, pour écarter les femmes de la succession dynastique et, le 15 novembre, pour confirmer leur incapacité à régner. La Déclaration du 7 août 1830 les exclue du trône à perpétuité, ainsi que leurs descendants. Si Condorcet passe à juste titre pour un homme préoccupé du sort des femmes, il manquait cependant d'enthousiasme pour ce qui concernait le droit de suffrage et son discours demeura théorique. Par contre, Pierre Guyomar, un député à la Convention, qualifié d'obscur parce qu'il ne s'illustra pas par de hauts faits politiques, rédigea un texte remarquable au printemps 1793: *Le Partisan de l'égalité politique entre les individus, ou problème très important de l'égalité en droits et de l'inégalité en fait*, essentiellement consacré aux droits des femmes (Guyomar, 1793). Il y réclame l'égalité complète entre hommes et femmes: 'De deux choses l'une, ou la nation est composée d'hommes et de femmes, ou elle ne l'est que d'hommes ... ; dans le second cas, les femmes sont des illotes de la république'. Le 'préjugé du sexe' est une 'erreur féodalement ridicule', tout comme l'était celui de la couleur de la peau. Remarquons que c'est justement la question du droit de vote accordé aux noirs à la fin de la guerre de Sécession, qui durcit le combat des Américaines anti-esclavagistes, déçues qu'on refuse ce droit aux femmes. Comme l'affirme encore Guyomar, si l'on exclut la moitié de la population, il n'existera plus que des *'femmes* ou *filles* de citoyens, jamais (des) *citoyennes*. Ou retranchez le mot, ou accordez la chose'. Le contraire prévalut: le 30 avril 1793, les femmes furent exclues de l'armée; le 30 octobre, on interdit les clubs féminins; le 20 mai 1795, la Convention leur ferma l'entrée des tribunes; le 24 mai, il leur fut interdit d'assister aux assemblées politiques et de se réunir à plus de cinq dans la rue (Arnaud-Duc, 1990). Mais si on a peu écrit, peu discuté, peu légiféré sur la pleine citoyenneté des femmes, ce sont des femmes mythiques—elles n'effraient pas—qui personnifient les acquis révolutionnaires (Agulhon, 1979).

Le problème se reposa en France quand fut restauré, en 1848, le suffrage universel. Les socialistes préférèrent, partout en Europe, lutter d'abord pour l'obtention de ce droit, promettant qu'ils penseraient ensuite aux femmes (Sowerwine, 1978). Mais le 28 juillet 1848, en leur interdit à nouveau d'être membres d'un club politique et quand le député socialiste Pierre Leroux proposa qu'elles votent aux élections municipales, il fut copieusement hué par ses collègues. Face au principe de l'égalité contenu dans la *Déclaration des droits* de 1789, la Cour de Cassation n'aura aucun embarras à condamner une femme coupable de vol simple, pour n'avoir pas déclaré cette con-damnation privative de droits civiques, qui l'écartait du métier de colporteuse de journaux: elle sanctionne ainsi le défaut de déclaration des conséquences infâmantes d'une condamnation la privant de droits qu'elle ne possède pas![5] Des projets, jugés ambitieux par leurs auteurs, virent le jour: comme donner au mari deux bulletins de vote (1874)! En France, il faut signaler le combat mené par Hubertine Auclert, directrice du journal *La Citoyenne*, qui refusa de payer ses impôts, puisqu'elle ne participait pas au vote du budget. Mais elle se retrouva en définitive très isolée (Auclert, 1982). Des femmes, telle Marguerite Durand, tentèrent, lors de la victoire des Républicains, de se faire inscrire sur les listes électorales, en arguant du caractère général du mot *citoyen*: en pure perte.[6] Le *citoyen* est toujours mâle, même si le *souteneur* ne l'est pas forcément.[7] Maurice Hauriou, professeur de droit, appliqua au problème la célèbre théorie des nullités de mariage chère aux civilistes: la femme est un citoyen *inexistant* et non un citoyen *nul*, comme est nul, par exemple, un mariage incestueux et inexistant le mariage entre deux individus du même sexe.[8] Si les féministes françaises furent attentives à la conquête des droits publics par les Américaines, elles ne suivirent pas l'exemple britannique, où l'entêtement des conservateurs provoqua des incidents très violents. Cinquante propositions de lois avaient été déposées à la veille de la guerre, l'agitation ayant débuté en 1832, avec l'appui de John Stuart Mill. Les Françaises préférèrent user des meetings, des pétitions, des congrès, de la presse. Le mouvement fut mené par les institutrices, type de la femme qui doit travailler pour vivre mais se sent coupée de ses racines. Elles s'allièrent pour cela aux radicaux. L'idée gagnait du terrain chez un certain nombre de jeunes juristes, d'intellectuels. A la veille de la guerre, trois cents députés paraissaient favorables au droit de vote, le problème de l'éligibilité divisant plus les sympathisants. A vrai dire, à part en Angleterre, le féminisme ne fut pas très suffragiste. Si les Allemandes obtinrent le droit de voter dès après la guerre, comme les Anglaises et les Scandinaves, les pays latins résistèrent et la France s'illustra en ce domaine: c'est par souci électoraliste qu'un général donnera ce droit aux femmes en 1946.

b)   Le droit à l'instruction et au travail

Prendre sa place dans la cité, c'est aussi pouvoir accéder à l'instruction et au travail. Dès l'époque de leur *Pétition ... au Roi*, en 1789,[9] des femmes, beaucoup par conviction, un peu par stratégie, ne réclamèrent le droit à l'instruction que pour devenir de meilleurs mères et éducatrices, et travailler plus facilement. Cette attitude présente un aspect positif: les femmes estiment avoir dans ce domaine plus de qualités que les hommes. Mais l'aspect négatif est d'importance: conscientes de leur place en retrait dans la société, elles ne voient qu'une issue convenable pour elles, se marier. S'instruire, c'est trouver plus facilement un travail honnête, ne pas tomber dans la prostitution, qu'elles évoquent longuement, avec cette attirance/répulsion qui marque les rapports entre femmes 'respectables' et celles qui s'adonnent au 'vice', attitude que l'on retrouve même chez des féministes.

Si la politique scolaire de la Révolution n'améliora en rien la condition féminine, il faudra attendre la loi Camille Sée de 1880 pour que l'enseignement secondaire soit organisé, et on l'envisagera comme le moyen de faire de la jeune fille un 'intime compagnon' de son futur mari. La médaille commémorative de la loi portera la devise: 'La République instruit les jeunes filles qui sont les mères des hommes'. Cependant, toute revendication économique ou sociale des femmes doit aussi être envisagée comme un désir de participer à la vie de la cité. Leurs conquêtes seront autant de grignotages des privilèges masculins.[10]

En ce qui concerne le droit au travail, on sait combien l'Etat répugna à intervenir dans le 'contrat de louage de services', conclu entre patrons et ouvriers, pour que soit respectée la 'liberté' des contrats. Dans le dernier tiers du dix-neuvième siècle, un peu partout en Europe, des lois protégèrent le travail des enfants mineurs dans les usines et ateliers, leur interdisant, comme aux femmes, les travaux souterrains (loi du 5 mai 1874). La loi de 2 novembre 1892 réglementa le travail de nuit, imposant le repose hebdomadaire et la journée de 11 heurs, avec une heure de repos. Elle fut mal appliquée; on renforça la réglementation le 22 décembre 1911. Une loi de 29 décembre 1900 obligea les patrons à mettre un siège à la disposition de leurs employées. Les femmes enceintes obtinrent un congé non payé de huit semaines avec garantie d'emploi le 27 novembre 1909, les institutrices et les employées des PTT bénéficiant de droits plus importants. Il ne peut être question ici de décrire les conquêtes féminines en ce qui concerne l'accès aux métiers de l'administration, de l'education etc. On rappellera simplement la victoire obtenue en 1900 par la loi qui autorisait les femmes à devenir avocat, la possibilité d'élire aux tribunaux de commerce (1898); d'être électrices et éligibles au Conseil supérieur du Travail (1903); l'admission aux commissions communales d'assistance (1905); l'élection et l'éligibilité aux tribunaux de Prudhommes (1907 et 1908). Nous ajouterons qu'il fallut attendre 1897 pour que les femmes puissent témoigner dans les actes d'état-civil et notariés, droit reconnu un temps pendant la Révolution.

L'égalité truquée

Il faut parler de soumission de la femme à l'homme en droit civil. En effet, si le principe de l'égalité des droits de la femme sujet civil ne fut pas remis en question, la femme majeure célibataire, veuve ou divorcée demeurant capable de les exercer, la femme mariée, par l'effet de la puissance maritale, est totalement incapable de les faire valoir du seul fait du mariage: ou le mariage n'est-il pas l'établissement *naturel* de la femme?

a) Le droit révolutionnaire

Pendant la Révolution, certaines mesures qui visent les deux sexes profiteront quelquefois plus largement aux femmes. La loi du 26 mars 1790, en abolissant les lettres de cachet, les libère, tout à la fois, des abus des pères et des maris. Le décret des 8–15 août 1791 supprime le droit d'aînesse et donc interdit d'exclure les filles des successions. Ce texte précède celui du 17 nivôse an II (6 janvier 1794), qui, dans son article 82 (reprise par l'art. 745 du *Code civil*), établit l'égalité dans les successions *ab intestat*. L'abolition de la puissance paternelle et la limitation aux mineurs des pouvoirs sur les enfants les concernent évidemment. Les deux premiers *projets* de code civil de Cambacérès parlent du consentement des père *et* mère au mariage. Contre les pères et maris, la loi des 16–24 août 1790 crée les tribunaux de famille, coup porté à la toute puissance du père de famille. Le nouveau régime d'état civil fixe, en 1792, la majorité à 21 ans. Mais la loi (comme celle sur les successions) qui déchaînera les passions des ennemis de la Révolution est celle sur le divorce, des 20 et 25 septembre 1792. Le décret du 23 avril 1794 confirmera les divorces antérieurs à la loi, admettant ainsi sa rétroactivité. Outre la possibilité de rompre le line matrimonial, qui n'est plus qu'un contrat, la mesure véritablement révolutionnaire est la consécration du divorce par consentement mutuel, véritable expression de la volonté symétrique des époux. Aucun texte révolutionnaire ne sanctionnera l'adultère. En 1792, le divorce est conçu comme une mesure destinée à rétablir l'excellence du mariage et de la société conjugale. Mais peu avant Thermidor, les modérés le rendent plus difficile. Bonaparte suivra cette voie et il faudra attendre 1975 pour que le divorce par consentement mutuel réapparaisse dans notre droit. Il semble que ce sont surtout les femmes qui en usèrent, essentiellement pour cause de sévices.[11]

Si l'on excepte la loi sur les successions et les mesures concernant le partage des communaux, d'abord conçues comme destinées à abolir les privilèges, le droit révolutionnaire contient peu de dispositions sur les biens. En particulier, le temps a certainement manqué pour que soit réglé le sort des biens entre époux. Mais l'analyse des projets successifs est révélatrice de l'évolution politique des assemblées, en ce qui concerne la femme. Le premier projet du Code civil par Cambacérès, discuté en 1793, admet l'administration commune sous le régime légal et rend nécessaire le concours des époux pour disposer de leurs propres, supprimant la puissance maritale. Merlin de Douai le repousse au nom de la suprématie *naturelle* de l'homme.[12] Il fera école puisque les autres projets sont tous en retrait, jusqu'à ce que le Code de 1804 consacre l'incapacité totale de la femme mariée.

b) *La femme mariée dans le Code civil de 1804*

Le sort des épouses sera scellé pour longtemps par cet 'infâme Code civil', devant lequel 'nous les femmes sommes toutes des esclaves mineures par les droits et majeures par les fautes', comme l'écrivait en 1921 la féministe française Nelly Roussel (Roussel, 1932, p 233).

i) La femme est une mineure La doctrine juridique s'exprima avec complaisance et force détails sur les fondements 'justifiés' de l'incapacité de la femme mariée qui, par le seul fait du mariage, devient totalement soumise à son époux. L'article 213 du *Code civil*, dont Napoléon a personnellement imposé la lecture publique au moment de la célèbration du mariage, est sans ambiguïté: 'Le mari doit protection à sa femme, la femme obéissance à son mari'. L'épouse, plus fragile physiquement et intellectuellement, investie d'une mission rituelle, doit laisser au mari la direction de la cellule familiale et se soumettre à sa surveillance, afin que l'ordre social soit maintenu dans ce groupement d'individus, fondement de la communauté nationale.

Protecteur et directeur moral, le mari pourra corriger sa femme: seuls les excès constituent un délit et une cause de divorce ou de séparation de corps. Il peut ne pas l'autoriser à exercer une activité salariée, ouvrir un compte d'épargne (jusqu'en 1875) ou en banque. Elle ne peut, sans son consentement, s'inscrire à l'universitè, faire établir un passeport, passer un examen, aller séjourner dans un établissement de cure. Elle n'a qu'un nom, celui du mari, même si aucun texte juridique ne l'y oblige. Elle doit habiter le domicile choisi par son époux, qui l'y faire ramener par la force.[13] Aucune vie privée ne lui est permise; les lettres qu'elle écrit ou qu'elle reçoit risquent d'être interceptées légalement par son époux, en contradiction avec le principe d'inviolabilité de la correspondance, reconnu en 1790.[14] Si en France, n'existait pas, comme dans les pays scandinaves, en Suisse et en Allemagne, une tutelle des femmes, le Code de 1804 les rendit civilement incapables par le seul fait du mariage et, jusqu'en 1893, la mesure visait même les femmes séparées judiciairement. Le Code civil envisage la situation d'une femme dotée d'immeubles, mariée à une propriétaire ou un locataire. Le régime légal, la communauté de meubles et acquêts, celui du plus grand nombre, est destiné par préférence à des époux partageant un travail (artisans, petits commerçants, petits paysans propriétaires). C'est dire que les textes ne sont guère valables pour la majorité des Français, qui ne possèdent rien et se mariant, et vivent par la suite des salaires des époux, la femme courant le risque de voir le sien dissipé par le mari qui en dispose librement. Comme le mineur, elle doit être autorisée pour tout acte important, ne peut agir seul en justice, même s'il agit de demander la nullité de son mariage ou d'intenter une action en réparation contre son marie.[15] Elle est cependant responsable de ses délits. A la suite de longs débats (Arnaud-Duc, 1989), la communauté de meubles et acquêts calquée sur le modèle de la Coutume de Paris, devint donc le régime légal et le mari en était le chef, jouissant de tous les pouvoirs sur les biens communs, qu'il pouvait vendre ou donner. Mais c'est sous le régime contractuel de la séparation de biens que se vérifient le mieux les effets de l'incapacité générale de l'épouse, encore augmentée par la jurisprudence des tribunaux, qui restreignirent au maximum les pouvoirs d'administration reconnus à la femme sur ses biens, ne l'autorisant à accomplir que des actes purement conservatoires.

Les revendications féministes furent très vives en ce qui concerne les produits du travail des épouses. A la suite de mesures semblables prises en Europe, la France admet, par la loi du 13 juillet 1907, que ces *biens réservés* demeurent la propriété de la femme, tout comme les économies réalisées ou les biens acqui grâce à ces salaires ou bénéfices commerciaux. Cependant, en tant que revenus, ils tombent en communauté et sont administrés par le mari. De plus, la preuve de propriété est difficile à rapporter au moment de la dissolution de l'union. Les praticiens ne mirent pas beaucoup de conviction à l'appliquer et cette première loi féministe demeura quasiment lettre morte. Le pouvoir reconnu à l'épouse de représenter le mari dans les achats courants nécessaires à la tenue du ménage ne doit pas faire illusion: au cas de désaccord des époux, le mari est libre de retirer ce 'mandat domestique'.

ii)   La femme est d'abord une mère La finalité du mariage interdit à la femme de repousser un mari qui l'oblige à avoir des rapports sexuels 'normaux', c'est-à-dire visant à la procréation.[16] Ces principes justifient l'ensemble des mesures prises par le droit pour s'assurer de la fidélité féminine. La 'bonne reproduction' est celle qui donne de héritiers légitimes au mari. Portalis est très clair quand il présente au Corps législatif le titre *Du mariage*, le 7 mars 1803 (Fenet, IX, pp 178–79):

> l'infidélité de la femme suppose plus de corruption, et a des effets plus dangereux que l'infidélité du mari ... Toutes les nations, éclairées en ce point par l'expérience et par une sorte d'instinct, se sont accordées à croire que le sexe le plus aimable doit encore, pour le bonheur de l'humanité, être le plus vertueux ... Ce n'est donc point dans notre injustice, mais dans leur vocation naturelle, que les femmes doivent chercher le principe des devoirs plus austères qui leur sont imposés pour leur plus grand avantage et au profit de la société.

Le droit révolutionnaire, on l'a dit, ne punit pas l'adultère. A l'opposé, l'article 337 du *Code pénal* en fera un délit pour les deux époux. Mais cette égalité apparente ne résiste pas à l'examen de la mise en œuvre de la procédure et des conséquences de l'action. Le mari pourra fair punir sa femme pénalement et civilement sur simple constat de la matérialité des faits. L'épouse et son complice risquent trois mois à deux ans de prison, plus une amende pour l'amant. Au contraire, l'adultère du mari ne sera pris en compte que s'il est aggravé par l'entretien d'une concubine au domicile conjugal, très strictement défini. La peine ne sera que d'une amende de cent à deux cents francs. Si les tribunaux, en jouant sur la notion d'injure grave, rendirent moins intouchable l'attitude des maris quand on s'avance dans le siècle, il ne faut pas exagérer la portée de ces correctifs jusqu'en 1914. De 1816 à 1884, il ne s'agissait d'ailleurs que de séparations de corps, et quand le divorce réapparut, il n'existait que pour des motifs stricts, sanction d'une faute. Comme pendant la Révolution, ce sont surtout les femmes des milieux issus de la bourgeoisie moyenne qui demandèrent une séparation judiciaire, notamment à partir de la création de l'assistance judiciaire (1815). Les ménages les plus fortunés ne recouraient guère à ce type de procédure 'scandeleuse', tandis que les ouvriers préféraient souvent le concubinage, dans la mesure où ils ne disposaient pas de biens suffisants pour s'établir, suivant l'idée que l'on se faisait alors du mariage. Ajoutons à ce tableau le célèbre *article rouge* du *Code pénal* (art. 324) qui excuse légalement le mari qui tue l'épouse et l'amant surpris en flagrant délit au domicile conjugal. Si les textes concernant l'adultère tombèrent en partie en désuétude au vingtième siècle, la France est le seul pays occidental à avoir conservé cette inégalité de traitement jusqu'en 1975. L'interdiction du remariage entre les complices, qui subsista jusqu'en 1904, pénalisait surtout la femme. Sur l'ensemble de ces problèmes, qui consacraient l'inégalité de traitement, les féministes se mobilisèrent. Dès la fin du dix-neuvième siècle, l'adultère tendra à se banaliser et on en parlera beaucoup, reproduisant les clichés, grivois quand il s'agit des maris, excessifs quand ils insistent sur la 'nature' inconsistante, frivole, hypocrite des femmes, il n'en demeure pas moins que, comme le remarue un juriste, la scène devint 'une succursale de l'Ecole de droit' (Granotier, 1909).

Evoquer le rôle reproducteur de la femme, agent de transmission des biens, c'est aussi poser le problème des droits de la mère sur ses enfants. La fidélité de l'épouse allant de soi, le mari de la mère est réputé être le père de l'enfant. Favorable en principe à l'enfant, cette mesure confirme le fait qu'il 'appartient' au père. S'il n'est pas criticable d'empêcher le père de se soustraire à ses devoirs, en restreignant les possibilités de désaveu, on interdit par là, en contrepartie, la possibilité pour la mère de désigner le véritable père, qui pourrait reconnaître et légitimer son enfant par mariage subséquent: ainsi la reconnaissance de l'enfant né d'une femme adultère peut valoir comme aveu de culpabilité du délit, mais non comme preuve de paternité.[17] La puissance paternelle appartient au père qui l'exerce seul, sauf s'il est absent, interdit, déchu de ce droit (à partir de 1889). La père décédé, la mère est en principe tutrice légale mais il peut désigner un conseil. Remariée, le conseil de famille devra l'autoriser à conserver la tutelle, qu'elle partagera avec son nouveau mari. Ses pouvoirs sont également réduits par rapport à ceux du père en matière de droit de correction. Si elle a la garde de l'enfant après un divorce, les garçons étant plus facilement confiés au père après 7 ans, ce dernier conserve un droit de surveillance et son consentement demeure prépondérent pour autoriser le mariage. Si le père meurt alors que sa femme est enceinte, jusqu'en 1964, un 'curateur au ventre' était nommé pour protéger l'enfant contre sa mère.

Qu'en était-il des 'mauvaises reproductrices', des mère d'enfants naturels? Si la Révolution avait accepté comme 'enfants de la Patrie' tous les enfants abandonnés, les législateurs ne s'étaient pas pour autant montré favorables à la recherche de paternité. Le *Code civil* l'interdit solennellement jusqu'au 18 novembre 1912 (art. 340), où les conditions de mise en œuvre de l'action sont très restrictives: enlèvement ou viol contemporains de la conception, 'séduction dolosive' (abus d'autorité, promesse de mariage, fiançailles corroborées par des preuves écrites émanées du père présumé); ou enfin une preuve déterminante et précise, tel un aveu écrit du père, un concubinage notoire, l'entretien de l'enfant, à titre de père, par un homme qui ne se trouvait pas dans l'impossibilité d'engendrer. Seul l'enfant, représenté par sa mère pendant sa majorité, et dans des délais très brefs, pouvait l'intenter, à condition que la mère fût à l'abri de tout soupçon, menant une vie irréprochable. Dans un domaine voisin, celui des violences sexuelles visant les femmes, c'est seulement en 1832 que le viol sera distingé de l'attentat aux mœurs, la violence demeurant un élément constitutif du crime. La conséquence de cette politique est évidemment le très grand nombre d'avortements et d'infanticides. Les jurys populaires répugnaient à prononcer la peine de mort prévue. En 1911, les juristes en firent un délit, jugé par des magistrats professionnels, plus rigoureux: une peine de prison se substituait ainsi aux trop nombreux acquittements. Les campagnes néo-malthusiennes qui se développèrent à la fin du dix-neuvième siècle furent mal reçues et les féministes elles-mêmes n'étaient pas prêtes à réfléchir sur ces problèmes qui touchaient de trop près au rôle de la femme dans la société. Le trouble est également perceptible en ce qui concerne la prostitution. La France, depuis le Consultat, avait mis en place un système qui livrait les prostituées à la toute puissance de la police et de l'administration, entretenant un milieu clos, caché aux regards des honnêtes mères de famille, sauvegarde de l'ordre public puisque satisfaisant à la fois la morale et les besoins masculins (Corbin, 1978).

Le sort réservé à la femme mariée ne doit pas laisser croire pour autant que la femme seule avait forcément une situation enviable (Bordeaux, 1984). Certes, en droit, elle jouissait en principe de l'égalité civile. Mais socialement, elle était une 'vieille fille' ou une veuve. Non mariée, elle devait travailler et le vivra souvent mal. Veuve, elle se retrouvera du jour au lendemain confrontée à des héritiers agressifs, et sans ressources propres le plus souvent: jusqu'en 1891, il n'existe aucun droit pour le conjoint survivant. Mariée sous le régime légal, elle pourra refuser sa part de communauté ou ne l'accepter que jusqu'à concurrence des dettes qui la grèvent, courant le risque de tomber dans la misère par suite d'une mauvaise gestion maritale. Certes, sous tous les régimes, des garanties étaient prévues: hypothèque sur les biens du mari, possibilité de demander la séparation de biens, mais ces mesures étaient souvent illusoires. C'est pourquoi il convient de remettre à leur juste place les craintes qu'ins piraient, au travers de la littérature, les 'veuves abusives', brimant des héritiers pressés de vendre.

Pour une conclusion provisoire

La Révolution française a incontestablement posé la question de la place des femmes dans la cité. Mais cette mutation est traumatisante pour le pouvoir masculin qui avait toujours cru que le pouvoir politique n'appartenait qu'aux hommes. Historiquement, les applications ne seront pas à la mesure des espoirs suscités. Mais la réaction, qui fait mesurer la peur ressentie, sera extraordinairement virulente, et pour longtemps, alimentant tous les fantasmes. Faire de la femme un sujet de droit est en soi subversif, comme le pensent le monarchiste Bonald et le libéral Burke. Trahison de la *nature* et dangereuse pour la société, la reconnaissance de la femme comme individu ouvre la voie à tous les débordements, renforcés par la sécularisation du mariage et l'instauration du divorce. Face à la régression sociale, commencée dès Thermidor, mise en place dès le Directoire, magnifiée par l'autoritarisme napoléonien, triomphante dans la France bourgeoise de l'ordre moral, les femmes comme les ouvriers, devront, à travers les bouleversements socio-économiques de l'âge capitaliste, tenter d'aménager cet espace de liberté entrevu en 1789.

Dans le domaine du droit, les avancées favorables aux femmes sont bien minces à la veille de la guerre de 1914–18. Soixante-dix ans après, dans sa *Déclaration sur l'égalité des femmes et des hommes* du 16 novembre 1988, le Comité des Ministres du Conseil de l'Europe rappelle que la démocratie ne saurait ignorer le principe de l'égalité des femmes et des hommes et que doivent être garantis aux individus 'un traitement égal en droit' et une 'égalité de fait'.[18] Aujourd'hui en Europe, il s'agit plutôt d'inscrire dans les faits des principes établis par le droit, de hâter les prises de conscience, de lutter contre les pesanteurs sociales et contre les mœurs. Les féministes les plus réalistes avaient bien compris, au dix-neuvième siècle, qu'il fallait, tout à la fois, agir sur les principes juridiques en tentant de faire promulguer des lois, et, moins ouvertement, combattre sur le terrain. La lutte est aussi cruciale qu'il y a un siècle. Le fossé est tel entre la volonté d'égalité affirmée et la réalité sociale, qu'il est peut-être bon de s'interroger sur les principes. Comme le remarque bien Elisabeth G Sledziewski (1989b, p 6), le discours semble ignorer qu'il existe à la fois un déni et une dénégation dans l'universalisme des droits, aujourd'hui de mise. Par le déni, on semble ignorer qu'il existe deux sexes; la discrimination, plus insidieuse, rassure de manière explicite et rationnelle. Il convient de prendre en compte la diversité ontologique des sujets de droit, parce qu'ils ne peuvent être assimilés: hommes et femmes doivent 'recevoir la garantie que la différence des sexes et la communauté des droits ne s'annulent pas réciproquement' (Sledziewski, 1989b, p 9).

Pendant la Révolution, c'est la carence du politique qui a privé les femmes de l'exercice de leur citoyenneté, en tant que véritables sujets de droit, capables de choix politiques modelant les structures de la société. Le 29 octobre 1793, le conventionnel Fabre d'Eglantine dénonce ces femmes qui réclament des droits de citoyen, et qui ne sont point 'occupées du soin de leurs ménages, des mères inséparables de leurs enfants ou des filles qui travaillent pour leurs parents et prennent soin de leurs plus jeunes sœurs; mais ... une sorte de chevaliers errants, ... des filles émancipées, des grenadiers femelles'.[19] En 1902, un juriste fustigeait également ces femmes qui veulent mettre fin à l'inégalité: celles 'qui réclament l'égalité totale, tarées quelquefois, irrégulières presque toujours, qui constituent le corps le plus bruyant de l'armée féministe, ne parlent pas la même langue que nos mères de famille' (Martin, 1902). La première *Conférence ministérielle européenne* sur l'égalité entre les femmes et les hommes (Strasbourg, 4 mars 1986) souhaite voir le Conseil de l'Europe 'élaborer de nouvelles politiques et stratégies destinées en particulier à réaliser la participation des femmes, sur un pied d'égalité avec les hommes, dans tous les domaines et à tous les niveaux de la vie politique et du processus de la prise de décision'.[20] Ces textes nous font prendre conscience de l'extraordinaire résistance des mentalités, des sensibilités collectives. Dans les démocraties occidentales, aujourd'hui, il importe d'imposer une véritable parité sexuelle, de dépasser l'universalisme, de reconnaître la différence des sexes pour que disparaisse, dans les faits, une discrimination qui favorise toujours l'individu masculin: 'on dirait qu'à la conjuration de la peur de l'égalité succède la conjuration de la peur de la différence' (Fraisse, 1989, p 201). A une démocratie d'acquiescement doit succéder une démocratie participative, ne reposant ni sur le concept tranquillisant d'une prétendue *nature* féminine hier source d'incapacité, aujourd'hui vue comme un désintérêt pour le droit ou la politique—ni sur la négation de la parité sexuelle.

NOTES

1 Sur la condition de la femme, on lira Duby et Pettot. Pour la condition juridique au dix-neuvième siècle, cf. Nicole Arnaud-Duc, 1989, V.
2 Exposé des motifs de la loi du 14 juillet 1866, sur les droits d'auteur des conjoints survivants, Recueil Sirey, *Lois annotées*, 1866, p 53.
3 Viviani, rapporteur de la loi du 1er décembre 1901, Sirey, *Lois annotées*, 1901, p 1.
4 Cité par Antoine Martin, 1902.
5 Sirey, 1879.1.433, *Cass. crim.*, 11 juillet 1879.
6 Dalloz, 1885.1.105, *Cass.*, 16 mars 1885; Sirey, 1893.1.384, *Cass.*, 21 mars 1893.
7 Sirey, 1910.1.600, *Cass. crim.*, 17 février 1910.
8 Note dans Sirey, 1913.3.89, *Conseil d'Etat*, 26 janvier 1912.
9 *Pétition des Femmes du Tiers-Etat au Roi*, 1er janvier 1789, Bibliothèque Nationale, Lb 39 920.
10 Cf. M Albistur et D Armogathe, 1978 et L Klejman et F Rochefort, 1989.
11 Cf. D Dessertine, 1981.
12 *Archives parlementaires*, Première série, 70, p 674.
13 Sirey, 1812.2.414, Turin, 17 juillet 1810; Sirey, 1825–27.1.434, *Cass.*, 9 avril 1826; Sirey, 1863.2.97, Paris, 11 mars 1863.
14 Sirey, 1877.2.161, Bruxelles, 28 avril 1875, *note*.
15 Sirey, 1851.1.102, *Cass.*, 10 février 1851.
16 Sirey, 1839.1.817, *Cass. crim.*, 21 novembre 1839.
17 Sirey, 1825–27.2.208, Paris, 13 mars 1826.
18 *Note et programme* du Séminaire sur 'La démocratie paritaire. Quarante années d'activité au Conseil de l'Europe', Strasbourg, 6–7 novembre 1989, p 1.
19 *Moniteur*, XVIII, p 290; *Archives parlementaires*, première série, 78, pp 20–22.
20 Cf. note 19.

REFERENCES

Léon Abensour, *Histoire générale du féminisme des origines à nos jours* (Paris, 1921).

Maurice Agulhon, *Marianne au combat, l'imagerie et la symbolique républicaines de 1789 à 1880* (Paris, Flammarion, 1979).

Maité Albistur et Daniel Armogathe, *Histoire du féminisme français*, 2 vols (Paris, Edition des femmes, 1978).

Philippe Ariès et George Duby, eds, *Histoire de la vie privée* (Paris, Seuil, 1987).

Nicole Arnaud-Duc, 'La genèse du titre V du livre III du Code civil', dans *La famille, la loi, l'état*, Irène Théry, Roger Rotmann, Christian Biet, eds (Paris, Centre G Pompidou et Imprimerie nationale, 1989).

——'La mise en question du rapport de sexes dans la cité', dans *Conditions féminines à l'époque de la Révolution française*, Centre Interdisciplinaire d'Etudes Philosophiques de l'Université de Mons (à paraître en 1990).

Hubertine Auclert, *La Citoyenne* (articles de 1881 à 1891), préface, notes et commentaires de Edith Taïeb (Paris, Syros, 1982).

Michèle Bordeaux, 'Droit et femmes seules. Les pièges de la discrimination', dans *Madame ou Mademoiselle? Itinéraires de la solitude féminine. XVIè–XXè siècles*, Arlette Farge, Christine Klapisch, eds (Paris, Montalba, 1984), pp 19–57.

Nathalie Chambelland-Liebault, 'La durée et l'aménagement du temps de travail des femmes de 1892 à l'aube des conventions collectives', thèse, Faculté de droit et des sciences politiques de Nantes, 1989.

Alain Corbin, *Les filles de noce. Misère sexuelle et prostitution aux 19è et 20è siècles* (Paris, Aubier, 1970).

Alfred Dessens, *Les revendications des droits de la femme au point du vue politique, civil, économique pendant la Révolution* (Thèse de droit Toulouse, Paris, 1905).

Dominique Dessertine, *Divorcer à Lyon sous la Révolution et l'Empire* (Lyon, PUL, 1981).

Georges Duby et Michelle Pettot, *La Storia delle donne*, 5 vols (Bari, Roma, Laterza, et édit française, Paris, Plon, a paraître).

Paule-Marie Dihet, *Les femmes et la Révolution* (Paris, Julliard, 1971).

Christine Fauré, *La Démocratie sans les femmes. Essai sur le libéralisme en France* (Paris, Presses Universitaires de France, 1985).

P A Fenet, *Recueil complet des travaux préparatoires du Code civil*, 15 vols (Paris, 1836).

Geneviève Fraisse, *Muse de la raison* (Aix-en-Provence, Alinéa, 1989).

Louis Frank, *Essai sur la condition politique de la femme. Etude de sociologie et de législation* (Paris, 1892).

Dominique Godineau, *Citoyennes tricoteuses. Les femmes du peuple à Paris pendant la Révolution* (Aix-en-Provence, Alinéa, 1989).

Paul Granotier, *L'autorité du mari sur la personne de la femme et la doctrine féministe* (Thèse de droit Grenoble, Paris, 1909).

Pierre Guyomar, 'Le partisan de l'égalité politique entre les individus, ou problème très important de l'égalité en droits et de l'inégalité en fait', *Archives Parlementaires* (Paris, 29 avril 1793), Première Série, 63, pp 591–9.

Laurence Klejman, Florence Rochefort, *L'égalité en marche. Le féminisme sous la Troisième République* (Paris, Presses de la Fondation Nationale des Sciences politiques, Edition des femmes, 1989).

Yvonne Knibiehler, Catherine Fouquet, *La femme et les médecins, analyse historique* (Paris, Hachette, 1983).

Marie-Françoise Lévy, *De mères en filles. L'éducation des Françaises 1850–1880* (Paris, Calmann Lévy, 1984).

Jocelyne Livi, *Vapeurs de femme. Essai historique sur quelques fantasmes médicaux et philosophiques* (Paris, Navarin, 1984).

Antoine Martin, *La situation politique des femmes* (Thèse de droit Paris, 1902).

Françoise Mayeur, *L'enseignement secondaire des jeunes filles sous la Troisième République* (Paris, Presses de la Fondation Nationale des Sciences politiques, 1972).

Stéphane Michaud, *Muse et madone. Visages de la femme de la Révolution française aux apparitions de Lourdes* (Paris, Seuil, 1985).

Thérèse Moreau, *Le sang de l'Histoire. Michelet. L'Histoire et l'idée de la femme au XIXè siècle* (Paris, Flammarion, 1982).

Michelle Perrot, 'De Marianne à Lulu. Les images de la femme au XIXè siècle', *Le débat*, 3 (1980).

Nelly Roussel, *Derniers combats* (Paris, L'Emancipatrice, 1932).

Elisabeth G Sliedzewski, *Révolutions du sujet* (Paris, Méridiens Klincksieck, 1989).[a]

—— *Rapport sur les idéaux démocratiques et les droits des femmes*, présenté au Comité européen pour l'égalité entre les femmes et les hommes au Conseil de l'Europe, Strasbourg, 6–7 novembre 1989 (Séminaire sur 'La démocratie paritaire. Quarante année d'activité du Conseil de l'Europè).[b]

Charles Sowerwine, *Les femmes et le socialisme, un siècle d'histoire* (Paris, Presses de la Fondation Nationale des Sciences politiques, 1978).

Louise A Tilly, Joan W Scott, *Les femmes, le travail et la famille* (Marseille, Rivages, 1978).

CHAPTER 3

Natural Law and Gender Relations: Equality of all People and Differences between Men and Women

Ginevra Conti Odorisio

Abstract

My paper is an analysis of how natural law theorists trace the evolution of the position of women within a particular conceptual framework. This framework is presented as a critique of traditional authority in its affirmation of the laws of human reason and in its claim to the discovery of natural laws. Within this framework, these natural laws are said to conform to the rational capacity of man; they are neither the product of custom nor the expression of positive law, on the grounds that positive law does not always coincide with natural law.

From a historical and ideological point of view, the theory of natural law has the appearance of being very innovative and revolutionary. My conclusion, however, is that this appearance is deceptive. The problem of sexual difference is not passed over. On the contrary, natural law theory asserts that nature is not contrary to sexual inequalities. That is why all attempts at the creation of a positive law more in conformity with natural laws for women become translated into the opposite endeavour. This endeavour is the demonstration that, in the case of women, positive law does correspond with natural law. Whereas for men natural laws tend to be identified with reason, with the critique of traditional authorities, when it is a matter of the female human being, then natural laws are bound up with custom and with all kinds of cultural, religious and legal traditions.

25

Sur l'universalisme de la Déclaration des droits de l'homme

Le bicentenaire de la Révolution française célébré dans un cadre politique européen en profonde transformation, a suscité un intéressant débat sur la signification de la Déclaration des droits de l'homme. Devant l'étendue des problèmes affrontés je voudrais souligner quelques aspects relatifs au caractère abstrait et universaliste de la Déclaration. En particulier G Gusdorf a soutenu son caractère universaliste car 'elle interpelle chaque individu, sans distinction de situation géographique, de race ou de religion, d'appartenance politique ou de contingence historique'; il s'agit, conclut donc Gusdorf 'd'un appel aux citoyens du monde' (Gusdorf, 1989, p 26). Et voici donc un premier aspect du problème posé. On parle d'universalisme et on ne fait pas mention des droits de la femme ou d'un possible appel aux citoyennes du monde. Or il n'est pas douteux qu'aujourd'hui, comme l'a affirmé R Badinter 'une des grandes causes des droits de l'homme ce sont les droits de la femme' (R Badinter, 1989, p 2). Mais, continue Badinter, cela ne veut pas dire qu'on puisse envisager une déclaration des droits de la femme car 'nous aboutirions alors à la destruction du concept d'être humain' (R Badinter, 1989, p 2). Nous sommes donc ici, encore une fois dans une position sans issue, car l'acceptation d'un universalisme théorique fait disparaître la femme, son inclusion fait disparaître l'être humain.

Je crois, Qu'à ce stade il faut faire quelques distinctions entre la forme et le contenu, entre sa valeur en soi et sa signification historique.

Quant à la forme, on ne peut pas nier que l'énonciation des droits de l'homme soit faite d'une façon abstraite, générale et universelle et c'est cela, sans aucun doute, qui a déterminé son succès et sa durée. C'est-à-dire que le neutralisme aurait pu (aurait dû) s'appliquer indifféremment aux deux sexes et cela est prouvé par le fait que, toujours d'un point de vue historique, le recours aux droits naturels, à la liberté, à l'égalité, etc, a été une des armes dans la conquête de l'émancipation féminine. Cela est vrai pour la culture féminine et féministe du seizième et dix-septième siècle (M de Gournay, L Marinelli A Tarabotti, Poulain de la Barre) (G Conti Odorisio, 1979) et cela s'applique aussi au féminisme du dix-neuvième (voir E Varikas, 1987).

Mais quant à sa signification historique il serait beaucoup plus difficile, sinon impossible d'affirmer que dans la déclaration la notion de droits de l'homme était applicable, *sic et simpliciter*, egalement aux droits des femmes. Tout d'abord on discute beaucoup sur le fait si les droits envisagés dans la déclaration sont ceux de l'homme ou ceux du citoyen (S Goyard-Fabre, 1988, pp 42–7) ce qui nous porte encore une fois au point central que si les femmes auraient pu être des hommes, elles n'étaient certainement pas des citoyennes (Condorcet 1791).

Les rapports entre les sexes dans les théories du droit naturel

Je crois donc nécessaire de remonter à une des sources idéologiques plus importantes de la Déclaration pour examiner quelle était dans la théorie des droits naturels le rapport entre les droits de l'homme et la position de la femme.

Je dois préciser que cette étude fait partie d'un travail plus vaste sur le rapport entre famille et Etat dans la pensée politique moderne (Conti Odorisio, 1989) dans laquelle je me propose de suivre les changements théoriques et idéologiques intervenus dans les rapports entre la famille et l'Etat dans le passage de l'Etat absolutiste à l'Etat libéral, ou en d'autres termes dans le passage d'une conception du pouvoir dérivé de Dieu, à celle d'un pouvoir basé sur la volonté des hommes.

A travers l'étude du rapport entre la famille et l'Etat il y a différentes questions qui se posent à notre attention et sur lesquelles je serais obligée de m'exprimer avec une certaine concision pour des raisons objectives d'espace. D'abord il s'agit d'étudier les rapports que se forment dans la famille et dans l'Etat, les théories sur l'origine de la première et du second, les rapports entre les genres, le problème de l'origine du pouvoir politique, de l'origine du pouvoir de l'homme sur la femme et ses différentes explications. En deuxième lieu, mais ici cet aspect ne sera pas touché, il s'agit de comprendre comment, à propos des formes de gouvernement, le pouvoir paternel, défini comme l'autorité la plus ancienne et la plus naturelle, donc la plus juste et respectable dans la famille devient, appliquée à la société à travers bien des modifications et des changements, depuis Kant jusqu'à Tocqueville, la pire des formes de gouvernement.

Dans sa signification la plus vaste, le jusnaturalisme se proposait de critiquer l'authorité traditionnelle et de faire appel à l'autonomie de l'esprit humain pour la fondation d'une nouvelle forme de société humaine basée sur le principe de la raison humaine. Selon N Bobbio (N Bobbio–M Bovero, 1979, p 20) la caractéristique commune de ces penseurs, au delà de leurs différences, c'est dans la méthode, c'est à dire dans la croyance qu'avec une méthode rationnelle, le droit, la morale et la politique pouvaient devenir des sciences. En deuxième lieu ils croyaient que le devoir du juriste n'était pas celui de l'interprétation de loix et des normes existantes, mais la découverte des règles universelles et morales de la conduite humaine à travers l'étude de la nature humaine. C'est donc à partir de ces considérations générales que nous verrons dans quelle optique et si ces règles ont été respectés dans l'analyse des rapports des genres et des droits et devoirs des deux sexes par rapport à la raison humaine.

Historiquement donc, le jusnaturalisme, comme soutient aussi G Fassó (Fassó, 1966, pp 432–7), eut un effet laïque et antithéologique en proclamant l'indépendance de la raison et de l'histoire humaine de la volonté divine. De ce point de vue donc les questions que nous avons posé sont d'un extrême intérêt pour comprendre à fond les différences idéologiques et politiques liées à la différence sexuelle dans le rapport avec la nature et la société.

Grotius et l'excellence du sexe

Dans la conception du jusnaturalisme, fondamentale pour la compréhension de la société moderne, il faut distinguer au moins deux types de jusnaturalisme, le premier l'absolutisme contractualiste d'Hobbes, le deuxième le contractualisme libéral de Locke.

Par rapport à ces deux types de jusnaturalisme, et en particulier sur le sujet qui nous intéresse, il faut reconnaître que la pensée du 'père du jusnaturalisme' comme Grotius vient le plus souvent *défini*, n'a pas une valeur très innovatrice. Comme beaucoup d'interprètes ont noté, Grotius est très combattu et indécis entre une attitude que est une combinaison de rationalisme et d'empirisme et il faut dire qu'une grande partie de son empirisme est concentrée sur la question féminine. Pour faire un exemple de caractère général il serait suffisant de citer que dans sa définition de la Jurisprudence comme de la science sur la connaissance de ce qui est juste et de ce qui est injuste, il affirme qu'elle s'occupe des personnes, des choses et des actions. En ce qui concerne les personnes, il propose une représentation graphique qui vaut la peine d'être reproduite:

> Les personnes sont: Nobles ou
> roturiers,
> libres ou
> sous la puissance d'autrui comme:
>
> Les enfants,
> les esclaves
> les mineurs
> les femmes mariées
> les fous
> (H Grotius, 1625, p 90)

Les possibilités donc d'innovation de Grotius sont très limitée une fois qu'il a convenu et approuvé l'inévitable tradition aristotélicienne de la séparation entre une société où domine l'égalité (entre frères, citoyens, amis, alliés) et la société où règne l'autorité (entre le père, les fils et les esclaves). Il y a donc un droit civil que est à la base de l'Etat, défini comme une 'assemblée parfaite de personnes libres, associées pour être sous la protection des lois et pour leur utilité commune' et un 'droit particulier' qui concerne 'l'autorité paternelle, celle du maître sur son esclave et autres semblables' (Grotius, 1625, p 90).

L'autorité sur les personnes, pour Grotius s'acquiert ou par la procréation, ou par le consentement, mais dans les rapports entre les sexes on découvre une troisième sorte d'autorité basée sur 'la noblesse du sexe'. En cas de discussion entre les parents, le principe juridique sur lequel Grotius se base pour définir la justice est que l'autorité du 'père doit prévaloir, à cause de l'excellence du sexe' (*ibid.*, II, V, I, p 21). Grotius ajoute même que cela est un principe de droit naturel, donc éternel et immuable, mais que certainement d'autres lois concernant le mariage comme celles des lois Hebraïques qui considéraient nulle toute volonté d'une femme où la possibilité de disposer complètement de ses biens dérivait des lois positives et non du droit naturel.

La famille donc est une société entre les deux sexes, mais toute particulière, parce que à cause de la différence sexuelle, il y a des obligations différentes. La femme est placée 'comme sous les yeux et à la garde du mari ... elle est obligée de garder la foy à son mari' (*ibid.*, II, V, VIII, p 217).

Hobbes: égalité et pactes

Les vraies innovations théoriques et politiques naissent du contractualisme absolutiste de Hobbes. Hobbes accepte la similitude entre famille et Etat dans le sens que le pouvoir paternel et marital a les mêmes caractéristiques du pouvoir souverain. Mais le problème qui nous intéresse ici, c'est de découvrir quelle est l'origine du pouvoir de l'homme sur la femme, quelle est donc la place de la femme et quels sont ses droits dans la famille et la société. Il faut reconnaître que la construction de Hobbes est tout à fait rationaliste, extrêmement cohérente, bien qu'elle ne manque pas d'une bonne dose d'un rationalisme qu'on pourrait définir cynique et absolument manquant d'un principe d'équité et de justice.

Comme il est bien connu, Hobbes prend comme point de départ la description d'un état de nature. L'état de nature de Hobbes est un état où règne la liberté la plus extrême et l'égalité entre tous les hommes et toutes les femmes. De la liberté et l'égalité naissait l'état de guerre de tous contre tous, l'absence de certitude quant au travail, à la propriété, à la vie même, qui comme nous savons est le bien le plus précieux. Dans cet état il n'y a aucun principe certain et le philosophe anglais critique le principe de Grotius de l'excellence du sexe. 'Ceux qui attribuent le pouvoir à l'homme' écrit-il 'comme au sexe plus excellent, se trompe, car il n'y a pas toujours cette différence de force et de prudence entre l'homme et la femme pour qu'on puisse déterminer le droit sans la guerre' (Hobbes, (1651), tr.it. 1976, II, XX). Pour comprendre à fond la pensée de Hobbes il ne faut pas croire qu'il soit un défenseur de l'égalité des genres. Son but principal était de peindre l'état de nature dans les couleurs les plus noires possibles, d'en rendre la viabilité impossible, de détruire toute certitude dans le but de rendre désirable l'abandon de ce chaos, l'aliénation de tous les droits humains au souverain et, à travers le pacte, la création d'un pouvoir absolu. C'est à partir de là qu'après avoir établi que dans l'état de nature il n'existe aucune certitude quant à la propriété, que tous ont droit à tout, que l'usurpation et la guerre sont licites, il ajoute, comme dernière et plus effrayante note, qu'il n'existe non plus aucune supériorité basée sur la noblesse et l'excellence du sexe. Cela veut dire que c'est un état que tout homme raisonnable veut abandonner, parce que la loi de nature lui ordonne de chercher la securité, la paix et l'ordre et de faire tout ce qui est nécessaire pour l'obtenir (Hobbes, (1640), tr.it., 1968, I, XIV).

Ce qu'il faut toutefois ajouter et reconnaître est que bien que la critique de la théorie de l'infériorité biologique des sexes avait déjà été élaborée et exprimée dans des œuvres qui ne faisaient pas partie de la culture politique officielle, comme celle de 1600 de L. Marinelli (G Conti Odorisio, 1979, pp 47–68), avec Hobbes la critique de cette partie d'Aristote, c'est à dire que par nature il y a des hommes nés pour gouverner et d'autres pour obéir, devient aussi officielle et sera partagée par Poulain de la Barre. Pour Hobbes cette théorie pouvait être cause de discussions et rendre plus faible la construction de la société politique, parce que il n'était toujours pas si évident qui possédaient ces qualités et qui en manquaient.

Le seul principe capable de rendre la paix et l'ordre était celui du pacte et de la convention, soit dans la constitution de l'Etat soit dans les relations entre les sexes. Pour la constitution de l'Etat les hommes attribuent tous leurs pouvoirs à un homme ou à une assemblée d'hommes. On l'autorise au gouvernement et au pouvoir la condition d'égalité, c'est à dire que tout le monde en fasse autant (Hobbes, (1651), XVII, p 167). Pour les relations des sexes il s'agit là aussi d'un pacte entre les sexes, par lequel la femme perd sa liberté originelle, le pouvoir qu'elle avait sur le fils, et l'égalité: ce pacte est le mariage ou, comme dit Hobbes, l'union permanente avec un homme. Dans ce pacte il n'est pas question d'égalité, la femme perd tous ses pouvoirs à cause des lois qui règlent le mariage: la raison est très simple. Il ne s'agit pas de la supériorité ou de la noblesse du sexe, mais de la simple connaissance du réalisme politique, c'est à dire parce que les 'états ont été institués par les pères et non par les mères de famille' (*ibid.*, II, XX). Le principe fondamental donc est que 'dans tous les Etats qui ont été constitués par les pères de famille et non par les mères de famille, le pouvoir familial est attribué à l'homme' (Hobbes, (1642), IX, VI).

Pufendorf et Locke: droit naturel, intérêt social et pluralités des pouvoirs

L'œuvre de Pufendorf mériterait une analyse à part, que je renvois à une autre occasion, car elle se situe entre l'absolutisme de Hobbes et le liberalisme de Locke. Pufendorf est certainement un des plus systématiques interprètes de la théorie du droit naturel et toute son œuvre est particulièrement marquée par les difficultés théoriques d'établir une raison naturelle et de garantir en même temps la dépendance civile de la femme. En cette occasion je conclurais ma relation avec l'examen général de l'œuvre de ces deux penseurs, en soulignant toutefois quelques différences fondamentales. Pufendorf et Locke ne pouvaient pas accepter la théorie hobbesienne d'un pacte avec lequel les hommes aliénaient complètement leurs droits au souverain. Ils soutenaient

avec force l'idée d'un pacte ou d'une convention comme constitution de la
société, la validité duquel était garantie seulement si les hommes gardaient
une partie de leur pouvoirs naturels et s'ils donnaient naissance à un pouvoir,
qui bien loin d'être absolu, était limité et respecteux des droits individuels.
Dans ce cadre comment se posent les problèmes des droits naturels des
femmes et de leur subordination dans la société?

Pufendorf étudie la loi naturelle dans l'esprit de la formation des sociétés.
'Le mariage' selon Pufendorf 'est le fondement de la société' (Pufendorf,
(1670), tr. fr. 1734, p 189). Mais ce qu'il faut absolument mettre en relief c'est
que Pufendorf reproduit apparemment la pensée hobbesienne sur l'égalité
naturelle entre homme et femme dans l'état de nature, mais, sans la partager
ou sans la comprendre, il la renverse complètement (Pufendorf, *op. cit.*, ch I,
IX). Hobbes avait affirmé qu'il n'y avait pas dans l'état de nature cette grande
différence de force et de prudence entre homme et femme, pour que le
droit puisse se déterminer sans la guerre. Pufendorf au contraire donne cette
prédominance comme assurée, car il écrit: 'Quoi que d'ordinaire les hommes
surpassent les femmes en force de corps et d'esprit, cet avantage par lui-même
ne donne au sexe masculin aucun empire sur le féminin' (*ibid.*, p 192), ce qui
est la même conclusion hobbesienne mais en y arrivant par des prémisses
complètement différentes. Par la suite, Pufendorf en parlant du mariage dans
lequel 'le mari est le chef et le directeur pour tout ce qui concerne les affaires
du mariage et de la famille' (*ibid.*, p 194), déclare qu' en vertu de la convention
du mariage la condition du mari est plus avantageuse de celle de la femme et
que d'ailleurs, telle est donc sa conclusion avec laquelle il retourne décisement
à Grotius 'le sexe masculin est naturellement plus noble que le féminin' (*ibid.*,
p 196) et oublie complètement l'égalité hobbesienne. Il n'est pas contraire au
droit naturel, ajoute Pufendorf, qu'une femme dépende de l'empire du mari,
sujétion qui n'est pas incompatible avec l'amitié conjugale. Il faut remarquer
encore une fois comme le défaut d'une analyse des relations entre les genres
porte souvent à des conclusions élargies de la pensée de notre auteur et
fondamentalement fausses. En effet quand Pierre Laurent écrit que 'la condition humaine, c'est-à-dire d'être libre, appartient à chacun des membres de
l'humanité' évidemment il n'a pas considéré le lien particulier qui existe entre
la femme et le mari, mais d'autre part, en ne considérant pas le problème et
en parlant d'une façon universaliste il autorise une comprehension de la
pensée de l'auteur différente de la réalité (P Laurent, 1982, p 133 et aussi p
135). Toutefois pour Pufendorf l'autorité du mari sur la femme ne vient pas
directement de la nature, ni de l'ordre divin donné par Dieu aux femmes
d'obéir à leurs maris, mais d'une convention 'par laquelle la femme s'y soumet
et qui rend immédiatement le mari maître de la femme' (Pufendorf *ibid.*,
p 197). L'éclectisme de la pensée de Pufendorf est bien évident sur ce sujet à
propos duquel il prétend concilier toutes les théories, divines, naturelles,
contractualistes. D'un côté donc il prétend que 'l'autorité du mari vient
naturellement de ce que la femme y a consenti: de l'autre, que Dieu, pour
punir les femmes, leur a rendu cette autorité désagréable' (*ibid.*, p 198). Mais
en tout cas il doit être clair que l'égalité tant proclamée entre les hommes ne

demande pas la réciprocité. Aucun homme de bon sens—par exemple—précise Pufendorf, pourrait soutenir qu'en vertu de l'égalité naturelle le mari et la femme devraient commander tour à tour dans la famille (Pufendorf, *ibid.*, p 205). Et cela est vrai aussi dans la société, dans laquelle 'on se moque des femmes qui veulent se mêler du Gouvernement de l'Etat: on n'oserait dire du moins, que les hommes leur aient fait tort de les en exclure' (*ibid.*, p 205). D'ailleurs le consentement de la femme est toujours accompagné de la considération réaliste, d'origine hobbesienne, que le pouvoir appartient aux pères 'parce que tous les gouvernements civils ont été établis par des hommes, l'autorité domestique appartient à chaque père de famille' (Pufendorf, *op. cit.*, L.VI, II, p 234). L'analyse de la théorie de Pufendorf de la société conjugale, par exemple, nous permet de comprendre soit sa vision de la femme soit la souplesse avec laquelle les juristes codifient, sur le plan des relations sexuelles, des contracts et des principes juridiques qu'ils considéreraient répugnants d'un point de vue public.

En général, et cela est très évident dans la polémique avec Milton à propos du divorce, Pufendorf affirme que le mariage est un devoir pour la procréation, car si le seul but était celui d'avoir une compagnie agréable, les hommes 'se plaisent plus à être avec des hommes qu'avec des femmes' (*ibid.*, VI, I,m p 216) et 'se seraient mieux accordés ensembles et auraient pu se rendre les uns aux autres plus de service qu'ils n'en tirent des femmes' (*ibid.*) Cela dépend d'un côté de la réalite de l'esprit féminin, peu cultivé, mais la pensée de Pufendorf est contraire d'autre part aussi à l'idéal de la femme savante et il ne pense pas que l'étude puisse améliorer les qualités intellectuelles ou morales des femmes, ou que céla soit même désirable.

Dans une autre étude j'ai déjà analysé la critique de Locke au patriarcalisme de Filmer (Conti Odorisio, 1978, pp 46–56; 1983, pp 37–56, pp 166–9). Je voudrais ici seulement essayer de résumer la partie relative au droits des femmes, et à leur rapport avec la société et les profonds changements qui interviennent.

Les modifications les plus marquantes dans la pensée de Locke relèvent de la fonction de la famille et du pouvoir du père de famille. Locke ne pouvait pas accepter ni l'hypothèse d'un pouvoir patriarcal, origine du pouvoir souverain, détaché et supérieur à la volonté humaine, ni l'hypothèse de Grotius d'un pouvoir paternel fondé sur la procréation. Pour Locke l'acte de procréation ne pourrait donner aucun pouvoir parce que, bien souvent, il n'était pas accompagné d'une véritable volonté de procréation, mais seulement de jouissance. D'autre part on ne pourrant pas parler d'un pouvoir paternel, mais on devrait parler d'un pouvoir des parents, car la femme aussi avait son rôle dans la formation d'un enfant. Mais pour Locke, bien qu'il ne fût pas contraire à l'hypothèse de la séparation des pouvoirs, l'idée d'un pouvoir de la femme était une idée tellement absurde que, par elle même, elle aurait fait s'évanouir l'idée d'un pouvoir des parents. La grande révolution pédagogique qui commence par Locke se situe exactement dans le principe qu'il ne faut pas parler de 'pouvoirs' des parents, mais de 'devoirs' vis-à-vis de l'enfant.

Mais une fois refuté le problème des rapports de l'autorité du père à l'intérieur du mariage, il restait le problème bien plus compliqué de définir la nature de la société conjugale et l'origine du pouvoir marital, ce qui n'est jamais adressé ni contesté.

Pour Locke, en ce qui concerne la famille, des fois il s'agit d'une société naturelle déjà établie dans l'état de nature, avec des rôles et des fonctions codifiés pour lesquelles la constitution de la société civile n'apporte aucune modification sinon l'institution d'un magistrat civil avec la fonction de décider sur des éventuelles questions qui puissent surgir entre mari et femme (Locke, (1690) tr. it. 1948, I, VI, 53). Mais ce qui est étonnant c'est que le rôle du magistrat soit fixé d'avance, et donc il s'agit d'un rôle purement formel, car Locke écrit que, si le mari et la femme ont des volontés différentes, il est nécessaire d'attribuer le gouvernement à une seule personne et que c'est naturel que ce soit l'homme 'étant plus capable et plus fort' (*ibid.*, p 82). Le principe que le pouvoir du père de famille, en cas de discussion, doit toujours prévaloir, est en contraste avec toute la théorie lockienne qui établit que les hommes entrent dans la société civile pour la sauvegarde de leurs droits naturels et que, avec le contrat, ils trouvent le moyen juridique de mettre des bornes au pouvoir du souverain. Or dans la famille, s'il y a un contrat, il prévoit que le père ait toujours raison; si c'est une association naturelle elle est basée toujours sur le droit du plus capable et du plus fort. Les femmes n'ont aucun droit parce que elles n'entrent pas dans la constitution de la société, non plus crée, comme dans Hobbes par les pères de famille, mais par les hommes.

Avec Locke nous assistons à une pluralité des sources du pouvoir qui n'est plus seulement politique, mais civile, maritale, économique, mais qui dans les relations entre les sexes, ne perd aucune des caractéristiques primitives, sinon le droit de vie et de mort.

Notre examen ne serait pas complet dans une dernière mention d'un problème qui continue à tourmenter les jusnaturalistes contractualistes, tels que Pufendorf et Locke. Quel est, selon le droit naturel, le fondement de l'autorité du mari sur la femme et quelle place donner aux Ecritures sacrées dans ce problème? Et finalement cette autorité était basée sur une convention et donc était de droit positif ou bien d'une infériorité naturelle? La question n'était pas si simple et se prêtait à bien des subtilités. Si la femme était inférieure et n'avait aucune volonté, comment pouvait elle manifester un pouvoir qu'elle n'avait pas à travers un contrat? Et d'autre part si la soumission divine était considéré comme une punition, cela signifiait qu'au début la femme avait été crée libre.

Quant à Locke, c'est aussi sur ce point qui se réunissent beaucoup de contradictions. Pour Locke, Dieu ne donna aucun pouvoir politique à l'homme sur la femme, mais il se limite à faire une prévision, un acte prophétique et divinatoire sur la sujétion de la femme à l'homme, 'principe qui est accepté et pratiqué par les lois des hommes et les coutumes des nations, desquels je reconnais qu'il y a un fondément dans la nature' (Locke, ivi, V, 47).

Je ne veux pas terminer sans indiquer quelques conclusions et les possibles aboutissements et continuations de ma recherche. On peut déjà avancer une conclusion après notre analyse: c'est-à-dire combien est erronée l'affirmation des penseuses qui en Italie se reconnaissent sous la diction de la pensée de la diférence sexuelle, selon lesquelles la pensée politique moderne est caracterisée par une amnésie fondamentale sur la différence sexuelle. C'est-à-dire, comme le système moderne de domination, dans sa structure théorique, oublie la différence sexuelle féminine en la faisant confluer dans le paradigme abstrait de l'individu pris comme mâle universel (A Cavarero, 1987). Cette thèse peut avoir une certaine validité en ce qui concerne une certaine historiographie. Mais, comme je crois l'avoir démontré, les philosophes jusnaturalistes n'ignorent absolument pas les problèmes de la différence sexuelle. Il faut même ajouter qu'ils sont tourmentés par le problème de trouver un fondement pour la subordination politique et individuelle de la femme qui coincide avec l'ensemble de leur doctrine.

D'abord pour ce qui concerne donc la théorie des droits naturels, si innovatrice et révolutionnaire dans le cadre historique et idéologique, nous devons conclure qu'elle est bien décevante pour ce qui concerne les relations entre les genres, car, loin d'ignorer le problème de la différence sexuelle, on établit que la nature n'est pas contraire aux inégalités de sexe. Donc tous les efforts pour créer un droit positif plus conforme aux droits naturels pour la femme se traduisent dans la tentative opposée, c'est-à-dire démontrer que dans ce cas le droit positif correspond au droit naturel. Tandis que pour les hommes les droits naturels tendent à s'identifier à la raison, à la critique des autorités traditionnelles, quant il s'agit de s'occuper de l'être humain féminin, les droits naturels se rattachent à la coutume et à toutes sortes de traditions culturelles, religieuses, juridiques.

Il y a, à mon avis, une autre forme de jusnaturalisme rationaliste et paritaire, qui est rarement etudié, à côte des auteurs dont nous nous sommes occupés. Il s'agit de philosophes qui mériteraient d'être recupérés dans leur dimension de penseurs politiques et non pas dans celle bien plus réductive de 'défenseurs des femmes' ou de penseurs 'féministes'. Il s'agit du mouvement d'idées qui, à partir de Marie de Gournay, chez laquelle à vrai dire, on trouve à peine une courte référence à la nature, comme raison, qui impose l'égalité, arrivera à la grande œuvre de Poulain de la Barre. Dans son système, qui pour P Hoffmann, a le risque de tarir les sources de l'intensité heureuse des sentiments (Hoffmann, 1977, p 291) comme si elles pouvaient se trouver seulement dans l'inégalité et l'incompréhension, le problème de l'infériorité féminine dans la société n'est qu'un prétexte. Certes, c'est un des plus nobles et évidents, que pour l'ordre de la nature et de la raison il n'y a que l'idée d'égalité qui soit raisonnable et que la coutume, non pas comme affirmait Grotius, 'une seconde nature', même quand elle ne correspondait pas au droit naturel, était utile pour éviter des contestations et des disputes. Pour Poulain, au contraire, la coutume est quelque chose qui arrive à nous faire trouver naturelles les choses les plus irrationnelles et absurdes; elles deviennent ancrées dans la société à cause des préjugés et du prestige social accordé à ceux qui défendent des causes desquelles on est déjà convaincu. Il arrive donc qu'à la coutume on joint l'autorité des savants; et Poulain écrit que 'je trouve qu'à l'égard du sexe, ceux qui ont de l'étude et ceux qui n'en ont point, tombent dans une erreur pareille qui est de juger que ce qu'en disent ceux qu'ils estiment est véritable, parce que ils sont déjà prévenus ... au lieu de ne se porter à croire qu'ils disent bien, qu'après avoir reconnu qu'ils ne disent rien que de véritable' (Poulain de la Barre, 1673, p 80).

REFERENCES

R Badinter, *L'Universalité des Droits de l'Homme dans un Monde Pluraliste* (Strasbourg, Conseil d'Europe, 1989).

N Bobbio et M Bovero, *Società e Stato nella Filosofia Politica Moderna* (Il Saggiatore, 1979).

A Cavarero, *Eguaglianza e Differenza Sessuale: le Amnesie del Pensiero Politico*, relation pas publiée. Voir *Il Pensioro della Differenza Sessuale* (Milano, La Tartaruga, 1987).

Condorcet, *Sur l'Admission des Femmes au Droit de Cité*, 1790, dans R Badinter, *Condorcet, Prudhomme, Guyomar: Paroles d'Hommes 1790–1793* (Paris, POL, 1989). Voir Thomas A L Diderot et Mme d'Epinay, *Qu'est ce qu'une Femme?*, Préface par E Badinter (Paris, POL, 1989).

G Conti Odorisio, 'Matriarcato e patriarcalismo ne pensiero politico di Hobbes e Locke', a cura di Ida Magli, *Matriarcato e Potere delle Donne* (Milano, Feltrinelli, 1978) et *Matriarcat et/ou Pouvoir des Femmes* (Paris, Ed de Femmes, 1983).

—— *Donna e Società nel Seicento* (Roma, Buizoni, 1979).

—— 'Famiglia e stato nella République de J Bodin', a cura di S Rota Ghibaudi e F Barcia, *Scritti in Onore de L Firpo* (Milano, F Angeli, 1989).

G Fassò, *La Legge dell Ragione* (Bologna, Il Mulino, 1966). Voir N Bobbio e N Matteucci, 'Giusnaturalismo', *Dizionara di Politica* (Torino, UTET, 1976).

M Gauchet, 'Droits de l'homme', F Furet et M Ozouf, *Dictionnaire Critique de la Révolution Française* (Paris, Flammarion, 1988).

S Goyard-Fabre, 'La Déclaration des droits ou le devoir d'humanité: une philosophie de l'espérance', *Droits*, 8 (1988).

G Gusdorf, 'La France, pays des droits de l'homme', *Droits*, 8 (1988).

H Grotius, *Le Droit de la Guerre et de la Paix*, Vol I, 1625.

T Hobbes, *Leviatano*, 1650, tr G Micheli (Firenze, La Nuova Italia, 1976).

—— *Elementi di Legge Naturale e Politica*, 1640 (Firenze, La Nuova Italia). Voir *Sul Cittaddino*, IX, VI.

P Hoffmann, *La Femme dans la Pensée des Lumières* (Paris, Ophrys, 1977).

—— 'La Déclaration de 1789', *Droits*, 8 (1988).

J Locke, *Due Trattati sul Governo*, 1690 (UTET, 1948).

F Poulain de la Barre, *De l'Egalité des Deux Sexes* (Paris, Du Puis, 1673).

S Pufendorf, *Le Droit de la Nature et des Gens*, 1670, tr J Barbeyrac (Amsterdam, V ve de P de Coup, 1734).

E Varikas, 'Droit naturel, nature féminine et égalité des sexes', *Revue Internationale de Recherches et de Synthèses en Sciences Sociales*, 3–4 (1987).

CHAPTER 4

Scottish Communitarianism, Lockean Individualism, and Women's Moral Development

David E Cooper

Abstract

If human rights are conceptually linked to fundamental human needs, then the Scottish moralists have a significantly different vision of human needs than do the economic liberals of the Lockean individualist tradition. In terms of historical acceptance, the Lockean individualist conception of rights has won the battle for Western social acceptance. Historical transcendence, however, does not entail philosophical superiority. Recent studies of woman's moral and epistemological development give us good reasons to believe that the Lockean liberal tradition is deficient as a final account of human rights. Women's needs would be better served by a universalised Scottish moralist conception of rights. Since any adequate conception of human rights must serve the needs of both sexes, theoretical accounts of human rights should judiciously blend the insights from both these Enlightenment traditions.

Enlightenment philosophy was characterised by an optimistic search for transcendent universal moral truths. Whether philosophers of the period relied on a divine light of reason or moral sense theory the goal was the same: to transcend social and cultural idiosyncrasies by grounding moral judgements in universal principles or rights which would be self-evident to all rational moral agents. For example, Scottish moralists believed that because all men of good will shared a common moral sense, the ploughman was as capable as the scholar of apprehending moral truth. These thinkers did not believe, however, that the capacity to apprehend universal moral truths was a simple genetic gift. Faulty nurture could corrupt a man's natural capacity to comprehend moral truths, thus it was important that everyone experience a healthy moral heritage.

We can create a useful analogy by comparing the Enlightenment's faith in natural development with modern ethological ideas about the development of genetic predispositions. In response to a debate about the possibility of *in utero* (or in the egg) learning, Lorenz agreed that a chicken might have to learn element of pecking behaviour prior to hatching by having its embryonic head passively bounded up and down by the beating of its heart (Lorenz, 1965, pp 23–7, 79–83). But this learning may in turn require that the embryo position itself properly, a behavioural predisposition which may itself be a genetically determined adaptation to a stable nest. Evolutionary theory assumes that the development of complex skills always depends upon a sequence of mutually supportive genetic and environmental factors.

Now suppose we intervene in the chick's nest (its normal species environment) by periodically rolling the developing egg so that the heart cannot properly stimulate the nodding movement in the chick's head. Because the chick would miss the developmental stage in which it should learn elemental behaviours required for pecking, when the time for hatching arrived the chick would not be able to peck its way out of the egg. Clearly, the existence of normal adult chickens testifies to the fact that their eggs were not rolled, that is, we can presuppose they experienced normal nesting conditions that 'naturally' prepared them to escape from their eggs. In an analogous manner, Enlightenment philosophers believed men would naturally develop a rational capacity (or alternatively, a moral sense) for apprehending universal moral truths as long as no one figuratively rolled their eggs at some time when they were especially vulnerable to maladaptive learning. By appealing to such developmental misadventures, Enlightenment thinkers could explain away obvious moral deviants, e.g. people with sociopathic personalities. Because sociopaths are exceptions to the norm, we presuppose their early environments were morally dysfunctional. Like blind men, they did not develop the equipment for 'seeing' the ethical truths that are self-evident to 'good' men, that is, men who experienced a normal tribal heritage that prepared them for moral life.

But what about philosophical differences between people who apparently experienced stable nests? MacIntyre argues that the plurality of philosophical traditions proves that the Enlightenment philosophers were overly optimistic:

> ... both the thinkers of the Enlightenment and their successors proved unable to agree as to what precisely those principles were which would be found undeniable by all rational persons. One kind of answer was given by the authors of the *Encyclopédie*, a second by Rousseau, a third by Bentham, a fourth by Kant, a fifth by the Scottish philosophers of common sense and their French and American disciples. Nor has subsequent history diminished the extent of such disagreement.

It has rather enlarged it. Consequently, the legacy of the Enlightenment has been the provision of an ideal of rational justification which it has proved impossible to attain. And hence in key part derives the inability within our culture to unite conviction and rational justification (MacIntyre, 1988, p 6).

Because of the considerable formal agreement between these traditions, I am not yet ready to abandon the Enlightenment's optimism. It may be useful, however, to modify the Enlightenment goal to emphasise a hermeneutic[1] search for increasingly better transcendent 'truths' which in their own turn would need to be historically transcended. A general scepticism about any particular historical conception's claim to be the ultimate truth is healthy and does not entail that progress toward an ultimate or more transcendent conception is impossible. The rest of this paper indirectly assesses the idea of transcending a point of view by comparing how the different developmental paths of men and women create a need for a theory that can transcend their respective conceptions of human rights.

Since males and females typically begin life under fairly 'normal' but different 'nesting conditions', we should expect differences in their world view. It may be instructive to analyse those differences to see what they can tell us about the Enlightenment goal. Does the fact that there appears to be a significant difference between the ethical orientations of women and of men suggest that we should abandon the Enlightenment agenda? Or is it possible that a transcendent position can unite important insights which are found in each orientation? I will argue that although at various times men and women focus on different ethical truths, it is possible to transcend these differences by reflecting on them, assimilating them, and accommodating them. The power of reason to subject reason itself to a critique is the key to keeping an Enlightenment optimism, but it must be tied to a hermeneutical search for successive transcendent 'truths', that is, we must learn to peck our way out of our early nests through a process of comparative self-criticism. Like philosophical traditions, sexual orientations are tribal in a provincial sense only if they truncate our ability to go on and become critically self-reflective. A sexual heritage, a tribal heritage, and a philosophical heritage are all stages in the process of a natural human development that ought to (and can) lead to a series of transcendent experiences.

Piaget's and Kohlberg's research carried on the habit in psychological research of focusing almost exclusively on males, so for years the typical modern description of moral development emphasised the 'content' areas that are of primary interest to men, e.g. justice and individual rights (Piaget, 1932; Kohlberg, 1973).[2] Perhaps it is not surprising, then, that most of the historical refinements of Enlightenment philosophy (which were developed primarily by men) also emphasised this content. It is only in the last couple of decades that academics have begun fascinating research studies on how women come to know about the world (Belenky, et al.). Some of these studies reveal that women typically focus on different ethical content from men, and this in turn suggests that there may be ways to pursue the Enlightenment dream without following the historical path of liberal individualism which was taken by so many male philosophers. Before turning to these content differences, however, it will be useful to review a common developmental path that is shared by both men and women.

Research data indicate that women experience the same 'forms' of intellectual moral development as men (Gilligan, 1982; Kohlberg, 1973, n 5). That is, after an initial amoral stage of infancy, male and female children both move through a form of development characterised by a preconventional egocentric orientation to social rules. At this first level, ought-statements are based on simple desires for rewards and attempts to avoid punishment. Gilligan found that young women with an egocentric orientation focused on pragmatic concerns and personal survival:

> From this perspective, *should* is undifferentiated from *would*, and other people influence the decision only through their power to affect its consequences ... the self, which is the sole object of concern, is constrained by a lack of power that stems from feeling disconnected and thus, in effect, all alone. (Gilligan, 1982, p 75)

Since rules at this level are experienced only as external constraints placed on impulse, a society of these egocentric individuals would resemble a gang of pirates rather than a Kantian 'kingdom of ends' (Kant, 1964, pp 100 ff). This is, of course, to be expected, since it does not make sense to use the terminology of 'political or moral' autonomy with people who have not yet experienced some kind of stable social structure. As Peters points out, 'before one can choose a rule, one must first learn what it means to follow a rule' (Peters, 1973, p 46). Only after we learn to follow imposed rules do we have the necessary experiences upon which to build a transcendent qualitative understanding of the higher social purpose behind rules. To transcend the level of mere acquiescence to imposed rules, males as well as females must come to care about the rules that have been imposed on them. Peters argues that a moral agent:

> must be sensitive to considerations such as the suffering of others or fairness which are to serve as principles for him. For it is not sufficient to be aware that actions have certain types of consequences; he must care about the consequences. (Peters, 1973, p 99)

If caring is one of the prerequisite capacities for full moral understanding, then the tribal heritage that imposes rules on us must also, in some sense, provide each of us with a sense of social identity that can help us transcend our initial egocentric mode. When people are raised in a 'nurturing' tribal system (the stable nest analogy) they should develop what Kohlberg calls a second level conventional oritnetation to social rules, in which loyalty and social commitment become primary motives. Gilligan's research shows that this orientation becomes a dominant theme in the development of many women:

> Whereas from the first perspective, morality is a matter of sanctions imposed by a society of which one is more subject than citizen, from the second perspective, moral judgment relies on shared norms and expectations. The woman at this point validates her claim to social membership through the adoption of social values. Consensual judgment about goodness becomes the overriding concern as survival is now seen to depend on acceptance by others. Here the conventional feminine voice emerges with great clarity, defining the self and proclaiming its worth on the basis of the ability to care for and protect others. (Gilligan, 1982, p 79)

After mastering the conventional skills that allow them to experience social commitment, many people find that the conflicting demands experienced in pluralistic environments push them to develop a third orientation which is based on a postconventional autonomous capacity critically to reflect on and improve the social norms with which they had identified earlier. At this level people finally achieve full moral agency. They become morally autonomous ends with the capacity critically to judge and choose the moral rules that will govern them. This level of individual autonomy should not be confused with the preconventional person's ability to complain about the norms he sees as external constraints on his personal desires. Since the preconventional person has not experienced the other orientations, he lacks qualitative understanding of social relations. His egocentric emotional ignorance amounts to a psychological incapacity which deprives him of the actual freedom to 'choose' moral rules, that is, we cannot choose between options until after we experience them as options. In contrast, third level autonomy combines a new rational theoretical understanding of norms with the previous level's conventional capacity to care about social norms. Together these two developments give people a new capacity simultaneously to evaluate both the rational and the social quality of values. Gilligan says that in women, this third perspective is characterised by

> a new kind of judgment, whose first demand is for honesty ... the criterion for judgment thus shifts from goodness to truth when the morality of action is assessed not on the basis of its appearance in the eyes of others, but in terms of the realities of its intention and consequence. (Gilligan, 1982, p 83)

During the developmental transition, then, for both males and females rules are first encountered as external constraints, then embraced as a source of identity, then criticised and reformed so that they will be compatible with the individual's 'principled' conscience. However, while women and men appear to share these same 'forms or perspectives' during intellectual transitions, the 'content' that receives emphasis in their respective ethical nests is quite different. Typically, women treat relational virtues like 'caring and social responsibility' as ultimate moral values, in contrast to the typical male emphasis on 'impartial justice and individual rights'. Of course some women approach morality in ways that do not appear to be different from men. But in recent studies of men and women who do take up one orientation or the other, it was found that while 50 per cent of the women focus on justice and 50 per cent focus on care, nearly all the men focus on issues of justice (Held, 1989, p 222). The interesting consequence of this distribution of content is that 'if women were eliminated from the research sample, care focus in moral reasoning would virtually disappear.' (Gilligan, in Held, 1989, p 222) We can clearly see this difference in focus in the following quotations from Gilligan's text. She claims that

> ... a principled conception of justice is illustrated by the definition of morality given by Ned, a senior in the college student study:
>
> 'Morality is a prescription, a thing to follow, and the idea of having a concept of morality is to try to figure out what it is that people can do in order to make life with each other livable, make for a kind of balance, a kind of equilibrium, a harmony in which everybody feels he has a place and an equal share in things. Doing that is kind of contributing to a state of affairs that goes beyond the individual, in the absence of which the individual has no chance for self-fulfilment of any kind. Fairness, morality, is kind of essential, it seems to me, for creating the kind of environment, interaction between people, that is prerequisite to the fulfilment of most individual goals. If you want other people not to interfere with your pursuit of whatever you are into, you have to play the game.'
>
> In contrast, Diane, a woman in her late twenties, defines a morality not of rights but of responsibility, when explaining what makes an issue moral:
>
> 'Some sense of trying to uncover a right path in which to live, and always in my mind is that the world is full of real and recognizable trouble, and it is heading for some kind of doom, and is it right to bring children into this world when we currently have an overpopulation problem, and is it right to spend money on a pair of shoes when I have a pair of shoes and other people are shoeless? It is part of a self critical view, part of saying "How am I spending my time and in what sense am I working?" I think I have a real drive, a real maternal drive, to take care of someone—to take care of my mother, to take care of children, to take care of other people's children, to take care of my own children, to take care of the world. When I am dealing with moral issues, I am sort of saying to myself constantly, "Are you taking care of all the things that you think are important, and in what ways are you wasting yourself and wasting those issues?"' (Gilligan, 1982, pp 98–9)

Ned emphasises impartial principles of justice and individual rights because like most males he presupposes that moral agents are separate but equal people with individualised goals. These assumptions fit with the concept of male maturity defined by the ideal of autonomy, where individualism and social separation are accepted as basic elements in adult life. In the male orientation, relationships have extrinsic value as a means for facilitating the male's 'success Dream' (Levinson, 1978, pp 93ff). Morality is seen as a game of reciprocity that each individual must play to protect his right to do whatever he is 'into'. It seems natural in this perspective to characterise obligations to others negatively as 'non-interference', since human rights are treated as the kinds of claims that would be made by rational autonomous individuals whose primary need is to be protected from external interference. As Ned points out, the purpose of ethics is to create a balanced social world where individual self-fulfilment is possible.

Since males also typically see individual interests as naturally conflicting, it makes sense for them to define social justice in terms of the kinds of procedural rules or contracts that are used for resolving conflicts. Kohlberg claims that typical first attempts at contract theory do not have a complete integration of rights and duties, since these theories say that a person in danger has a right to life but that people in a position to help do not have a specific duty actively to aid in protecting the right (I am not my brother's keeper) (Kohlberg, 1973, n 5). It seems to me that Hobbesian and Lockean social contract theory take this male perspective and convert it into a full social theory. Since obligations are contractual in nature, one's specific duty is to avoid violating contractual or natural rights. As long as a person does not directly violate rights, he has no other specific positive or perfect duties. There is indeed a general imperfect obligation to help others, but actions based on an obligation to care about the welfare of others are classified as charity or mercy, i.e. supererogatory actions that go beyond what is required by positive duties. Nozick is the most current and perhaps the most impressive advocate of this approach (Nozick, 1974). He argues that we have positive duties to avoid violating the natural rights of others but that no-one has a positive duty to help others satisfy their rights (unless of course, one has voluntarily taken on positive duties of station by making explicit additional contractual commitments).

In contrast to the male emphasis on principles that protect autonomous individuals by calling for equal treatment, women define themselves in terms of their actual relationships and their obligations to care for those who depend upon them. They emphasise particularised interventions designed to meet the differing needs of unique individuals who depend on the network of relationships. That is, rather than being concerned with legal fairness or due process equality between abstract individuals, women are more likely to be concerned with finding particularised exceptions to the rules to alleviate the differing needs of unequals (a concern that gets called charity or mercy in the male perspective). Goodness is not so much impartiality as it is the willingness to accept positive obligations to help others in the relational net in whatever way the context calls for:

> Care becomes the self-chosen principle of a judgment that remains psychological in its concern with relationships and response but becomes universal in its condemnation of exploitation and hurt ... This ethic, which reflects a cumulative knowledge of human relationships, evolves around a central insight, that self and other are interdependent. (Gilligan, 1982, p 74)

Responsibility or duty to others is defined by the psychological logic of relationships. This means rights and responsibilities are conceptually linked to protecting the social net upon which relationships depend rather than protecting the separate status of individuals. The emphasis is on positive duties to identify and alleviate needs in the relational network. This is especially true during the conventional orientation, since these women see a focus on 'individual' rights as selfish. When rights are associated with 'selfish' fulfilment, however, a conceptual disparity between responsibility and rights is created that must be resolved before one can develop an integrated theory. As Gilligan says,

> ... women's insistence on care is at first self-critical rather than self-protective, while men initially conceive obligation to others negatively in terms of non-interference. Development for both sexes would therefore seem to entail an integration of rights and responsibilities through the discovering of the complementarity of their disparate views. (Gilligan, 1982, p 100)

Because women have historically been a disenfranchised class, they must be freed from the 'intimidation of inequality' (Gilligan, 1982, p 95) before they can fully exercise their right to take a place in the moral world. In a world dominated by male authority, a supporting web of social relations becomes essential for female survival. Thus, women have learned to define themselves in terms of their supportive relational network at the same time that they are being discouraged from participating as individual decision-makers in the world controlled by competitive males. This nest experience teaches them to think that: 'The moral person is one who helps others: goodness is service, meeting one's obligations and responsibilities to others, if possible without sacrificing oneself' (Gilligan, 1982, p 66). From the point of view of moral agency this is not necessarily a positive development. Too often what emerges from the traditional female experience 'is a sense of vulnerability that impedes these women from taking a stand' (Gilligan, 1982, p 66). This deprives them of their right to be moral agents since:

> The essence of moral decision is the exercise of choice and the willingness to accept responsibility for that choice. To the extent that women perceive themselves as having no choice, they correspondingly excuse themselves from the responsibility that decision entails. Childlike in the vulnerability of their dependence and consequent fear of abandonment, they claim to wish only to please, but in return for their goodness they expect to be loved and cared for. This, then, is an 'altruism' always at risk, for it presupposes an innocence constantly in danger of being compromised by an awareness of the trade-off that has been made. (Gilligan, 1982, p 67)

What women need, then, is a social world that allows them to develop as autonomous moral agents, not by acting as men, but by building on their unique capacity to care. Men, in a corresponding way, need a world that allows them to care and be responsible without putting them at risk of losing the autonomy they had thrust upon them by their different nesting experience. As Gilligan says about her research subjects:

> ... she, assuming connection, begins to explore the parameters of separation, while he, assuming separation, begins to explore the parameters of connection. But the primacy of separation or connection leads to different images of self and relationships. (Gilligan, 1982, p 38)

> Development for both sexes would therefore seem to entail an integration of rights and responsibilities through the discovery of the complementarity of these disparate views. For women, the integration of rights and responsibilities takes place through an understanding of the psychological logic of relationships. This understanding tempers the self-destructive potential of a self-critical morality by asserting the need of all persons for care. For men, recognition through experience of the need for more active responsibility in taking care corrects the potential indifference of a morality of noninterference and turns attention from the logic to the consequences of choice. (Gilligan, 1982, p 100)

It is important to be sensitive to voice when we interpret ethical issues. Voice has a powerful influence on the practical interpretations we give to theory and on the theoretical interpretations we give to practice. Is there an Enlightenment tradition that can help both sexes transcend their respective voices by creating a social vision where these lines of development can merge without doing damage to the gains made by either sex? If so, it would be instructive to consider it. Perhaps the tendency in liberal philosophy to deny that there are positive duties of charity is only characteristic of males who have been torn from their tribal roots. Males in tribal settings typically speak with a voice that places a stronger emphasis upon positive obligations to the community. So, if we want to consider a philosophical tradition that is more compatible with both voices, we will do well to consider a male heritage that has strong tribal roots. It seems to me that the Scottish communitarian perspective on rights should be more compatible with both male and female voices than is the liberal individualistic perspective that has evolved out of Locke's social contract theory. Members of the Scottish Enlightenment were careful to contrast their approach with what they called the selfish school of morality behind the theories of Hobbes and Locke (Wills, 1978, p 215). Since Hobbes, Locke, and Rousseau all began with an assumed original self-rule, they emphasised the utility of a social contract for protecting the self's interests. In contrast, theories in the Scottish Enlightenment based morality on man's social nature. They assumed we each possess a 'moral sense' which functions as a principle of social connection. Where moral sense rules, the basis for social intercourse is a bond of affection. For example, Hutcheson argued that moral sense gives us the capacity to see as well as approve of benevolence. It is like an aesthetic sense in that it leads to disinterested approbation, that is, we take pleasure in witnessing benevolent acts even if they in no way benefit us individually (Hutcheson, 1961, pp 42–53). When the main focus in moral life is benevolence toward others, rather than a duty not to interfere in other people's plans, then impartial justice does not serve as the basis for morality.

Scottish philosophy portrays a world that is not based on competition and individual struggles for a place in a hierarchy of private profit. With its emphasis on the universalisation of tribal feelings it can see the possibility for a kind of personal success that does not have to be purchased at the expense of relationships, but instead, can contribute to the well-being of community relations. In this perspective, even the definition of individual rights places emphasis upon the interconnection between self and others. Since individuals are not conceived of as being endowed with pre-govern-mental inalienable rights that need to be protected from the social order, rights can be defined by referring to the conditions that give us the opportunity to be benevolent (to care or help others). For example, individual rights to life and liberty are justified by showing how they are necessary prerequisites for the possibility of benevolence (Wills, 1978, p 213). 'Good men' insist on these moral rights because they function as preconditions for a benevolent life. We can also judge other social forms, like the market-place, exchange of goods, competition, etc according to how they affect the opportunities for co-operative interdependence. They are morally justified because, in creating a need for community, they provide an opportunity for benevolence. So the assumed right to self-fulfilment behind Ned's account of morality (in the earlier quotation) takes on a social connotation when it is placed in the context of moral sense theory. One cannot seek self-fulfilment unless one is part of a social web that encourages the exercise of our highest faculties. But, as any 'good' Scottish communitarian would know, a good life is benevolent social life. Since moral sense is the source of the highest form of pleasure, even if a person is motivated by 'self'-fulfilment his moral sense will moderate any natural tendencies to be greedy.

It seems to me, that the Scottish Enlightenment communitarians come close to emphasising the same virtues as the women's perspective discussed above. And yet one of them, Adam Smith, has generally been considered to be one of the champions of the liberal negative rights approach to duties. Perhaps this is the result of interpreting his theory with the content concerns of the male voice? It would be useful to compare the more common masculine interpretation of Adam Smith with a woman's voice interpretation. Smith is probably best known in Western culture for his famous assertion that the prosperity of a nation is best advanced by allowing businessmen to pursue their own interests in a competitive market-place free of government regu-lation. Pursuing self-interest in a free market will maximise the social good just as though a fairly benevolent invisible hand were directing the outcome. Smith's apparent emphasis upon the individualistic pursuit of self-interest seems to fit nicely with the liberal male tradition that emphasises protecting negative rights to economic freedom among autonomous equals. There is indeed contextual evidence for the liberal interpretation of Smith:

Adam Smith's employment of self-interest in the *Wealth of Nations* ... merely means that Smith was preaching, in the economic world, the same gospel of individual rights and individual liberty which in one form or another was the burden of eighteenth-century social thought. It expresses his faith in the value of the individual and in the importance of freeing the individual man from the fetters of outworn economic institutions. (Morrow, 1927, p 33)

When 'Smith was conscripted to individualist uses by nineteenth century liberalism' (Wills, 1978, p 232), however, his language received an emphasis that was far more individualistic than Smith probably intended. Certainly as a male, Smith shows the usual concern for individual autonomy and justice, but this emphasis is softened when one uses the woman's voice to focus on the contextual elements that reflect his Scottish moral sense heritage. G R Morrow argues persuasively that there is only one Adam Smith:

> ... in the *Moral Sentiments* Adam Smith opposes the egoistic doctrine that man acts only from self-love, and exalts benevolence as the highest virtue. But there are other, inferior virtues recognized, such as prudence, frugality, industry, self-reliance. These virtues must be restrained and regulated by justice, but when so regulated they are conducive to the welfare of the general public as well as of the individual. The important consideration is that these self-interested activities must be regulated by justice. Very little is said in the *Wealth of Nations* about the principles of justice (that was to have been the subject of Adam Smith's projected work on jurisprudence); but justice is of course always presupposed as necessary for the existence of nations at all ... In short, unregulated self-interest is no more advocated in the *Wealth of Nations* than it is in the *Moral Sentiments*, whereas in the latter work the moral value of the inferior virtues, when properly regulated, is fully recognized. (Morrow, 1927, pp 330 ff)

How should inferior values be regulated? R B Lamb claims that:

> In *Moral Sentiments* as in the *Wealth of Nations* Smith makes exactly the same assertion, that he expects men to act first in accordance with their self-interest before thoughts of benevolence. Yet ... in neither book does self-interest eliminate sympathy. The two are universal human sentiments experienced by all men. ... They often exert simultaneously their influence upon individuals engaged in property relations. Sympathy means being able to comprehend and enter into the situation of others, especially into their property and self-interested situation and sensing and then judging our approval or disapproval of their acts. (Lamb, 1974, p 682)

Notice that the ability to enter into the condition of others is a very well-developed social ability. Smith cannot be talking about an egocentric self-interested individual. Smith's economic man is a Scottish communitarian. He cannot only sympathetically understand the lot of other economic agents, he can exercise 'self-command' over his selfish impulses. (Self-command is Smith's way of referring to the capacity to restrain selfish inclination and do what is right). If Smith believes that economic agents do not need government regulation, it is because he assumes that they are already regulated by an 'impartial spectator' in their own breast. To understand the social, caring nature of this concept we must look more closely at Smith's theory of the moral sentiments.

How do moral agents develop self-command? Smith's development of the idea of 'the man within' evolves along lines that are very similar to Kohlberg's and Gilligan's account of the development of the formal levels of moral reasoning. That is, at first Smith says we exercise self-command to gain the approval of others, later he says it is to gain the approval of our own conscience. Consider the following statement from the 'first' edition of Smith's *The Theory of Moral Sentiments*:

> we must imagine ourselves not the actors, but the spectators of our own character and conduct, and consider how these would affect us when viewed from this new station ... We must enter, in short, either into what ought to be, or into what, if the whole circumstances of our conduct were known, we imagine would be the sentiments of others, before we can either applaud or condemn it.
> A moral being is an accountable being. An accountable being, as the word expresses, is a being that must give an account of its actions to some other, and that consequently must regulate them according to the good-liking of this other. Man is accountable to God and his fellow-creatures. (in Hope, 1984, p 159)

In this first edition of his work Smith is pointing out that conscience is tied to the attitudes of our external fellows. In the sixth edition of his work, however, Smith's theory evolved to the point where he contrasted this primitive conception of self-command with a much more mature conception of conscience. Raphael points out that

> The rudimentary stage of the virtue of self-command, found in the child or the man of weak character, depends on the feelings of actual spectators. The higher stage, reached by the man of constancy, depends entirely on conscience. (in Hope, 1984, p 158)

As we saw earlier, developmental research shows that this higher conscience develops only after people pass through two previous stages of (1) forced obedience and (2) social identification with the social order. The 'sixth' edition's 'man within' may represent an autonomous conscience, but it is a conscience that fully understands and sympathises with social existence. Of course, Smith did not have access to modern developmental theory, so he was always uneasy with the elevation of the inner 'impartial spectator' to the level of an ideal observer. He continually emphasised that ethics must be based on the sympathy felt between 'real' people. Because of his communitarian roots Smith also seemed uncertain about how to characterise the relation between conscience and convention. Hope summarises Smith's dilemma as follows:

> If conscience is conventional, the ordinary man can be conscientious, but duty is the slave of fashion. If conscience requires perfection, duty is freed from

public opinion, but the ordinary man cannot be conscientious. His confusion is indicated, perhaps, by his reference in the second edition to 'this inmate of the breast, this abstract man, the representative of mankind', the latter phrases suggesting someone who is not real, yet somehow epitomizes real attitudes. (Hope, 1984, p 161)

Hope then goes on to give a male voice interpretation of Smith's problem. He says that

Smith unfortunately confuses mere dutifulness with virtue, of which, indeed, it forms a part, and hence precludes the possibility of being more than dutiful ... he should recognize the difference between mere dutifulness and true virtue, between meeting an obligation and acting supererogatively. There is no inconsistency between conscience agreeing with a minimum laid down by convention while advocating that more be done. How much more the individual does is up to him and his natural virtue. (Hope, 1984, pp 161 ff)

But, perhaps as a good communitarian speaking in a more relational caring voice, Smith did not want to make use of the male voices' version of the supererogatory distinction at this point in his theory. Perhaps he was being sensitive to the need to maintain the sympathetic relations that protect the conventional order. The impartial spectator must be sensitive to everything that is relevant to a complete ethical judgement. His judgement is supposed to be informed by 'the whole circumstances of our conduct', and a concern with protecting the relational context is an important part of the circumstances to a communitarian. The fact that a moral spectator is impartial does not mean he is blind to the interdependent nature of social life. Smith may have wanted the protection of tribal relations to be a duty rather than a supererogatory act.

Speaking in what I would characterise as a transcendent woman's voice, Onora O'Neill says that when making decisions we should ask ourselves what 'rational needy beings' would choose (O'Neill, 1989, p 306). It seems to me that this is the emphasis we would find in an impartial spectator who was from the moral sense school. The impartial spectator who understands relational 'needs' is going to be speaking with a different voice than that found in an abstract autonomous male. He will have a more sympathetic and caring interpretation of how to best draw the line between perfect and imperfect obligations.

Smith says that 'the rules which she [nature] follows are fit for her, those which he [man] follows for him: but both are calculated to promote the same great end, the order of the world, and the perfection and happiness of human nature' (in Lamb, 1974, p 671ff). What is the perfection of human nature? 'To feel much for others, and little for ourselves, that to restrain our selfish, and to indulge our benevolent affections, constitutes the perfection of human nature ...' (in Lamb, 1974, p 675). A man with this sense of self must have benefited from a rich moral heritage. This is not an isolated social atom hiding from responsibility behind his negative rights. This is a mature social being concerned about the quality of social relations. As Lamb says, for Smith

> ... morality begins with society, the field of moral training is provided for a man in the family first, and then in society and the state; the range though not the intensity of his sense of duty expands as he finds himself rising from small groups to large ones. (in Lamb, 1974, p 681)

Thus, it is possible to see both an individualist in Smith who might speak with Ned's masculine voice, but it is also possible to see elements of a more relational but caring voice in Smith:

> Although Smith gives numerous indications that self-interest is men's rational motive for their acquisition of wealth, their fundamental desire is to receive sympathy from other men for their material as well as their moral situation. They seek wealth to acquire approval. They seek dignity because this will ensure the continuous approval of other men. Therefore 'sympathy' rather than self-interest is the basis of property in Smith's system. (in Lamb, 1974, p 682)

Finally, Smith's focus on self-interest in *Wealth of Nations* may just be part of his empirical approach. He is a practical man who understands how social life functions. We must express our duty in the way that will be most effective, by taking care of those close to us first, since we can affect them the most. As Hope says:

> Equality of interest does not mean, however, equality of attention by one person to others. ... Each person should look to himself first, then to his family, friends and associates. Impartiality asks that everyone's interests are open to the same means of satisfaction, though each person gives prominence first to himself, then his family and so on. So self-interest combines with altruism under the general direction of sociableness. (Hope, 1984, pp 164–5)

It seems clear that the voice one uses to interpret Smith does matter. Elements of Smith's philosophy that recognise our interdependence have been marginalised in popular Western writings. Perhaps it is due to the tendency of male writers to focus on those feaures of his philosophy which are of special interest to the male voice. But, this may not be the best historical interpretation of Smith. Even more important, it is not the best descriptive use of Smith's rich philosophy. An impartial spectator with a moral sense heritage will emphasise our social interdependent nature and our need to support and maintain the network of relationships that make a community of autonomous beings possible. From this perspective it seems simplistic to think of Smith as a modern Lockean economic liberal focusing only on a conception of negative rights. We can get greater normative insight from Smith if we either read him with both the male and female voice or, better yet, with a transcendent voice that incorporates the insights from both the male individualist perspective and the woman's relational caring perspective.

As a developmentalist Smith understood our need for tribal roots. If the Scottish business-man's egg has not been rolled, it will not seem 'natural' to him to benefit himself at the expense of the community's good. He knows his own self-interest is tied to his identification with the community's good, so in acting on self-interest he would be regulated more thoroughly than if the govenment was regulating him. I think it was his faith in moral sense that led Adam Smith to the optimistic belief that an economy based on self-interest would serve the public good just as if it were being guided by an invisible hand. The invisible hand is not so invisible, since it is found in the breast of every business-man who has a developed moral nature.

At the higher stages of development, men and women will both need to imitate Adam Smith and experiment with abstract perspectives (like the 'veil of ignorance' or the 'impartial benevolent spectator'), because to achieve a transcendent vision an attempt must be made to characterise abstract individuals as social and social people as individuals. Just as women have trouble accepting the moral responsibility that comes with the autonomy presupposed in the male world, men have trouble remembering that they are obligated to care about the needs of others even if they are in a male world. Thus, in the search for transcendence, thinkers in the male individualist tradition found that they could account for positive obligations to care for others only if they developed intellectual devices like Rawls' 'veil of ignorance' (Rawls, 1971, p 136 f). Basically, this device forces us to acknowledge that rational, free, and equal abstract individuals would think as though they were governed by a disinterested moral sense. Theories like this one, that come close to uniting male and female perspectives, illustrate the kind of moral progress we should be looking for in Enlightenment philosophy. It may not be a final theory, but it is more enlightened than the individual heritages out of which it arose. In this regard, the world view of the Scottish moralists is more likely to keep us focused on the full range of social values than is the Lockean liberal tradition, because it draws our attention to a proper reverence for community while it acknowledges that individuals ought to be autonomous (or self-governed by a will that is dominated by a moral sense).

NOTES

1   For a good introduction to hermeneutics, see Wachterhauser (1986).
2   For a review of major criticisms of Kohlberg's theory as well as Kohlberg's response, see Kohlberg et al (1982).

BIBLIOGRAPHY

M F Belenky, B M Clinchy, N R Goldberger, J M Tarule, *Women's Ways of Knowing* (Basic Books, 1986).

Carol Gilligan, *In a Different Voice* (Harvard, 1982).

Virginia Held, 'Liberty and equality from a feminist perspective', in Neil MacCormick and Zenon Bankowski, eds (Aberdeen, 1989).

Vincent Hope, 'Smith's demigod', in *Philosophers of the Scottish Enlightenment*, V Hope, ed (Edinburgh, 1984).

Frances Hutcheson, 'Concerning the moral sense, or faculty of perceiving moral excellence, and its supreme objects', in *The Story of Scottish Philosophy*, Daniel Sommer Robinson, ed (Exposition, New York, 1961).

Immanuel Kant, *Groundwork of the Metaphysic of Morals*, translated by H J Paton (Harper and Row, 1964).

Lawrence Kohlberg, 'The claim to moral adequacy of a highest stage of moral judgment', *The Journal of Philosophy*, 70 No 18 (1973), pp 630–46.

——*et al.*, *Ethics: Special Issue on Moral Development*, 92 No 3 (1982).

Rober Boyden Lamb, 'Adam Smith's system: sympathy not self-interest', *Journal of the History of Ideas*, 35 (1974).

Daniel Levinson, *The Seasons of a Man's Life* (Knoph, New York, 1978).

Konrad Lorenz, *Evolution and Modification of Behavior* (Chicago, 1965).

Neil MacCormick and Zenon Bankowski, eds *Enlightenment, Rights and Revolution* (Aberdeen, 1989).

Alasdair MacIntyre, *Whose Justice? Which Rationality?* (Notre Dame, 1988).

G R Morrow, 'Adam Smith: moralist and philosopher', *The Journal of Political Economy*, 35 (1927).

Robert Nozick, *Anarchy, State and Utopia* (Basic Books, New York, 1974).

Onora O'Neill, 'The great maxims of justice and charity', in MacCormick and Bankowski eds (Aberdeen, 1989).

Richard Peters, *Reason and Compassion* (Routledge & Kegan Paul, Boston, 1974).

Jean Piaget, *The Moral Judgment of the Child* (Trubener, 1932).

John Rawls, *A Theory of Justice* (Harvard, 1971).

B R Wachterhauser, ed *Hermeneutics and Modern Philosophy* (New York, 1986).

Garry Wills, *Inventing America* (Doubleday, New York, 1978).

CHAPTER 5

The 'Physical Organisation', Education, and Inferiority of Women in Denis Diderot's *Refutation of Helvétius*

Letizia Gianformaggio

Abstract

This paper analyses certain extracts from a most interesting work of Enlightenment philosophy. In these extracts, Diderot attacks the rationalist and, in his view, pseudo-scientific, method which Helvétius uses for the analysis of the problems of equality in general and of the problem of sexual equality in particular. Diderot's attack is on Claude-Adrien Helvétius' work *De l'homme*. In this work, Helvétius had asserted the thesis of the natural equality of the sexes. This thesis had been derived from his principle that differences between men, with respect to 'physical organisation', did not necessarily result in differences with respect to 'aptitude of mind'. Helvétius went on to give the example of those women, who despite their differences from men with respect to physique, are nonetheless neither superior nor inferior with respect to 'aptitude of mind'. Diderot's response borders on the outrageous, but from a theoretical point of view it is weak. Indeed, his objection remains exclusively at the level of the empirical and, because of that, it is worthless in this case. Diderot simply presents the 'facts'. These facts are 'women's weakness, their delicate nature, their periodic illness, their pregnancies, their confinements'. He proceeds then to ask if all these constraints could possibly afford women the force and the continuity of meditation which Helvétius had called the creative power of genius, and to which he attributed all important discovery. Diderot's conclusion resumes Helvétius' reference to the Sapphos, the Hypatias, and the Catherines as women of genius. He adds, however, that from this small number he will infer only an equal aptitude for genius in both sexes. Diderot is not often so lacking in profundity and rigour in his reasoning. He takes seriously, although ultimately rejects, Helvétius' thesis that men are naturally equal. But when it comes to women, and the natural equality of the sexes, Diderot clearly decides that it is scarcely worth becoming seriously involved in the argument—the inequality is simply manifest.

Ce qu'on pourrait appeler 'la question des femmes' est posée en général, au dix-huitième siècle, en tant que question d'égalité: les femmes, sont-elles égales ou non aux hommes? Voilà le problème. L'homme constitue la mesure, le modèle auquel les femmes doivent être proportionnées à fin d'être évaluées, jugées.

A propos de cette question, dans la philosophie Lumières, l'attitude ration-aliste, l'esprit de géometrie l'emportent encore, de façon que, pour pouvoir attribuer aux femmes la même dignité qu'à l'homme, on cherche à retrouver dans les femmes—ainsi que dans les esclaves, ainsi que dans les sauvages— le trait distinctif de l'homme—à savoir du mâle bourgeois européen. C'est à cause de cela que l'émancipation des femmes, des esclaves, des sauvages est tellement difficile et tourmentée au dix-huitième siècle.

Il y a, cependant, certainement des exceptions; et cette communication vise à attirer l'attention justement sur l'une de ces exceptions. C'est-à-dire les thèses de Claude-Adrien Helvétius, l'auteur de *L'Esprit* et de *L'Homme*, à propos de l'égalité des sexes, et sur les réactions soulevées par ces thèses.

L'égalité naturelle des hommes est un principe absolument fondamental dans la philosophie d'Helvétius. Tous les hommes sont égaux par nature, les différences entre eux sont d'ordre culturel, elles sont le produit, l'effet de l'éducation et de la législation. L'instituteur et le législateur peuvent tout. Ce sont eux, pas la nature, par l'organisation physique, qui font des hommes ce qu'ils sont. L'homme, par sa nature, c'est-à-dire par son organisation physique, n'est qu'un être sensible, faible et apte à se multiplier. Le seul ressort de toutes ses actions est la recherche du bonheur, c'est-à-dire du plaisir physique. Le bon législateur et le bon instituteur sont ceux qui, éclairées par la science de l'homme, à savoir par la philosophie, moyennant habilement les peines et les récompenses, réussissent à rendre désirables esprit et vertue, et ainsi à conduire l'homme vers une conduite utile à lui-même et à la société.

D'après ces renseignements concis, on peut comprendre comment la thèse de l'égalité naturelle des hommes est absolument nécessaire à la justification du contenu et de la procédure du programme réformateur envisagé par Helvétius. Si les hommes sont doués d'un égal penchant à cultiver l'esprit et la vertu, indépendamment des différences qui peuvent subsister entre eux quant à l'organisation physique, l'éducation et la législation peuvent être des véritables instruments de réforme, peuvent espérer réussir à conduire l'homme (c'est-à-dire chaque homme, tous les hommes) à l'esprit et à la vertu.

Je ne peux pas montrer ici comment se déroule-t-elle, dans l'ouvrage d'Helvétius, la démonstration de cette thèse fondamentale. Je soulignerai seulement que cette thèse est proposée d'une façon particulière et suivant une méthode typiquement rationaliste cartésienne; mais je rappellerais encore qu'il n'y a pas seulement, dans les pages d'Helvétius, la démonstra-tion rigoureuse et géometrique (ou prétendue): il y a aussi de nombreuses exemplifications. Parmi ces exemplifications, on trouve la suivante:

> Les femmes, par exemple dont la peau plus délicate que celle des hommes, leur donne plus de finesse dans le sens du toucher, n'ont pas plus esprit qu'un Voitaire, que cet homme peut-être le plus étonnant de tous par la fécondité, l'étendue et la diversité de ses talents. (Helvétius, 1773, II, cap.XII, vol. 1°, pp 153–4)

Ce texte est suivi d'une note:

> L'organisation des deux sexes est sans doute très différente à certains égards: mais cette différence doit-elle être regardée comme la cause de l'infériorité de l'esprit des femmes? non: la preuve du contraire c'est que nulle femme n'étant organisée comme un homme, nulle en conséquence ne devroit avoir autant d'esprit. Or les Sapphos, les Hypathies, les Elisabeths, les Catherines ... etc. ne le cedent point aux hommes en génie. Si les femmes leur sont en général inférieures c'est qu'en général elles reçoivent une encore plus mauvaise éducation. (*ibid.*)

Dans les pages d'Helvétius, donc, la thèse selon laquelle l'infériorité des femmes par rapport aux hommes est due exclusivement à la 'encore plus mauvaise "education"' et nullement à la différence quant à l'organisation physique entre les deux sexes, est proposée dans le contexte du discours qui pose l'éducation en tant que cause unique des différences entre les hommes. On souligne donc que l'exemplification ci-dessus citée est tout simplement une exemplification. L'argumentation d'Helvétius se déroule de la façon suivante: tous les hommes sont égaux entre eux indépendamment de leur différente organisation physique et l'on peut en donner une preuve (empirique, sans doute) en alléguant le fait que les femmes sont égales aux hommes. On pourrait argumenter aussi, analoguement, de la façon suivante: tous les hommes sont égaux, et une preuve en est que les nègres sont égaux aux blancs.

Intentionnelle ou non, il s'agissait certainement d'une provocation déclen-chée envers la pensée des Lumières. Pour deux raisons entrelacées. La pre-mière est que ce passage de l'argumentation d'Helvétius montre que le mot 'homme', dans la thèse générale qui affirme l'égalité des hommes, doit être entendu comme comprenant le mâle et la femme; la deuxième raison est que la thèse particulière de l'égalité entre hommes et femmes est proposée seulement en passant, et elle ne constitue pas l'objet d'une argumentation spécifique. Bien au contraire, elle est proposée comme évidente, en tant que justification, non pas en tant que thèse nécessitante et digne de justification.

Quelle a été la réponse, la réaction du 'véritable esprit des Lumières' à cette provocation? Nous pouvons le contrôler dans une œuvre bien connue et importante, la *Réfutation suivie de l'ouvrage d'Helvétius intitulé L'Homme* par Denis Diderot. Il s'agit d'une réaction, d'une réponse extrêmement significative; d'un essai de confutation qui se prête merveilleusement à une analyse rhétorique, capable de rendre manifeste, de porter à la surface les 'lieux' de la confutation même, c'est-à-dire les prémi que l'auteur juge incontestées dans le milieu des destinataires de ses mots, et donc capables de fournir la base, le fondement de son argumentation.

La façon tout à fait différente d'aborder et de développer la question de l'égalité des hommes et la question de l'égalité entre hommes et femmes résulte frappante dès la première lecture du texte de la *Réfutation*. C'est-à-dire qu'un sujet qui avait été consideré un et unitaire par Helvétius—nous l'avons déjà vu et souligné—est partagé en deux par Diderot d'un coup net: d'un côté nous avons la question de l'égalité des hommes, de l'autre côté la question de l'infériorité des femmes (par rapport aux hommes, évidemment).

Il est à souligner, encore, que Diderot ne se donne pas de la peine d'expliquer aux lecteurs, à l'auditoire, la nécessité de cette division. L'auditoire simplement, à son avis, en est déjà fort persuadé: l'extravagance, la bizarrerie de la thèse et de l'argumentation d'Helvétius sont tout à fait évidentes.

Analysons, donc, le texte de la *Réfutation* plus en détail. Examinons tout d'abord le jugement et l'évaluation exprimées par Diderot sur l'ouvrage d'Helvétius dans son ensemble. Cette évaluation, ce jugement ne sont pas tout à fait négatifs; bien au contraire: ils sont fort équilibrés. Et, ce qui est de la plus grande importance, les argumentations qui justifient les jugements négatifs sont structurées sur la base de la méthode d'Helvétius. Diderot écrit:

> Pour tout lecteur impartial et sensé, avec ses défauts le livre d'Helvétius sera excellent ... J'en recommande la lecture à mes compatriotes, mais surtout aux chefs de l'Etat ... Je la recommande aux parents ... aux hommes vaines de leur talents, à tous les auteurs, etc ... (Diderot, p 358)

Où sont-ils donc, quels sont 'tous les défauts' de l'ouvrage d'Helvétius? Il s'agit surtout d'un défaut fondamental: le défaut de la méthode, on vient de le dire. Lisons:

> Et ainsi de toutes ses assertions, aucune qui soit ou absolument vraie ou absolument fausse. Il fallait être bien entêté ou bien maladroit pour ne s'en être pas aperçu et n'avoir pas effacé des taches légères sur lesquelles l'envie des uns, la haine des autres appuiera sans mesure, et qui relègueront un ouvrage plein d'expérience, d'observations et de faits, dans la classe des systématiques, si justement décriés par l'auteur. (Diderot, pp 357–8)

Dans ce passage on doit surtout remarquer l'opposition entre 'expérience, observations, faits' et 'système'. Nous y reviendrons mais, dès à présent, je voudrais souligner que, sous la plume de Diderot ainsi que celle d'Helvétius, dans le couple 'expérience/système' le mot négatif est le deuxième, et l'évaluation positive se concentre complètement sur le premier. Selon Helvétius et selon Diderot l'esprit de système est une attitude dépassée de la pensée; systématiques étaient les ouvrages du dix-septième siècle. Les philosophes savent bien, aujourd'hui, qu'une assertion, pour être absolument vraie, doit s'appuyer sur les faits. Helvétius s'exprime à plusieures reprises en faveur de cette dernière démarche, mais la méthode qu'il suit et non pas seulement déclare, se déroule d'une façon très différente.

Et Diderot? Sa tâche est plus facile, évidemment, dans la *Réfutation*; en effet, comme il s'agit justement d'une réfutation, il n'a qu'à réfuter les thèses qui ne lui semblent pas assez solidement fondées, il n'est pas tenu à les remplacer avec d'autres thèses. Lisons:

> Dans presque tous les raisonnements de l'auteur, les prémisses sont vraies et les conséquences sont fausses, mais les prémisses sont pleines de finesse et de sagacité. Il est difficile de trouver ses raisonnements satisfaisants, mais il est facile de rectifier ses inductions et de substituer la conclusion légitime à la conclusion erronée qui ne pèche communément que par trop de généralité. Il ne s'agit que de la restraindre
>
> *Il dit*: L'éducation fait tout. *Dites*: L'éducation fait beaucoup.
>
> *Il dit*: L'organisation ne fait rien. *Dites*: L'organisation fait moins qu'on ne pense.
>
> *Il dit*: Nos peines et nos plaisirs se résolvent toujours en peines et plaisirs sensuels. *Dites*: assez souvent.
>
> *Il dit*: Tous ceux qui entendent une vérité l'auraient pu découvrir. *Dites*: Quelques-uns.
>
> *Il dit*: Les femmes sont susceptibles de la même éducation que les hommes. *Dites*: On pourrait les élever mieux qu'on ne fait. (Diderot, pp 356–7)

Un autre passage de la *Réfutation* résume très bien, à mon avis, cette longue liste de thèses en opposition:

> D'où je conclus que toutes ces assertions sont hasardées, et que pour les accuser d'erreur ou les admettre comme des vérités, nous avons besoin d'observations très fines qui n'ont jamais été faites, et qui ne se feront peut-être jamais. (Diderot, p 322)

Nous avons déjà lu, dans la liste de thèses en opposition que nous venons de citer, un passage concernant la question des femmes. Dans ce passage Diderot expose son idée que l'on n'est pas en état de justifier le principe général selon lequel les femmes seraient susceptibles de la même éducation que les hommes. En effet, pourrait-on ajouter, il n'y a pas d'évidences empiriques de cette thèse générale, justement parce que nulle évidence empirique ne peut jamais suffire à fonder une thèse générale. Mais cependant, c'est l'avis de Diderot, le fait demeure que l'éducation des femmes pourrait bien être meilleure. Il s'agit d'une conclusion pleine de bon sens, ainsi que toutes les autres dans la liste.

Mais il n'y a pas seulement ces deux lignes, dans la *Réfutation*, sur l'éducation des femmes. Il y en a d'autres. Lisons:

> *Les femmes de génie sont rares.* D'accord. *Elles sont mal élevées.* Très-mal. Mais leur organisation délicate, mais leur assujettissement à une maladie périodique, à des grossesses, à des couches, leur permettent-ils cette force et cette continuité de méditation que vous appelez la créatrice du génie et à laquelle vous attribuez toute importante découverte? Elles font les premiers pas plus vite, mais elles sont plutôt lasses et s'arrêtent plus promptement. Moins nous en espérons, plus nous sommes faciles à contenter. Les femmes et les grands s'illustrent à peu de frais: ils ne sont entourés que de flatteurs. Le petit nombre de femmes de génie fait exception et non pas règle. (Diderot, p 319)

Et encore:

> Quoi donc! est-ce l'éducation et le préjugé seuls qui rendent en général les femmes craintives et pusillanimes ou la conscience de leur faiblesse, conscience qui leur est commune avec tous les animaux délicats, conscience qui met l'un en fuite au moindre bruit, et arrête l'autre fièrement à l'aspect du péril et de l'ennemi. (Diderot, p 330)

Et ensuite:

> *Il dit:* Les Sappho, les Hypatie, les Catherine furent des femmes de génie. *Ajoutez:* Et de ce petit nombre j'en conclurai une égale aptitude au génie dans l'un et dans l'autre sexe, et qu'une hirondelle fait le printemps. (Diderot, p 361)

Et enfin, ce morceau étonnant sur la dévotion des femmes:

> L'incrédulité est aussi commune chez les femmes que chez les hommes, elle y est un peu moins raisonnée, mais elle y est presque aussi ferme. (Diderot, p 436)

Dans tous ces passages l'allure et l'attitude demeurent les mêmes que dans la longue liste de thèses en opposition, les mêmes que dans toute la *Réfutation*. C'est toujours la réponse du bon sens, à savoir du sens commun, aux exagérations d'un esprit imbu d'un radicalisme outré. Or, on peut bien le comprendre, l'égalité absolue, l'égalité de tout le monde quant à une aptitude à l'esprit, à la vertu, au génie, est certainement une thèse dangereusement radicale, à laquelle le sens commun de la philosophie, au dix-huitième siècle, n'est pas prêt. Mais je voudrais souligner ici les lieux communs, c'est-à-dire les prémisses, de la *Réfutation* au sujet de l'égalité.

Nous avons parlé, ci-dessus, d'une dissociation operée par Diderot par rapport à l'argumentation d'Helvétius. En effet, on aura certainement remarqué que Diderot fait deux questions différentes (la question de l'égalité des hommes et la question de l'infériorité des femmes) de ce que Helvétius avait posé comme question et exemplification. Et il le fait sans le mettre en évidence. Le premier point à souligner par l'interprète est bien, donc, une manque de justification. Quoique le texte de la *Réfutation* suive en général l'allure de l'argumentation d'Helvétius, et quoique au contraire, dans ce cas particulier, Diderot modifie considérablement la structure de l'argumentation d'Helvétius, il juge qu'il ne vaut pas la peine de s'en justifier. La première conclusion qu'on peut tirer de l'argumentation de Diderot est, donc, celle-ci: que, en débattant la question de l'égalité des hommes, le mot 'homme' signifie mâle, rien que cela. Il en résulte deux questions différentes: la question de l'égalité des hommes et la question du rapport entre hommes et femmes.

De cette première remarque en découle aisément une autre; le lieu commun concernant la définition du mot 'homme' entraîne un second lieu: le lieu de l'infériorité naturelle des femmes. Puisque 'lieu' veut dire prémisse d'argumentation, encore une fois nous pouvons extraire le lieu d'un défaut d'argumentation.

Une caractéristique tout à fait évidente est commune aux trois passages de Diderot cités ci-dessus: le passage de l'exception, celui de l'hirondelle, celui des animaux craintifs et pusillanimes. Il s'agit là de l'apriorisme méthodologique, de cette déplorable attitude systématique rationaliste (à la place de l'attitude empirique qui avait été si louée jusquà ce moment là). Il s'agit au juste de cet apriorisme reproché à Helvétius, celui que Helvétius avait proclamé sans le suivre (et Diderot l'avait remarqué, bien sûr). Et Diderot? Diderot, on l'a vu, réussit dans la plupart des cas (grâce surtout au domaine étroitement borné de la confutation pure et dure) à être bien plus contrôlé et équilibré. Nous l'avons vu dans la longue liste de thèses en opposition.

Il y réussit souvent, mais pas toujours. Dans un cas du moins, Helvétius dit quelque chose d'énorme, de sorte que Diderot ne peut pas s'empêcher de riposter fâché:

> Une femme de génie? Quoi donc! C'est évidemment exception et non pas règle; C'est l'hirondelle qui ne fait pas le printemps; c'est un cas eventuel qui ne touche pas la thèse générale que toutes les femmes sont faibles, craintives et pusillanimes.

S'agit-il d'une thèse *générale*? *Toutes* les femmes? on peut rétorquer contre Diderot les même impeccables argumentations qu'il porte contre la méthode d'Helvétius. Ce que l'on doit souligner avec force, c'est la contradiction inhérente à la *Réfutation*. Diderot procède dans l'analyse de la thèse de Helvétius sur l'égalité des sexes d'une façon tout à fait différente de celle qu'il utilise pour analyser le principe de l'égalité naturelle et de l'omnipotence de la législation. En effet au moment où Diderot examine la thèse d'Helvétius sur l'égalité des deux sexes, il ne se borne pas seulement à la réfuter comme insuffisamment fondée, mais il avance, lui-même, une thèse générale opposée:

c'est-à-dire l'infériorité naturelle des femmes. Mais sur quelles évidences s'appuie cette thèse? Peut-on demontrer cette thèse avec des faits? Diderot ne répond pas.

Pourquoi l'existence des femmes de génie (en tant qu'exception) ne pourrait-t-elle démontrer la puissance, sinon l'omnipotence—selon l'opinion de Diderot—de l'éducation? Pourquoi donc, si le principe général qui admet que les femmes sont susceptibles de recevoir la même éducation que les hommes n'a aucun fondement, en aurait un la thèse opposée? Diderot ne semble pas se poser la question. Le bon sens, le sens commun des philosophes n'en a pas besoin. On ne discute pas l'évidence.

La manque de justification de cette thèse sur l'infériorité des femmes (et des corollaires qui en découlent) ressort particulièrement dans le dernier passage de la *Réfutation* ci-dessus citée: le passage de la dévotion des femmes. En vieillissant, avait-il écrit Helvétius, les femmes deviennent dévotes. Diderot répond: cela n'arrive plus. Aujourd'hui les femmes ont appris à tirer profit soit de leur beauté durant la jeunesse soit de l'expérience dans l'âge mûr. Elles préfèrent rire des sottises commises pendant leur jeunesse avec des amis intimes, plutôt qu'en pleurer aux pieds d'un prêtre. En effet—il conclut:

> l'incrédulité est aussi commune chez les femmes que chez les hommes, elle y est un peu moins raisonnée, ma elle y est presque aussi ferme.

Un peu moins raisonnée, donc. Cette remarque est dépourvue de toute justification dans le contexte. Elle est, en plus, gratuite parce qu'elle n'a pas été requise. En s'opposant à l'image grotesque évoquée par Helvétius, Diderot écrit que les femmes aussi participient de l'esprit des Lumières; toutefois sa réponse demeure comme réaction aux excès d'un philosophe foncièrement matérialiste. Il ne sait pas s'empêcher (et il ne le veut pas) d'estomper l'affirmation qu'il vient de faire en objectant immédiatement que avoir la même opinion n'entraîne pas nécessairement avoir la même abilité de la justifier rationnellement. Le peu de mots ('elle y est un peu moins raisonnée') n'ajoutent ni enlèvent rien au raisonnement au point de vue logique, mai au point de vue rhétorique cela est d'une efficacité extraordinaire. Ces mots servent et suffisent à confirmer que Diderot veut se ranger 'du bon côté'.

De ces 'lieux' de la *Réfutation* de Diderot découlent d'autres critiques adressées par le philosophe à quelques propositions d'Helvétius; critiques qui apparaissent en fonction d'objectifs de pure et simple conservation sociale. Diderot par exemple critique la thèse d'Helvétius de la supériorité de l'éducation publique sur l'éducation privée. Helvétius avait encore demandé l'institution du divorce sans limitations:

> Deux époux cessent-ils de s'aimer, commencent-ils à se hair? Pourquoi les condamner à vivre ensemble? (Helvétius, 1773, VIII, note 3, vol 2, pp 272–3)

A son avis, en effet, le mariage monogamique, indissoluble n'est pas la meilleure forme de mariage: c'est seulement ce qu'il convient à une communauté de paysans où:

> les conjoints occupés du même objet, c'est-à-dire de l'amélioration de leur terres, se voient peu, sont à l'abri de l'ennui, par conséquent du dégoût. (Helvétius, 1773, IX, note 6, vol 2°, p 490)

Devant cette affirmation Diderot s'indigne, cela va sans dire. Il se déclare naturellement contraire à l'introduction du divorce pour le bien des enfants, sans même se donner le mal de discuter la thèse d'Helvétius sur la relativité historique du mariage et de la famille en tant qu'institutions.

Et pourtant dans la théorie d'Helvétius demeure quelque chose qui, pour la plupart des critiques, nie carrément le principe de l'égalité entre les sexes. Helvétius propose des prix pour la vertu et le génie; et à côté des titres, des honneurs, des terres les plus fertiles, des mets les plus savoureux, il place en tant que prix les femmes les plus belles. Diderot s'insurge devant cette proposition, après avoir dit des femmes ce que l'on a vu précédemment:

> Quelque avantage qu'on imagine à priver les femmes de la propriété de leur corps, pour en faire un effet public, c'est une espèce de tyrannie dont l'idée me révolte, une manière raffinée d'accroître leur servitude qui n'est déjà que trop grande. (Diderot, p 294)

Sur son sillage, la plupart des exégèes se sont montrés à cet égard carrément et dûment scandalisés. Par contre les estimateurs d'Helvétius ont toujours préféré glisser sur ces passages, non sans un certain embarras. A mon avis cette proposition est tout simplement une conséquence évidente des thèses d'Helvétius sur les rapports entre bonheur et plaisir et entre droit et bonheur. En accusant, tout court, Helvétius d'antiféminisme—pour cette proposition—on décharge sur ses épaules le poids d'une culture et d'une civilisation antiféministe. Cette culture se réflète aussi sur les emplois linguistiques: d'un tout premier abord la polysémie du mot 'homme'.

Mais on a déjà vu précédemment que la définition explicite qu'Helvétius donne du mot 'homme' ne se prête pas à l'équivoque de vouloir signifier par 'homme' le mâle seulement. Et, encore, lisons ce passage d'Helvétius:

> Les femmes, chez les Gélons, étaient obligées par la loi à faire tous les ouvrages de force, comme de bâtir les maisons et de cultiver la terre; mais en dédommagement de leurs peines, la même loi leur accordait cette douceur, de pouvoir coucher avec tout guerrier qui leur était agréable. Les femmes étaient fort attachées à cette loi. (Helvétius, 1758, III, cap XV, p 364)

Diderot, on peut bien le comprendre, ne fait aucune mention de ce passage, tandis qu'il cite plusieures fois (pour étaler son dédain à leur égard, bien sûr!) les passages d'Helvétius sur les 'belles esclaves'.

REFERENCES

C-A Helvetius, *De l'Esprit*, A Paris, chez Durans, Libraire, rue de Foin, MDCCLVIII, avec approbation et privilège du Roi.

M Helvétius, *De l'Homme, de ses facultés intellectuelles, et de son éducation*, Ouvrage posthume, Londres, chez la Société Typographyque, 1773, 2 vols.

D Diderot, *Réfutation suivie de l'ouvrage d'Helvétius intitulé L'Homme*, in ID, *Oeuvres complètes*, ed Assézat et Tourneux, Paris, 20 vols, 1875–7, vol 2°, pp 275–456.

CHAPTER 6

Early European Feminism and American Women

Leslie Friedman Goldstein

Abstract

To early-nineteenth-century Europeans, the US offered an intriguing observation laboratory where the political values of liberty and equality were being
actualised. In addition, by the middle of the nineteenth century, Europeans
perceived America as the birthplace of a modern feminist movement. It is
perhaps no coincidence that two of the leading feminist theorists of the early
nineteenth century, Frances (Fanny) Wright and Harriet Martineau, both
participated in the rather widespread nineteenth-century practice of authoring
studies of democracy in America.

This essay examines these women's reflections on American women, American gender relations, and American democracy. The paper argues that these
two authors exemplify what have now come to be viewed as the two alternative intellectual traditions shaping American political history. Wright
(despite the radicalism of her communitarian utopian views) evidently shares
the heritage of the classical, virtuous republic tradition, while Martineau fits
easily into the tradition of liberal individualism that dates back to the doctrine
of Hobbes, Locke, and Hume. For both Wright and Martineau, their overarching political ideology appears to have shaped their feminism, rather than
the other way around.

To early-nineteenth-century Europeans, the US offered an intriguing observation laboratory where the political values of liberty and equality were being

actualised. In addition, by the middle of the nineteenth century, Europeans perceived America as the birthplace of a modern feminist movement (Rossi, 1970, pp 93–6; R Evans, 1977, p 44; Hecht, 1947, p 35; Koht, 1949, pp 45–54). It is perhaps no coincidence that two of the leading feminist theorists of the early nineteenth century, Frances (Fanny) Wright[1] and Harriet Martineau[2] both participated in the rather widespread nineteenth-century practice of authoring studies of democracy in America. It appears that for both of these authors, their feminism arose independently of their study of America. On the other hand, their feminism certainly informed their books on America, and one can gain useful insights into early feminist theory by a close look at these women's reflections upon American women, American gender relations, and American democracy.

Both Martineau and Wright were Enlightenment feminists; this is most plainly evident in their lengthy and frequent diatribes against the wave of 'superstitious' religious enthusiasm washing over particularly the women of America.[3] Moreover, each author was ahead of her time in the sense of predating, as well as wielding influence upon, the nineteenth-century feminist movement in America, which did not really gather momentum until the middle of the century.[4] Yet, peculiarly enough, despite their shared roots in British Enlightenment thought, these two authors exemplify what have now come to be viewed as the two alternative intellectual traditions shaping American political history.[5] Wright (despite the radicalism of her communitarian utopian views) evidently shares the heritage of the classical, virtuous republic tradition, while Martineau fits easily into the tradition of liberal individualism that dates back to the doctrines of Hobbes, Locke, and Hume. For both Wright and Martineau, their overarching political ideology appears to have shaped their feminism, rather than the other way around.

Frances Wright

Frances Wright's reflections on women and gender relations within American democracy went through at least three phases.[6] In her first phase, exhibited by the 1821 volume, *Views of Society and Manners in America*, Wright portrayed what she was later to describe as having been an idealised image of America. What is intriguing here is not so much the fact that she later reassessed the reality but rather that she rather dramatically altered her own vision of what would be ideal. In this phase the virtuous republic of Wright's idealisation was one displaying the virtue of a Christian Sparta. In America, young women were outspoken and remarkably independent, socialising freely and frequently with young men and nonetheless having the self-reliance to remain chaste. American men were, by European standards, remarkably deferential to women, shielding them from gross language, gross masculine habits like smoking and drinking, arduous outdoor labour, and masculine pursuits in general. In the same vein, American husbands were more faithful in marriage than Europeans, and American men refrained from rape to a degree that allowed women freedom to travel alone in safety. This was in marked contrast to the situation in European society. Americans were remarkably strict about sexual morality, both in word and deed (1821, pp 23–5, 33, 68, 69, 219–20).

It is not unusual that Frances Wright characterised American gender relations this way; one finds a striking consensus within the European travel literature of this period that these were indeed the facts of American life. What is at least a little remarkable is that Wright *praises* these chivalrous and strict gender relations. Only six and a half years later Frances Wright was to be advocating free love in the American press (see note 6 above).

In this 1821 phase, the feminist message in Fanny Wright's work centred on women's need for education. She noted that women's education 'Hitherto ... has been but slightly attended to' and endorsed the argument of Benjamin Rush to the effect that a successful republic must provide education in political principles to the future mothers of its male citizenry (1821, pp 22–3, 218). Although to date that had not been done, Wright noted that the New England states had made progress in that regard, and that 'public attention is now everywhere turned to the improvement of female education' (1821, pp 217–18).

Wright added another dimension, however, to Rush's woman-as-republican-mother argument. She noticed that American marriages often faced the problem that husbands had studied 'philosophy, history, political economy, and the exact sciences', while wives' learning had been limited to the supposedly 'ornamental' studies of 'French, Italian, dancing, and drawing'. Thus the married couple shared less in the way of common interests than was desirable in a marriage (1821, pp 218–21). The education of women for the improvement of marriage was to become a common theme in nineteenth-century feminism, and indeed, Wright continued to insist on the point in her later lectures (1834a, pp 24, 31).

In the midst of Wright's 1821 discussion of the need to improve both women's mental and physical education appears a truly extraordinary passage on the extent to which women are oppressed the world over:

> In the happiest country their condition is sufficiently hard. Have they talents? It is difficult to turn them to account. Ambition? The road to honorable distinction is shut against them. A vigorous intellect? It is broken down by sufferings, bodily and mental. The lords of creation receive innumerable, incaluable advantages from the hand of nature, and it must be admitted that they everywhere take sufficient care to foster the advantages with which they are endowed. ... [M]en husband with jealousy that which nature has enabled them to usurp over the daughters of Eve. ... [The majority of men] soothe their self-love by considering the weakness of others rather than their own strength. You will say this is severe; is it not true? In what consists the greatness of a despot? In his own intrinsic merits? No, in the degradation of the multitude who surround him. What feeds the vanity of the patrician? ... 'But what', I hear you ask, 'has this to do with the condition of women? Do you mean to compare men collectively to the despot and the patrician?' Why not? The vanity of the despot and the patrician is fed

by the folly of their fellow men, and so is that of their sex collectively soothed by the dependence of women: it pleases them better to find in their companion a fragile vine, clinging to their firm trunk for support, than a vigorous tree with whose branches they may mingle theirs. ... [When I think of women's suffering, I feel] ... disposed to sigh. Born to endure the worst afflictions of fortune, they are enervated in soul and body lest the storm should not visit them sufficiently rudely. Instead of essaying to counteract the unequal law of nature, it seems the object of man to visit it upon his weaker helpmate more harshly. It is well, however, that his folly recoils upon his own head, and that the fate of the sexes is so entwined that the dignity of the one must rise or fall with that of the other. (1821, pp 220–1)

Wright concludes this remarkable condemnation of manhood on the optimistic note:

In America much certainly is done to ameliorate the condition of women [referring apparently to the chivalrous deference toward women, which she had discussed just prior to this passage, at 218-220], and, as their education shall become, more and more, the concern of the state, their character may aspire in each generation to a higher standard. (1821, p 221)

Her awareness that men in a political republic might nonetheless behave despotically toward women evidently influenced a shift of emphasis in Wright's work. By 1834, Wright's understanding of the virtuous republic had evolved away from the emphasis on purity of morals and toward an emphasis on homogeneity of interest. This interest had to be prompted by an educational system that would be available nationwide, irrespective of class, race, gender, or religious creed. This educational system would have to be arranged by state legislatures (1834a, pp 114–15) and was necessary if America were ever to live up to the principles of her Declaration of Independence:

[E]qual rights must originate in equal condition ... equal condition must originate in equal knowledge, and that sound knowledge; in similar habits, and those good habits; in brotherly sympathies, and those fostered from youth [by the education system] ... (1834a, p 217)

To achieve *effective* equality of rights, Fanny Wright insisted, a society must provide 'a just and similar training of the thoughts, feelings, and habits of human beings.' 'Legislators may enact statutes, but wise education alone, by awakening just views, and forming just habits, can produce a rational and really republican state of society' (1834a, p 218). Her thinking was that if men and women were raised to feel themselves members of a single, homogeneous group, without opposed group interests, group oppression (whether of rich over poor or of men over women) could be ended.

Wright's emphasis on education in this second volume bespoke concerns that ranged far beyond the typical enlightenment faith in learning. Her concern with the providing for the habituation of a republican citizenry paralleled that of classical writers such as Plato and Aristotle. Moreover, she was simultaneously and explicitly attacking the economic uncertainties that beset the nuclear family in the epoch of the rise of industrial capitalism. Her argument was that children should be removed from their families at the age of two (although kept nearby for family visits) and totally provided for by the state (and eventually by the earnings of their own schools) until they reached the age of sixteen. At these schools children would acquire enough science, philosophy, rhetoric, political theory, and training in good habits, to fit them for life in a democratic republic and would also learn industrial skills sufficient to make their own way in life. The ultimate goal of this education, and one that she italicised, would be that

> the American people shall present ... but one class, and as it were, but one family— each independent in his and her own thoughts, actions, rights, person, and possessions, and all co-operating, according to their individual taste and ability, to the promotion of the common weal. (1834, p 216)

Although she denied that she favoured the equalisation of property (1834a, p 197), it is evident that Frances Wright aspired in her arrangements for societal care of children to protect all people against the most damaging consequences of personal economic failure. She believed that only in this way could genuine co-operation for the common good be possible.

By the time of her 1844 volume, Fanny Wright's views had evolved in two further directions. First, probably influenced, from her years in France, by the thinking of the St Simonians (see Goldstein, 1982, pp 92–7), she had begun to discuss the male and female as representing, as it were, two complementary principles of nature. Wright described human history as revealing that woman, 'the intellect, the soul, the providence of society' was subjugated by 'that sex who represent the selfish instinct of animal life—that which looks to individual conservation and selfish gratification.' In woman was 'enshrined' the 'nobler instinct'—'that which looks to conservation and happiness of the species'—but this was subjugated by the 'baser' [male instinct]. Thus, [male] 'brute force' quells [female] 'inspirations of the mind'; [male] 'law' usurps 'the place of [female] justice'; and [male] 'selfish interest that of [the female principle of] generous friendship' (1844, Letter III, p 16 and Letter VII, p 48).

Secondly, Fanny Wright by 1844 is clearly writing as a political feminist. Next, she denominates it as unjust and as a violation of the principles of the Declaration of Independence that America is a 'system founded upon male supremacy' (1844, Letter VI, p 32). Finally, she acknowledges that 'government by a male majority' was a practice in need of correction (1844, Letter V, p 25, her emphasis). As currently constituted, America was ruled by

a majority as of brute force, counted by numbers, and of the male sex. A worse rule ... could scarcely be devised ... [except for that which prevailed in Europe, viz.] control [by] ... *a minority* of landed and moneyed monopolists upheld by the brute force of armies, coercive law, and all the machinery and corrupting influences of Government. (1844, Letter V, p 27)

Although America contributed greatly to the world by embracing the principle of 'the practical sovereignty of the people' (1844, Letter V, p 29), Wright now faulted its system for arranging power and reward along the arbitrary lines of gender, race, and inherited class instead of according to an appropriate virtue. Economic reward ought to go, '*to every man, woman, and child, according to his and her works*' (1844, Letter V, p 26, her emphasis). And, while 'every sane, sound, and useful member of society' should be granted some 'voice in the affairs which regard him', she suggests that political rule should be determined not by brute numbers, race, and sex, but rather should go to those people, irrespective of sex or race, who comprise 'a majority of the experienced, the intelligent, the virtuous, the industrious' (1844, Letter V, p 27).

Thus, it is apparent that despite change of emphasis and conception, the feminism of Fanny Wright throughout her career was guided by a commitment to the idea of a virtuous republic.

Harriet Martineau

Harriet Martineau toured America in 1834–1836, beginning at the age of thirty-two, and she was not one to wait several years before noting that the US did not live up to its own political principles with regard to women. She promptly wrote three books based on that travel experience, *Society in America* (1837), *Retrospective of Western Travel* (1838) and *How to Observe Morals and Manners* (1838). In two of these she took America harshly to task: 'The Americans have, in the treatment of women fallen below, not only their own democratic principles, but [even] the practice of some parts of the Old World' (1962, p 291; see also 1985, pp 58–65). Unlike the young Fanny Wright, the young Harriet Martineau was not dazzled by the chivalry of men's manner toward women, nor by their 'protecting' women from arduous labour, nor by the relative chastity of American sexual mores (1962, pp 291–2, 300). Harriet Martineau asks for women in 1837 what John Stuart Mill was to request on their behalf thirty-two years later: justice rather than indulgence, a justice adumbrated in the principles of the Declaration of Independence. Martineau likens America's women to its slaves:

In both cases justice is denied on no better plea than the right of the strongest. In both cases, the acquiescence of the many and the burning discontent of the few, of the oppressed, testify, the one to the actual degradation of the class, and the other to its fitness for the enjoyment of human rights. (1962, p 292)

In other words, the fact that there were many contented women and many contented slaves proved only how degraded people's spirits could become under oppressive circumstances, not their natural fitness for those circumstances. That a rare few women and ex-slaves managed despite overwhelming oppression to perceive and demand those rights demonstrated, by contrast, the validity of the claim of women and of blacks to equality in natural rights.

Women's oppression in America took three forms: political, educational, and occupational. Martineau attacked all three in detail:

> One of the fundamental principles of the Declaration of Independence is that governments derive their just powers from the consent of the governed. How can the political condition of women be reconciled with this? (1962, p 125)

Martineau points out that governments in the US have the power to tax women; to divorce them; to fine, imprison, and execute them; to dispose of their property upon marriage.

> Whence do these governments derive their powers? They are not 'just', as they are not derived from the consent of the women thus governed ... The democratic principle condemns all this as wrong; and requires equal political representation of all rational beings. (1962, p 125)

She then proceeds systematically to rebut every argument she has heard or read against equal political rights for women. Thomas Jefferson gets the first round. His worry that permitting women to 'mix promiscuously in the public meetings of men' would bring about the danger of 'depravation of morals and ambiguity of issue', earns a scornful reply:

> As if there could be no means of conducting public affairs but by promiscuous meetings! As if there would be more danger in promiscuous meetings for political business than in such meetings for worship, for oratory, for music, for dramatic entertainment—for any of the thousand transactions of civilized life. (1962, p 126)

Next she takes up James Mill's argument from the 'Essay on Government', to the effect that women are virtually represented by their family members—either father or husband will guard their interest. To this Martineau replies, 'the true democratic principle is, that no person's interest can be, or can be ascertained to be, identical with those of any other person'. That we have laws protecting people against actions by their husbands or fathers proves the non-identity of interest. (1962, pp 126–7)

She then addresses the argument made by some otherwise egalitarian thinkers that women's having political voice would be 'incompatible with the other duties [they] ... have to discharge.' Martineau's answer is to assert the moral autonomy of each individual. If there were not time and power to discharge all moral duties, 'it would be for women to decide which they would take and which they would leave'. (1962, p 127)

Finally, the 'commonest' argument of all is the one hardest to address. 'One might as well try to dissect the morning mist.' (1962, p 127) That argument is the old saw about women's exercising the truly effective power in society, the supposed power behind the throne, the ability to pull men around via their hearstrings, etc. Martineau's only reply to what she views as an evident stupidity is to express the wish that the men making these assertions could change places with women, exchanging with them their 'duties and privileges' (1962, pp 127–8).

Beyond the blatant denial to women of the obvious political rights like voting and office-holding, Martineau faults American society for the more subtle deprivation of oppportunities to contribute to civic betterment by taking public moral stands. In the mid 1830s, during Martineau's stay, women were barred by social taboo from speaking in mixed gender meetings, even in radical, anti-slavery circles (Goldstein, 1982, pp 528–31). This denial to females of a public role for their expression of conscience could not help but stunt their individual moral development. Martineau concludes that in America, 'the morals of women are crushed' (1962, pp 292–6).

Women's political and civic disfranchisement was compounded by further injustices: they were denied both educational and occupational opportunity. These two denials were manifestly interdependent: since 'women have none of the objects in life for which an enlarged education is considered requisite, the education is not given' (1962, p 292). In this regard America was no worse than England. In both countries women were provided with a smattering of shallow accomplishments, aimed at making them companionable to men, but in fact educating them far beneath their spouses (1962, pp 292–3, 296–7: 1985, pp 64–8). No effort was made to develop the fullness of their individual faculties (1962, pp 292–3, 296).

With regard to occupational opportunity, women in America were in fact worse off than in either England or France. In England, poverty pushed many women into jobs; this opportunity for personal growth had notable beneficial effect.

> But the prosperity of America is a circumstance unfavorable to its women. It will be long before they are put to the proof as to what they are capable of thinking and doing: a proof to which hundreds, perhaps thousands of Englishwomen have been put by adversity, and the result is a remarkable improvement in their social condition. (1962, pp 295–6)

Similarly:

> In France, owing to the great destruction of men in the wars of Napoleon, women are engaged, and successfully engaged, in a variety of occupations which have been elsewhere supposed unsuitable to the sex ... Already, women can do more in France than anywhere else; they can attempt more without ridicule or

arbitrary hindrances ... [I]n France ... the independence and practical efficiency of women ... are greater than in any other country. (1985, pp 61–65)

In the US women's occupations, due to 'the old feudal notions about the sexes', are the most restricted of anywhere. Apart from prostitution, the only jobs open to females are teaching, sewing, menial factory work, domestic service, and running a boarding house (1962, p 306; 1985, p 62). Teaching jobs were evidently not plentiful, and the others not very fulfilling. Thus, Martineau summarises women's lot in America as follows: 'wifely and motherly occupation may be called the sole business of woman there. If she has not that she has nothing' (1962, p 300).

As for the lot of women without either wealth or a husband and unable to teach, Martineau bemoans their poverty in that land 'where it is a boast that women do not labor' (1962, p 306):

> During the present interval between the feudal age and the coming time, when life and its occupations will be freely thrown open to women as to men, the condition of the female working classes is such that if its sufferings were but made known, emotions of horror and shame would tremble through the whole of society. (1962, p 307)

In the midst of this compelling plea for opening occupations, as well as political, civic, and educational opportunities, to women, Martineau inserts a puzzling passage: 'it is not only that [in America] masculine and feminine employments are supposed to be different. No one in the world, I believe, questions this' (1962, p 294). In what sense Martineau believes that 'masculine and feminine employments are supposed to be different' is by no means obvious. One can only speculate that this referred to the traditional division of labour *within* marriage, the place where John Stuart Mill, too, would call a halt to equality (*On the Subjection of Women*, Ch II–III), and where Martineau's American contemporary, Sarah Grimké, did the same in her own 1838 feminist tract, *Letters on the Equality of the Sexes and the Condition of Women* (p 81). Martineau evidently was not anticipating a wholesale restructuring of family life, in the mode of Fanny Wright. Rather, she seems to have been emphasising the *personal freedom* to choose an occupation, with the occupation of wife and mother remaining for at least part of adult life as one option to choose.

What appears to upset Martineau most about women's treatment in the supposed land of opportunity was the denial to them of participation in political self-government and other avenues for individual growth—for the development of civic responsibility, self-reliance, moral fortitude, intellectual depth. In this sense a tone of liberal individualism pervades her work.

It *is* true that she did hopefully anticipate that American property arrangements would someday give way to some sort of 'community of property'. She believed that co-operative living arrangements, as in the style of the Shakers and Rappites, were much more cost-efficient than family-based households

(1962, pp 176–7). She also faulted the private property system for producing crime, disease, excessive anxiety about money, and inadequate leisure (1962, pp 177, 264–72).

On the other hand, whatever form this 'community of property' might take, it would, according to Harriet Martineau, have to conform to the following maxims 'required by justice', a justice that manifestly assured due regard and reward for individual attainments:

> [N]o one will ever be allowed to take from the industrious man the riches won by his industry, and give them to the idle; to take from the strong to give to the weak; to take from the wise to give to the foolish. Such aggression upon property can never take place, or be seriously apprehended in a republic where all, except drunkards or slaves, are proprietors, and where the Declaration of Independence claims for every one, with life and liberty, the pursuit of happiness in his own way. (1962, p 265)

Conclusion

Both Harriet Martineau and Frances Wright repeatedly called on America to be true to the principles of its own Declaration of Independence, and to spread the application of those principles to women (and also to blacks). These two early nineteenth-century feminists had dramatically different conceptions of what it would mean to put those principles into practice. What this paper has argued is that the differences between the approaches of these two feminist theorists are differences more broadly characteristic of two alternative strands of thought that have shaped the American political heritage: the virtuous republic tradition and the tradition of liberal individualism.

When Fanny Wright and Harriet Martineau produced feminist readings of the ideology of the republic of civic virtue and of liberal individualism, respectively, they were breaking with the masculinist versions of those ideologies only in the limited sense that the feminists were applying the principles in a more thorough-going manner than the prevailing versions of the theories did. Wright perceived correctly that devotedness to the public good properly included the whole public, not just the propertied, white, male piece of it. And Martineau perceived correctly that liberal principles properly understood required equality of opportunity for all people, not just for white males.

It is a commonplace that the reforms advocated by Martineau—an end to educational and occupational barriers against women and an opening up of political participation to women—have made more progress in America than has the totalistic, communal education, with its deep inroads into family life, that was advocated by Fanny Wright. This fact about the relative success of these women's ideas probably tells us less about the reception of feminism in America than about the relative impact of each of these broader intellectual traditions upon American political culture. Although the civic virtue tradition has always been in the background as a kind of counterpoint, the dominant theme, at least since 1800, has clearly been liberal individualism.

NOTES

1   Fanny Wright, born in Scotland in 1795, to a wealthy merchant family, was orphaned at two and a half years and raised in England. She wrote her first study of America (1821) as a European but moved at the age of twenty-nine to the US. Frequently thereafter, however, she resided in Europe for lengthy periods: spring 1827–spring 1828, 1830–1835 and 1839–1843. Although she more or less settled in Cincinatti, Ohio in 1843, she made thirteen transatlantic voyages in the thirteen years prior to her death in 1852 (Eckhardt, 1984, pp 270–83). In 1834 she was depicted in the American anti-abolitionist press as a 'British radical'. (L L Richards, 1970, p 67).

   Her works were both studied and admired by Elizabeth Cady Stanton, and Susan B Anthony, who used her portrait as the Frontispiece for their *History of Women Suffrage* (Eckhardt, 1984, pp 282–3).

2   Harriet Martineau (1802–1876) was a British woman of letters, author of more than fifty books, and of frequent articles in such eminent journals as the *Edinburgh Review* and the *Westminster Review*. As early as 1823 she published an article in the *Monthly Repository* advocating educational equality for girls. Her 1859 article, 'Female Industry', in the *Edinburgh Review*, discussing the demographic and economic reasons for women's entry into the labour force, is said to have resulted in a fundamental reappraisal of British public policy toward women (Weiner, 1983, pp 60–74). She supported a wide range of feminist reforms, and attempted unsuccessfully to establish a journal wholly devoted to that cause (Rossi, 1973, p 123). According to Allan Nevins (p 139) 'most educated Americans' of the mid nineteenth century were familiar with her writings. Her 1837 study, *Society in America*, aroused considerble controversy on both sides of the Atlantic, and played a major role in shaping British opinion. It was described by Charles Dickens as the best book written on the US and was cited as an authority by Sarah Grimké in her 1838 book, *Letters on the Equality of the Sexes* (Letters X and XII, pp 64 and 81), the first feminist tract published in the United States.

3   Both authors attributed American women's peculiar susceptibility to religious quackery to their lack of a sound education; Martineau, in addition, blamed women's lack of opportunities to pursue meaningful vocations.

4   For details on the earliest stages of feminism in America, see Goldstein, 1987, pp 528–31.

5   For the germinal work here, see Wood, 1969. For two recent discussions of the now sizeable literature on the subject of these two traditions, see Tushnet, 1988 and Sherry, 1986.

6   One could say four phases if one included her short-lived hope that voluntary experiments with communitarian, free-love villages would show America the path to an ideal future. She apparently abandoned this hope after a disastrous experience with her own attempt to launch such a community (Eckhardt, 1984, Ch 5–6; Perkins and Wolfson, 1939, pp 123–207). Only the barest hints of her earlier fascination with free love appear in her later writings. Her 1834 volume

suggests that developing a reasoned, social science of morals will enable humans eventually to

> govern and not crucify the appetites which, forming part of our being, can as little be stifled as palled, without injury to our physical, moral, and mental health. It has been the requiring the annihilation instead of the just government of the human passions, which has nourished the belief, so slanderous to our nature, that they were beyond the control of our reason. (pp 77–8)

In her 1844 volume, she made a cryptic reference to the unfortunate societal fact that, 'prostitution, contraband or legal, [has usurped the place] of love (Letter III, p 16).

BIBLIOGRAPHY

Celia Morris Eckhardt, *Fanny Wright, Rebel in America* (Cambridge, Mass, Harvard University Press, 1984).

Richard J Evans, *The Feminists: Women's Emancipation Movements in Europe, America, and Australasia 1840–1920* London: Croom Helm, 1977).

Leslie Friedman Goldstein, 'Europe Looks at American Women, 1820–1840', *Social Research* 54 (1987), pp 519–42.

—— 'Early Feminist Themes in French Utopian Socialism: the St. Simonians and Fourier', *Journal of the History of Ideas* XLIII (1982), pp 91–108.

Sarah Grimké, *Letters on the Equality of the Sexes and the Condition of Women* (reprint of 1838 edn) (New York, Burt Franklin, 1970).

David Hecht, *Russian Radicals Look to America 1825–1894* (Cambridge, Mass, Harvard University Press, 1947).

Halvdan Koht, *The American Spirit in Europe* (Philadelphia, University of Pennsylvania Press, 1949).

Harriet Martineau, *Society in America*, Seymour Martin Lipset, ed (New Brunswick, NJ, Transaction Books, 1982).

—— 1985, *Harriet Martineau on Women*, ed G G Yates. Excerpt from *How to Observe Manners and Morals* (1838), pp 58–65.

James Mill, 'Essay on Government', in *Utilitarian Logic and Politics*, Jack Lively and John Collwyn Rees, eds (Clarendon Press, 1984).

John Stuart Mill, *On the Subjection of Women* (Prometheus Books, 1986).

Allan Nevins, *America through British Eyes* (New York, Oxford University Press, 1948).

A J G Perkins and Theresa Wolfson, *Frances Wright, Free Enquirer* (New York and London, Harper and Row, 1939).

L L Richards, *'Gentlemen of Property and Standing' Anti-abolition Mobs in Jacksonian America* (New York, Oxford, University Press, 1970).

Alice S Rossi, ed, *The Feminist Papers* (New York, Bantam, 1973).

Susanna Sherry, 'Civic virtue and the feminine voice in constitutional abjudication', *Virginian Law Review*, 72 (1986), p 543.

Mark Tushnet, *Red, White, and Blue* (Cambridge, Mass, Harvard University Press, 1988).

Gaby Weiner, 'Harriet Martineau: A Reassessment (1802–1876)', in *Feminist Theories: Three Centuries of Key Women Thinkers*, Dale Spender ed (New York, Pantheon Books, 1983, pp 60–74.

Gordon Wood, *The Creation of the American Republic 1776–1787* (Chapel Hill, University of North Carolina Press, 1969).

Frances (Fanny) Wright, *Views of Society and Manners in America* (with a commentary by Paul R Baker) (Cambridge, Mass, Belknap Press, 1963).

——*Course of Popular Lectures with Three Addresses on Various Public Occasions and a Reply to the Charges Against the French Reformers of 1789*. In Frances Wright D'Arusmont, *Life, Letters and Lectures 1834–1844* (New York, Arno Press, 1972).

——*Supplement Course of Lectures, Containing the Last Four Lectures Delivered in the United States*. Reprinted in *Life, Letters and Lectures 1834–1844* (New York, Arno Press, 1972).

——*Biography, Notes and Political Letters*. Reprinted in *Life, Letters and Lectures 1834–1844* (New York, Arno Press, 1972).

CHAPTER 7

Feminist Jurisprudence as Women's Studies in Law: Australian Dialogues

Judith Grbich

Abstract

Through a critique of traditional legal scholarship, women's studies in law has sought to interrogate major presuppositions, such as the representation of law as norms or rules. Women's studies in law has also sought to displace the traditional focus on the legal subject through a concept of legal subjectivity as constituted within judicial practices of abstracting from and generalising from the actual social relations of litigants. This paper reviews and appraises current attempts, particularly with reference to Australian feminist writing, to move from these critiques to a common focus and a common tradition for women's studies in law.

Introduction

Women's studies in law are the disciplinary practices of writing and teaching from the perspective of women with the intention that these scholarly practices should form part of the politics of women's lives. Scholarship practices are always engaged in politics but women's studies in law makes the forms of these engagements a priority for investigation. The aim of this paper is to consider the questions about scholarship practices which women writing and teaching women's studies in law have been asking. Can we interrogate or question, our questions and find a common focus and a common tradition? The aim is to consider the practices of women's studies in law by joining the conversations begun by other women about the aims and priorities of undertaking feminist scholarship within the conditions of the law discipline.

Attention has already been drawn to the rarity of the 'legal perspective' within women's studies programmes but the aim of this paper is different; it is to give an account of women's studies scholarship within law and to investigate in what ways, if any, it might be understood as constituting a 'legal' perspective. 'Women and law' courses in law school programmes have already been identified as contradictory (Thornton, 1986, p 21), in the sense that an inquiry *for* women is everything that inquiry into 'law' is not.[1] This paper seeks also to investigate whether this contradiction is fundamental to theorisation about the nature of law or whether, instead, mainstream legal theory and legal research can be understood as social practices of scholarship aptly described as 'hegemonic masculinity'. (Thornton, 1989a; Thornton, 1989b, p 98)

I am engaging in those conversations begun by women who have understood their project to be a feminist one and who have been concerned with the conditions of women's lives. The scope of my narrative about feminist scholarship in the law discipline has national boundaries and institutional boundaries. I provide an account of Australian writing. This is not to suggest that these issues are distinctly Australian: it is to write a current history, it is to constitute and engage the conversants, an engagement which seems so crucial to our individual and separate endeavours. The process of engagement seems to give a validity which might otherwise be denied. My narrative provides an account of feminist scholarship carried out in institutions for the training of lawyers and other educational institutions in which the law discipline is regarded as an objective form of knowledge. So my narrative is bounded by the conditions under which a feminist scholar is required, as teacher, researcher or student to live the practices of disparagement and where deference to objectivity is the norm.

Women's studies in law shares with other women's studies research a questioning of its disciplinary modes and practices. As elsewhere this questioning seems to be an effect of the conditions of survival and a dilemma created by fundamentally oppressive institutions. The teaching of women's studies in law by simply adding the category woman to existing legal doctrine has been understood as replicating a masculinist tradition in which woman was at best 'other' (Graycar, 1986b; Rosser, 1988; Morgan, 1988, p 757; Thornton, 1989b), and at worst, outside the forms of human understanding. Constructing courses about women by focusing upon present categories of knowledge was understood as marginalising the feminist inquiries which such a course made possible for students (Graycar, 1986b), while preserving traditional scholarship as an account of men's lives. Mainstreaming women's studies within the traditional categories of legal knowledge around which most law teaching is organised is now understood as having the potential to disrupt those forms of knowledge in ways which will make feminist inquiry possible. Feminist inquiries ask different questions and constitute different knowledges (Grbich, 1989). Women's studies in law is beginning to be understood as a different mainstream, as a different discipline. It is certainly concerned with legal scholarship and legal practice and like all disciplines, it seeks institutional boundaries. A women's law department is being posed as one practice for maintaining the integrity of the feminist research project within institutions for the training of lawyers, and is being understood as the condition for facilitating the introduction of different kinds of legal education—educational practices with the potential to produce lawyers who are not solely the organic intellectuals (Gramsci, 1971; Cain, 1979) of capital. A women's law department is envisaged as the institutional boundary of a mainstream women's studies in law which is capable of educating students to become the organic intellectuals of gender. The aim of women's studies in law is to construct 'a feminist cultural image' (Thornton, 1986, p 15), a culture in which women are visible as images of productivity rather than as endlessly representing that which is private and outside what is valued, and a culture in which women are visibly the producers of images.

Women's studies in law looks like a new discipline, it has more in common with feminist scholarship in the humanities, social sciences or natural sciences than it does with traditional legal scholarship. Women's studies in law shares a focus upon understanding the cultural practices which constitute what women's lives mean and it shares the awareness of the situated character of knowledge.[2] This commonality with the concerns of other discipline is of course a feature which traditional legal scholarship itself displays. Traditional legal scholarship is like much of the research and scholarship of other disciplines in its focus upon understanding the practices of constituting the meaning of men's lives and its disbelief that knowledge is situated; instead, legal knowledge is understood to be objective, an account of 'what is', which could be found by any legal researcher properly trained in the conventions of the discipline. The researcher's standpoint in sexual relations, or relations of class or ethnicity are, by convention, personal and outside what is understood to be legal methodology or 'technique'.

Women's studies in law is concerned with questioning the 'naturalness' of legal power and the foundational character of beliefs about law. It seeks to develop a theory about the nature of law which is sensitive to women's experience of authority. Theory is built around the meanings which women attribute to many different relations of authority. In this sense it is like traditional legal scholarship which assumes a theory about law which has been built around those meanings of authority relations which have emerged from men's lives. The male experience of authority is called 'law' and it is the maintenance and reproduction of these representational practices which the new discipline of women's studies in law seeks to understand as legal power.

The critique of traditional legal scholarship

Traditional legal scholarship has been understood within women's studies as that practice which represents law as the rule-creation and rule-following behaviour of various officials—judges, legislators, bureaucrats and police— and legal meaning as the interpretation which these officials give to human and corporate behaviour (Kerruish, 1985). Truth within traditional scholarship is understood to be that meaning which most nearly conforms to the meaning which the rule creator must have originally intended. Legality then becomes the adherence in human behaviour to the legal meaning of the rules.

Feminist scholarship has pointed out that this practice of representing law as a system of rules, norms, principles, commands or standards of human behaviour is a conscious political activity of drawing boundaries which differentiate the legal mode of social ordering from other forms of social ordering. Feminist writers have differed in their estimation of which aspect of this political practice they consider in need of challenge, engagement, dismantling or support. They concur, as participants in a new discipline, in understanding these practices of representation as fundamentally important to the task of changing the social conditions of women's lives.

The identification of traditional scholarship as political activity has been important to the task of understanding the specific practices of the politics of writing legal theory, undertaking research into the meaning of law reform and the need for law reform, the merit of espousing legal rights strategies for changing women's subordinate social position and the difficulties which feminist writers and teachers have experienced in the law discipline. Understanding traditional legal scholarship as politics has meant understanding also as political struggle the tasks of writing feminist legal theory, research into the meaning of law reforms to women (Graycar, 1987), utilising legal rights for the empowerment of women (Morgan, 1988, p 752), achieving predictable employment for feminist writers and remaining employed within the law school (Thornton, 1986, p 14).

The representating of law as norms or rules has been challenged as a political practice which privileges the perspective of those social groups from whom the rule makers and offical interpreters are systematically recruited (Duncanson, 1982; Duncanson, 1984). The objection to the claims of traditional scholarship is not that this perspective is not normative or rule-like, nor that mainstream legal theory or jurisprudence does not give a good description of the practice but instead, that this perspective about authority relations—legal relations—misrepresents the consensus or political obligations and morality of a section of the society as that perspective, consensus or morality of the whole (Duncanson, 1989; Kerruish and Hunt, 1990). It has been understood to represent the perspectives and ethical standards created within the male standpoint as if they were gender-neutral or gender-inclusive standards (Thornton, 1986, p 12; Grbich, 1989), and it has also been understood to represent the perspective and ethical standards of the bourgeoisie as if they were class-inclusive (Duncanson, 1989). The objection is not to mainstream jurisprudence as scholarship but to it as a political practice which systematically demands obedience by women to authority relations constructed from the male standpoint in the name of legality.

If mainstream jurisprudence is understood as those representations of the meaning of authority relations from the male standpoint, the question is raised as to whether the concept of law is essentially a representation in which the meanings of authority portrayed will always privilege the beliefs of the theorist. Do the practices of producing and disseminating the concept of law simply justify and validate a range of knowledge practices maintained by others who share the theorists' standpoint? Can feminist representations of the meaning of authority relations provide a notion of law which does not necessarily disempower those who do not share this understanding of authority? Must a feminist concept of law—one that is sensitive to women's experience of authority—necessarily constitute another hierarchical relation in which others are portrayed as less knowledgeable, as having needs which are irrelevant, and in which others are subordinated by the practices of the theory?

Feminist writing in law has nevertheless included support for the task of inquiring into a 'general theory of law' (Kerruish, 1987) in the belief that the idea of law is not essentially a hierarchical relation of authority in which the perspective from which the meaning of authority relations is drawn will remain differentiated and partial. Val Kerruish sees this task as one of finding

> an alternative general theory which produces an idea of law which accepts and explains the sense in which law is norm, but which goes beyond this to the generative mechanisms in social formations and the particular modes of reason which produce and legitimise the power to normalise the orthodox practices of a particular sort of social order. (Kerruish, 1987, p 19)

The task of working towards a general theory of law has been understood as activity capable of enriching the ideal of legality. These practices and ideals are the emancipatory potentials of law, an emancipation ultimately dependent on a transition to a socialist society (Kerruish, 1985, p 76).

However the problems remain of whether the ideal of legality is essentially a hierarchical relation of authority, and whether the practices of constructing ideals of consensus of normative morality must always position representations from the standpoint of women as meanings of authority relations to be contested. Does women's studies in law support the inquiry into the possibility of knowing what law 'is' only as one more cultural practice? The focus might remain an epistemological one of searching for the criteria or practices through which certainty is possible, ultimately a matter of the conditions of ideals and the knowing of ideal conditions, but nevertheless accepting that it is only the search which is possible (Grbich, 1990a; Grbich, 1990b). This may not necessarily be as pessimistic a task as it appears; post-structuralist methodologies in which the subject of knowledge is an active and imaginative participant in the symbolic meanings of a culture provide good reason for optimism.

Women's studies in law differ of course in the emphasis they place upon the importance of constructing a theory of the nature of law which surpasses the partiality of traditional legal theory. Whether the task is conceived of as a matter of constructing theory (Thornton, 1986; Morgan, 1988), or of including women in the research endeavour (Graycar, 1986b, p 371; Grbich, 1989), the misrepresentation of the male perspective as 'law' and legality is understood as a practice to be contested.

However, the adoption of post-structuralist methodologies by feminist writers has contributed to the understanding that the practices of representing the meaning of authority relations which could be differentiated as 'law' do not essentially differ from those practices of representing the meaning of other kinds of authority relations—practices understood as science, medicine and, perhaps, the humanities.

The issue in question here arises from the post-structuralist methodological commitment to the theoretical strengths of the notions of the subject, subjectivity, the symbolic and the imaginary, and a commitment to finding theoretical strategies for working through the difficulties which the concepts of ideology and agency appear to have presented. Writing feminist theory in law using the concepts of ideology and hegemony has led to a profound pessimism that the political practices of feminst writing are ultimately capable of only piecemeal reforms which will have the effect of legitimising the patriarchal order.[3]

The issue is whether one can ever theoretically accept or work with an idea of law in which 'law' means normative standards or ideals even if one holds a belief that in a society in which norms are democratically constructed an emancipatory and empowering legality can be achieved for all citizens. This idea of law as normative consensual standards, however democratically constituted, seems to leave little room for a theory of subjectivity in which modes of 'reason' can be explored and work begun upon the particular practices by which the subject constitutes the legitimacy of power.

The dialogue within feminist jurisprudential writing in Australia around the notion of 'transforming the normative tradition' (Graycar, 1986b; Mossman, 1986; Morgan, 1988, p 757), therefore contains two quite separate themes. One theme is of changing the tradition, the understanding that the rules or norms of law have been constituted from all social standpoints and, instead, understanding present law as that morality or normativity constructed from the male standpoint. The other theme is of changing the idea of law as norm or rule and, instead, beginning to explore the different kinds of representational practices involved in subjectivity and implicated in both positive and negative ways in the constitution of hierarchical relations.

(a) *Changing the tradition*

Feminist writers have differed in their understnding of the issues involved in changing the tradition, in some part due to working with different theories of what has been called the relation of law to society. Sociological theories have presented the most difficulty because some of these theories have borrowed from traditional positivist legal scholarship the idea that law is rules created by officials, and this has led to the argument that judges and legislators can instrumentally cause society to change; although it has been recognised that it is often difficult to know if an observed change in human or institutional behaviour was the effect of the legal rule or the origin of the legal rule. The adoption of historical materialism has been important for locating a process of change which allows full consideration to be given to the social and material conditions under which different kinds of legal rules are created by judges and legislators. But it has only been the development of the epistemological issue within the marxist theory of knowledge which has provided the theoretical skills for coming to grips with the issues of standpoint involved in the law tradition (Thornton, 1986, 1989; Kerruish, 1987, 1989, 1990). The theoretical work upon developing a specifically feminist historical materialism by feminist scholars in North America and the United Kingdom—in the disciplines of political theory, philosophy, and sociology—appears to have been the impetus for these developments.

A major problem which remains in feminist projects which work with the theoretical premises of historical materialism is the base-superstructure metaphor for understanding legality and other hierarchical authority relations. If 'law', the legal rules or norms, are understood as part of the superstructure, as epiphenomenal, as ideological in its false sense, how does one explain the practices of resistance to these 'illusions', or the practices of creating 'illusions' of one's own? The problem appears to be inherent in marxist epistemology although there is much to suggest that such interpretations have just missed the point! If ideology is understood as illusion or 'false consciousness', one is representing the real as elsewhere, traditionally in the social relations of the mode of production. The idea of law as ideology has led to arguments that some legal rules are false, which does not fit comfortably with the notion that laws are nevertheless contingent upon the social relations of their creation.

Marxist theory contains another 'real', the 'real men who make history'. Understanding ideology as the masking of the reality of social relations seems to imply that the real men who live these social relations will inevitably be misled by the ideological. One could assume the gender specificity of 'real men' in the marxist text and comfortably accept this conclusion; while written in jest this interpretation seems to acquire a plausibility in the re-reading. The more usual interpretation is that ideology is a distortion of social relations and that it distorts understanding, in that ideology is negative and oppressive. This epistemological position on ideology, and law as ideology, seems to have contributed to the pessimism of some feminist writing in law and led some feminists to conclude that legality will always oppress women and that law reform is pointless. This pessimism is nourished in institutions where feminist writing is risky at the best of times, and usually professional death for the untenured.

Feminist writings located within the theoretical assumptions of historical materialism have begun to confront the materiality of legal ideologies in different ways. Legal rules and legal concepts have been challenged as inappropriate objects of theoretical inquiry (Kerruish, 1985; Grbich, 1989; 1990a,b) and of practical reform strategies, but changing the tradition has been understood as retaining the idea of law as a consensual normativity. Legal rules are understood as ideologies which are real and which constitute the social knowledge of being legal subjects (Kerruish, 1985, p 85), but the object of inquiry becomes the actual social relations and conditions within which the legal forms of knowledge are generated (Kerruish, 1985). The legal subject, so central to traditional scholarship, is understood as a subjectivity which actively marginalises an individual's own understanding of authority relations (Kerruish, 1985, 1987). Legal subjectivity is constituted within judicial practices of abstracting from and generalising from the actual social relations of litigants.

The traditional focus upon the legal subject, and even the relations between legal subjects, is understood as subverting any real inquiry into other ideological or political practices in which the subject resists understanding authority relations in terms of the legal categories of knowledge. It seems that by conflating those practices in which the subject represents the meaning of authority relations with the practices of subjects making claims or not making claims on other citizens, we might disable inquiry into how some 'associative obligations'[4] are understood as legally claimable and others as more informally due, according to different moralities. Also at stake is understanding the practices of initiating law reforms—what are the social practices whereby oppressed peoples perceive the illegitimacy of the behaviour of others. This is not to assume that law reform is essentially liberating; rather, it is an attempt to understand why oppressive social relations can be accepted as legitimate.

Whether law reform can be in any sense liberating is a question repeated in feminist inquiries into the materiality of legal ideologies, a question most often repeated with a faith that 'piecemeal reform' does not inevitably maintain oppressive gender relations. If the participation of women in the dialogues on the real problems and meanings of social relations is part of the process of change, how can the conversation be maintained when the official agenda, often constructed by statutes and other legal rules, is not the feminist agenda (Graycar, 1987)? If legal concepts are no longer to be the appropriate objects of inquiry, where does that leave the reform practices of consultation and participation in government inquiries? If the policy questions of proposed reforms are not conceptualised in feminist terms is engagement in the reform process inevitably oppressive (Graycar, 1986c)? Feminist inquiries in which legal ideologies are no longer understood as false, illusory, or 'barriers' to change seem better able to continue the research endeavour beyond matters of faith and simple optimism.

Changing the tradition of writing jurisprudence is now understood as questioning one's own political practices in doing jurisprudence. The mainstream jurisprudential tradition in which social practices were included only as the hypotheticals for analysing abstract questions of legality and morality can now be understood as an imaginative style adopted by writing communities whose members were invariably drawn from positions of social privilege, or whose members were institutionally implicated in maintaining relations of privilege. Membership for some appears to require a rigid adherence to the traditional style.

The questions which arise in the new tradition of women's studies in law have only begun to link the scholarship practices of hypotheticals with the different systematic exclusions of women's voices and other 'others' (Kerruish and Hunt, 1990). The questions concern the different forms in which the mainstream tradition has maintained the male standpoint as one of legal power and political power, if such a distinction can be maintained. Women writers are becoming attuned to the ways in which the traditional boundaries of jurisprudence have not only formed the legal texts as we know them, but have delineated the cultural knowledge of what can count as an authority, in both its textual and human bodily meanings.

(b) *Changing the normative in the tradition*

Recent writing has begun understanding 'law as ideology', in ways capable of acknowledging the positive or constitutive aspect of representational practices. In this work law is one more representational practice, legal rules become knowledges and the representation of the meaning of authority relations is understood as discursive regularities or perhaps the conversations of mankind (Grbich, 1990a,b). Where women have been included in these discussions they have been situated as conversations of humanity. The male perspective, which comprises the legal rules, is understood as having a reality and a materiality which must be contended with. Legal rules are no longer false or masking the real but are understood as that symbolic order or code of meaning which has been constituted by the imaginary male a symbolic order which constitutes each subject as male. These changes to a post-structuralist or perhaps a pre-structuralist methodology seem to have created a more optimistic political practice for women's studies in law (Berns, 1988; Howe, 1989; Grbich, 1987, 1990a,b).

In post-structuralist writing, theorisation of the position of the subject in the social constitution of the legitimacy of power has begun. As in other feminist writing there is a reflexive methodology in which it is understood that the writer is part of the representational practice of constituting the subject as a unity, so it is understood that subjectivity is always a divided and disorganised being. The human condition is that which seeks to make it appear certain and known. This theorisation of the subject of power is the second theme of the feminist writing project of 'transforming the normative tradition' (Graycar, 1986b). Tradition is understood as an invention, and the idea of law as normativity as a male vision of consensus, in the sense that the notion that there can be a common morality is the masculine imaginary. The legal rules which are traditionally understood as abstract reason or objectivity are theorised as an imaginary signifier, as the symbolic whose referent is perhaps woman as unknowing, or perhaps the unknown, if the theorist is generous.

Theorisation of the subject of power or hierarchical relations has the related themes of the subject as an authority and the subject as subjected. The theme of the subject as an authority has a focus upon the legal text and the practices of texuality. The new questions began as inquiries into the 'sexism of legal language' (Scutt, 1985), they now place traditional legal scholarship as the writing of 'word-histories', as coherent patterns of legal reasoning which contribute to the authority relations of the present by providing a teleological account of past word-progress. Questions asked about sexism in judicial interpretive language disrupted the coherence of present justifications for present arrangements of power. Inquiries into the word-histories written by judges on women as persons (Scutt, 1985; Mossman, 1986, 1989) have revealed more than a time and a place for the writing of each legal text/judgement. They have located the cultural constraints which these texts place upon the female subject and female subjectivity. They locate scholarship practices which delineate 'How we have been led to imagine ourselves ...' (Rich, 1975, p 90) as women. The theme of the subject as subjected includes a focus upon the details of the masculine imaginary, here legal rules, as abstracted reason and objectivity, are understood as an embodied imagination that is situated in the male experience of disconnectedness from others, a disconnectedness understood as autonomy. The male understanding that bodies are not reliable forms of social knowledge is the Cartesian tradition in which reality must be abstracted reason (Grbich, 1990a,b).

This focus has provided optimistic research directions for feminist writing. Spaces are being made for the female imaginary. The female imaginary created different visions and different metaphors for constituting the meaning of human practice. Women's experience of connectedness to others, not essentially, but through their actual life practices, has provided a different imaginary. The metaphors of vision recede and new metaphorical modes take their place. Human practice is imagined as nourishing, knowledge as having a fluidity or circularity and 'law' as that sense of authority which comes with being 'in touch'.

This project of theorising the nature of legality and the constitution of the legitimacy of power appears to allow space for the female imaginary to be nourished and supported within a symbolic order in which the female subject continues to be represented as male. She can contest these symbolic representations of woman as 'the other', as outsider, without lapsing into understanding female subjectivity as essentially true or the individual as a theoretical entity to which she should aspire. Her experience of subjectivity as provisional and disruptive seems to fit comfortably with the different representational modes of authority relations. The idea of law seems to have moved from normativity to the subject in its embodied imaginings (Grbich, 1990a,b): in a sense normativity has become an issue of subjectivity. Perhaps we could understood law as that embodied imagination by which we represent ourselves as authorities, we could understood law as not essentially consensus or order or normativity, but as a practice of finding the possibilities for order. The different representational practices in which order is imagined can be understood as expressions of an ideal of tranquility forever to be reworked by human disruption.

The common tradition which appears to emerge from women's studies in law is the persistent reflexive form of feminist jurisprudence. Theorisation of the nature of legality takes the form of questioning whether the scholarship practices of the writer are sensitive to women's experience of present politics. Women's representations of the meaning of authority relations are the politics which inform the scholarship of feminist jurisprudence. Whether women's studies scholarship 'within law can be understood as constituting a legal perspective must remain unanswered and unanswerable, as feminist jurisprudence has long since departed from the law discipline and joined the uncertain world of the humanities and the social sciences. Scholarship practices are now acknowledged as one of the cultural forms in which the politics of order are negotiated. Whether the idea of law can retain a specificity or boundary to separate it from other practices of finding the possibilities for order remains unanswered. Is it possible to imagine an idea of law which does not in practice necessarily constitute another as unknowledgeable, irrelevant and subordinate?

NOTES

This paper was delivered at the first Australian National Women's Studies Conference, Adelaide, 6–8 July 1989. Thanks are due to my colleagues in Melbourne, Adrian Howe and Jenny Morgan, for their support and assistance in the early stages of writing this paper. Thanks also to Ian Duncanson for reading drafts and providing critical and supporting responses.

1   Thornton argues that 'the idea of feminism and law is an oxymoron' (Thornton, 1989b, p 97).
2   The standpoint specificity of knowledge and elated issues of experience and justification have been widely researched in women's studies as well as in sociology, philosophy, political science, and history. The situated character of knowledge appears in the humanities and in the social sciences, so has been the epistemological focus of the 1980s. Australian writing includes :Graycar, 1986c; Thornton, 1989a, p 125; Grbich, 1989).
3   Thornton has written of the 'fierce individualism' which characterises academic appointments and argues that 'a paradigm shift would therefore be necessary to effect a radical rethinking of the role of women within the academy. Hegemonic masculinity, which is embedded in our social institutions, values and practices, ensures that this will not occur' (Thornton, 1989, p 127).
4   Valerie Kerruish and Alan Hunt provide a critical discussion of Dworkin's use of the term 'associative obligations' (Kerruish and Hunt, 1990).

BIBLIOGRAPHY

Sandra Berns, 'Hercules, Hermes and Senator Smith: the symbolic structure of *Law's Empire*', *Bulletin of the Australian Society of Legal Philosophy*, 12 (1988), pp 35–45.

Maureen Cain, 'The general practice lawyer and the client: towards a radical conception', *International Journal of the Sociology of Law*, 7 (1979).
—— 'Realism, feminism, methodology and law', *International Journal of the Sociology of Law*, 14 (1986), pp 255–67.
Ian Duncanson, 'Jurisprudence and politics', *Northern Ireland Legal Quarterly*, 33 (1982), pp 1–19.
—— 'Moral outrage and technical questions: civil liberties, law and politics', *Northern Ireland Legal Quarterly*, 35 (1984), pp 153–79.
—— 'The Politics of common law in theory and history', *Osgoode Hall Law Journal*, 27 (1989), pp 1–21.
Antonio Gramsci, *Selections from the Prison Notebooks*, Q Hoare and G Nowell Smith eds (Lawrence and Wishart, 1971).
Regina Graycar, 'Feminism comes to law: better late than never', *Australian Feminist Studies*, 3 (1986a), pp 115–20.
—— 'To transform the normative tradition of law: a comment on the feminist project in the law school', *Australian Quarterly*, 58 (1986b), pp 366–74.
—— 'Yes, Virginia, there is feminist legal literature: a survey of some recent publications', *Australian Journal of Law and Society*, 3 (1986c), pp 105–35.
—— 'Towards a feminist position on maintenance', *Refractory Girl*, 30 (1987), pp 7–11.
Judith Grbich, 'The position of women in family dealing: the Australian case', *International Journal of the Sociology of Law*, 15 (1987), pp 309–32.
—— 'The critical resources of feminist revenue law scholarship', *Canadain Journal of Women and the Law* (1990a) [forthcoming].
—— 'The body in legal theory', *Wisconsin Women's Law Journal* 91990b) [forthcoming].
—— 'The body in legal theory', in Martha Fineman, ed *At the Boundaries of Law*: *Feminism and Legal Theory* (Routledge, 1990c) [forthcoming].
Adrian Howe, 'Social injury revisited: towards a feminist theory of social justice', *International Journal of the Sociology of Law*, 15 (1987), p 423.
—— 'Chamberlain revisited: the case against the media', *Refractory Girl*, 31/32 (1989), pp 2–8.
Valerie Kerruish, 'Systematically misleading theory: legal positivism on law and legality', *Law in Context*, 3 (1985), pp 75–104.
—— 'Epistemology and general legal theory', in Gary Wickham ed *Social Theory and Legal Politics* (Sydney, Local Consumptions, 1987), pp 5–24.
—— 'Coherence, integrity and equality in *Law's Empire*: a dialectical review of Ronald Dworkin', *International Journal of the Sociology of Law*, 16 (1988), pp 51–73.
—— 'Reynolds, Thompson and the rule of law: jurisprudence and ideology in Terra Nullius' *Law in Context*, 7 (1) (1989), pp 120–33.
—— and Alan Hunt, 'Dworkin's dutiful daughter: gender disrimination in *Law's Empire*', in Valerie Kerruish and Alan Hunt eds *Essays on Dworkin* (OUP, 1990) [forthcoming].
Jenny Morgan, 'Feminist theory as legal theory', Melbourne *University Law Review*, 16 (1988), pp 743–59.
Mary Jane Mossman, 'Otherness and the law school: a comment on teaching gender equality', *Canadian Journal of Women and the Law*, 1 (1985), pp 213–18.

—— 'Feminism and legal method: the difference it makes', *Australian Journal of Law and Society*, 3, 30, reprinted in *Wisconsin Women's Law Journal*, 3 (1986), pp 147–68.

—— 'Invisible constraints on lawyering and leadership: the case of women lawyers', *Ottawa Law Review*, 20 (1988), pp 567–600.

Adrienne Rich, 'When we dead awaken: writing as re-vision', in Barbara Charlesworth Gelpi and Albert Gelpi eds *Adrienne Rich's Poetry* (New York, W W Norton, 1975).

Kim Rosser, 'Law and gender: the feminist project in action', *Legal Service Bulletin* (1988), pp 233–5.

Jocelynne Scutt, 'Sexism in legal language', *The Australian Law Journal*, 3 (1986), pp 163–73.

Margaret Thornton, 'Feminist jurisprudence: illusion or reality?', *Australian Journal of Law and Society*, 3 (1986), pp 5–29.

—— 'Hegemonic masculinity and the academy', *International Journal of the Sociology of Law*, 17 (1989a), pp 115–30.

—— 'Women and legal hierarchy', *Legal Education Review*, 1 (1989b), pp 97–9.

CHAPTER 8

Women, the Economy, and the US Constitution

Rita Mae Kelly

Abstract

This paper presents an overview of the role that patriarchical sex-role ideology has played in limiting the constitutional and legal status of women in the US economy. It traces how English common law traditions dominated Supreme Court interpretations until the 1970s. Decisions in the 1980s which opened previously closed options for women are highlighted. Finally, the paper presents several policy areas needing particular attention in the 1990s if women are to improve their relative position in the US labour force.

Battles in the US in the 1980s over the role of women in the US economy reflect centuries-old myths and ideological conflicts about the appropriate role of women in society. Implicit within popular notions of sex roles is an assemblage of Graeco-Judeo Christian beliefs about male-female differences and how each sex relates to the public and private roles in society. The essence of the Greek rationalisation of these beliefs that still influences us is as follows (Marshall, 1964, pp 71–2): (1) males and females are opposite in nature, the reconciliation of which brings order and harmony to society; (2) similarly, the roles of males and females are opposite and complementary in accord with the design of Nature. Society's needs can be divided into two distinct spheres which agree with the nature and capabilities of the two sexes; (3) the outdoor sphere, comprising heavy labour, military activity and deliberation over the protection and livelihood of the society, is assigned to the male, while the indoor sphere, where less strength but a greater share of love and nurture is required, is relegated to the female; (4) the outdoor nature of the male makes it appropriate for him to engage in the public, political, visible and official activities of his society; women's indoor nature excludes her from the above and places her in the private, publicly invisible functions; (5) the public sphere, concerned with the survival of the *polis* and the freedom of its members, is more dignified and sublime and more important than the private sphere, which is concerned with the most common of animal needs, the survival of the species—a care of slaves and even beasts; the male is stronger, more courageous, superior; the female weaker, deficient, irrational, inferior.

These views of how men and women were related to public and private space were carried over to views of the rights and prerogatives to which each sex was entitled. Full male citizens were entitled to three basic rights: social rights, civil rights, and political rights.

Throughout history women have typically been accorded social rights (the right to a modicum of economic welfare and security) only. Civil rights (liberty of person; freedom of speech, thought, and faith; the right to own property and to conclude valid contracts; the right to justice) and political rights (the right to vote and the opportunity to hold office) were available to women essentially only through their husbands, fathers, sons, or some other legally designated male protector as part of the patriarchal system. The French and American revolutions, with their emphasis on equality, liberty, and fraternity raised women's hopes for attaining all three rights of citizenship but these hopes were shattered by the conservative sex-role ideology of the male revolutionary leaders (Kelly and Boutilier, 1978, p 36).

The US Declaration of Independence stated that men were created equal. Though many often argued that 'men' subsumed 'women', the political and legal history of the US clearly contradicts this assertion. For example, the US Constitution of 1789 counted women as equal members of the population but restricted the franchise to white propertied males. The law of the land has strongly supported the view that the patriarchal nuclear family is the basic unit of the society. The law has also reinforced the control of males over females on the grounds that the maintenance of unity of interests was essential for the well-being of the state. Indeed, the commonality of interest was believed to be so great that English common law (the basis for US law) denied women legal identity once they were married. The opinion of Justice Bradley in the well-known 1873 US Supreme Court case of *Bradwell v Illinois*, which denied Bradwell the right to work as a lawyer even though she had the legal training, summarises the dominant ideology about the role of women prevailing in the eighteenth and nineteenth centuries of the United States:

> ... the civil law, as well as nature herself, has always recognized a wide difference in the respective spheres and destinies of man and woman. Man is, or should be, woman's protector and defender ... The constitution of the family organization, which is founded in divine ordinance, as well as in the nature of things, indicated the domestic sphere as that which belongs to the domain and function of woman-

hood. The harmony, not to say, identity of interests and views which belong, or should belong, to the family institution is repugnant to the idea of a woman adopting a distinct and independent career from that of her husband. So firmly fixed was this sentiment in the founders of the common law that it became a maxim of that system of jurisprudence that a woman had no legal existence separate from her husband, who was regarded as her head and representative in the social state. (*Bradwell v. Illinois*, 83 US (16 Wall) 130, 1873)

From Abigale Adams to the present, women have argued for separate political and economic legal identities. It is only in the twentieth century, however, that the feminist position that women are persons equal to men has come to have political and occupational significance. Indeed in 1868, the Fourteenth Amendment, which in the 1970s and 1980s became so central to advancing women's equality, introduced sex-specific language into the US Constitution for the first time, making women's position explicitly worse (O'Connor, 1990). This Amendment stated that, if the states denied males over the age of twenty-one the right to vote, then their proportional representation in the US Congress would be reduced. Given that the Fourteenth Amendment prohibits states from 'denying to any person ... the equal protection of the laws', this statement in effect denied that women were legal persons. In 1837 the US Supreme Court explicitly ruled in the Slaughter House cases that the Equal Protection Clause applied only to state laws discriminating against blacks.

This patriarchal view of women with regard to how God and Nature required laws restricting women from having careers, public roles, and separate identities and requiring them to accept male protection continued well into the 1960s. For example, even in the 1960s states prohibited women from keeping their maiden names and from getting driver's licences in their own names, arguing that such a practice would harm the interests of the state. In 1961, following precedent, the US Supreme Court reaffirmed that serving on jury could be restricted to men because 'woman is still regarded as the centre of the home and family life' (*Hoyte v Florida*, 1961). The necessity of the state to protect women from working for wages in particular capacities (via laws passed by male legislators, implemented by essentially male administrators, and interpreted by male judges) was politically accepted until the 1960s.

This logic of protection also applied to business owners. In 1948, the US Supreme Court upheld a Michigan state law that forbid women working as bartenders. In this case the woman who was working in the bar was also the owner whose husband had died. While he was alive, she could work as a bartender since he would protect her and her morals. Once he died, however, the Court ruled the state could prohibit her from such work and that such laws did not violate the Equal Protection Clause of the Fourteenth Amendment even though the woman owned the bar. Her sex overrode her rights as a citizen, as a worker in the capitalist free labour market, and as a business person (*Goesaert v Cleary*, 1948).

Economic and military necessity have been factors contributing to the changing ideology regarding women and work in the US. To illustrate, as early as 1942 the National War Board endorsed the principle of equal pay for equal work in an effort to encourage women to work during the Second World War. Nonetheless, not until the major political movements of the 1950s and 1960s focusing on civil rights and on women's rights did significant and numerous changes in both law and ideology occur. For example, it was in 1963 that the Equal Pay Act was passed, requiring that all employers subjected to the Fair Labour Standards Act pay women the same as men for similar work.

The most dramatic legal change for women was the last minute inclusion of sex in Title VII of the Civil Rights Act of 1964 which 'prohibits discrimination on the basis of sex, race, color, religion, or national origin in any employment condition, including hiring, firing, promotion, transfer, compensation and admission to training programs' (Powell, 1988, p 209). It is this Title VII that authorised 'affirmative action' as follows:

> If the court finds that the respondent has intentionally engaged in an unlawful employment practice ... the court may order such affirmative action as may be appropriate (Glazer, 1988, p 101).

In the 1970s and 1980s, as more women moved into the labour force and the pressures to incorporate women into all levels of work, management, and leadership increased, it became clear that discrimination in the labour market comes in many forms (Schmid, 1984). Three major forms are (a) pre-market types of discrimination, e.g. in socialisation, education, mobility, training, and family responsibilities; (b) employment discrimination, e.g. not hiring women at all or for certain, usually less favourable jobs only, and (c) wage discrimination, e.g. lower pay for the same or comparable job.

Title VII was insufficient to deal with all of these issues. To address some of the pre-market types of discrimination Congress passed several new laws. In 1972 the Equal Employment Opportunity Act became law; the Equal Rights Amendment cleared Congress, though it was never successfully ratified by a sufficient number of states to become law; Title IX of the 1972 amendments to the Education Act gave women more equal educational opportunities; the Equal Credit Opportunity Act of 1974 gave women independence for husbands, fathers, and guardians in obtaining credit; the Career Education Incentive Act of 1977 sought to reduce sex stereotyping in employment; and the Women's Education Opportunity Act of 1978 sought to expand educational options further. The sex bias of veterans' benefit and advantages open to males through military participation were reduced by the Defense Appropriations Act of 1976 which opened the service academies to women. In 1978 the US Pregnancy Discrimination Act modified Title VII of the Civil Rights Act of 1964 to prohibit employers from discriminating on the basis of pregnancy. However, there was no recognition that the workplace laws, structures, and policies are based on a male reproduction/child-bearing model.

Experience with differential treatment in hiring and promotion practices from the mid 1960s to the present revealed that addressing pre-market discriminatory laws and behaviour, while vital, was also insufficient. Discrimination in employment and its ideological underpinnings needed to be continually confronted.

A major boost to this effort came in 1971 when the US Supreme Court finally used—for the first time—the Equal Protection Clause of the Fourteenth Amendment to prevent a state law from discriminating against women (O'Connor, 1990). In *Reed v Reed* (1971) this clause was used to enable women to be appointed as administrators of estates. Since 1971, over fifty cases have been heard by the US Supreme Court on sex-based challenges under the Equal Protection Clause, among other things, against sex stereotyping and discrimination stemming from it in hiring, promotions, maternity leave, disability insurance, pension rights, and seniority issues.

Another major factor in the fight against sex discrimination was the Title VII of the 1964 Civil Rights Act. Title VII offered two conceptual frameworks for enforcing equality in the workplace: disparate treatment and disparate impact analysis. Disparate treatment doctrine prohibits practices motivated by discriminatory intent. It guarantees similar treatment for those who are similarly situated to each other. Most of the Title VII cases up to 1990 have been decided using this framework. This doctrine essentially takes the labour force and economic structures as they are, with all their built-in assumptions about job requirements, descriptions, and work hours—most of which have been devised when the work force was predominantly male.

In the 1980s objections arose (e.g. Eichner, 1988; West, 1988) to this implicit assumption by employers and the courts that employment standards ought to accept masculine traits and sex roles as the norm for job descriptions and work structures. Assumptions of gender neutrality and being similarly situated focused essentially on the individual. The problem often appeared, however, to be institutional structures and ideological assumptions that implicitly disadvantage women, allowing only those women who could assimilate to be or act like men to be viewed by the courts as 'similarly situated' (Williams, 1982).

To address male-biased ideology in the economy and job standards several legal scholars suggest examining female disadvantage rather than just sex differences. They suggest achieving this end by means of a more sophisticated use of disparate impact doctrine. This doctrine, established in *Griggs v Duke Power Co* in 1971, prohibits employment practices having a discriminatory effect and establishes that 'facially neutral employment practices that have significant adverse effects on protected groups may violate Title VII' (Eichner, 1988, p 1408). This doctrine goes beyond the disparate treatment doctrine in that it allows for dealing with prohibited practices such as 'male-biased job requirements [that] are "fair in form, but discriminatory in operation"' (Eichner, 1988, p 1397). To be successful in addressing these ideological biases the courts need to examine carefully the use of what is called the 'business necessity defense'. Eichner (1988, p 1413) suggests a two-part test, as follows:

> They should ask first whether the challenged requirement is essential to the core function of the job. If the answer is affirmative, courts should then consider whether the selection process screens for that requirement in an unbiased manner ... The core function test would require courts to look beyond stereotyped notions of how the job should be performed to the basic function of the job itself.

Once these tests are completed, the employer still needs to demonstrate that no other employment options of comparable business utility would have a less discriminatory impact. They also need to be most careful in accepting the idea that it would cost too much to restructure either job standards, the job environment, or job characteristics to remove impediments to women. Discrimination is not more tolerable because it is more profitable.

In the 1980s and the advent of the Reagan Administration opposition to affirmative action became more vocal. Attorney General Ed Meese attempted unsuccessfully to rescind Executive Order 11246, and many departments— most notably the Justice Department—refused to set numeric goals, quotas, or timetables. In addition, President Reagan appointed several conservative justices to the US Supreme—Antonio Scalia, Anthony M Kennedy, William A Rehnquist—who have not always revealed support for affirmative action in general and for women in particular. (Sandra Day O'Connor, though also a conservative appointed by Reagan, often has a different position on women-related issues than her male compatriots (O'Connor and Siegal, 1990). Despite these trends toward more vocal opposition to affirmative action, both the Courts, the business community, and the majority of the American people continued to support actions to remove disparate treatment and impact on women in the labour force.

In 1986, in *Wygant v Jackson Board of Education* the Court addressed the question of whether a race- or gender-conscious affirmative action plan developed with the idea of facilitating the removal of general sex and gender imbalances in the work force is legal. The Court affirmed such plans are constitutional and that affirmative action plans 'need not be limited to the remedying of specific instances of identified discrimination' (*Wygant v Jackson Board of Education*, 1985, p 1853).

In the 1986 case of *Johnson v Transportation Agency* the Court explicitly supported positive affirmative action plans for promoting women. In this case the Court supported a plan adopted by the Santa Clara District Board of Supervisors that encouraged sex to be considered a factor in promotion in those cases where women were significantly under represented compared to their percentage in the country labour force.

According to Minow (1987),

> *Johnson* should have far-reaching effects on employers' voluntary affirmative action. The Court explicitly rejected an employer's own discrimination as a

factual predicate to voluntary affirmative action, and required evidence only of a current manifest statistical imbalance in the representation of women in a job category in the employer's workforce. The Court's decision in effect allows employers to use affirmative action to redress statistical imbalances regardless of their cause.

In 1989, the US Supreme Court made several rulings that appeared to move back from the earlier strong support for affirmative action. In one case (Wermiel, 1989, p A3) the Court allowed a group of white fire-fighters in Birmingham, Alabama, to challenge a plan adopted in 1981 with federal court approval to settle law suits filed by blacks against the city for discriminatory hiring and promotion practices. The white fire-fighters used Title VII to argue that they were being denied promotions on the grounds of their race. It is unclear the extent to which this more conservative Court will negatively address affirmative action. Reagan's new appointees were obviously more likely to accept the negative consequences of traditional sex-role ideology on gender equality in the labour force as the normal result of basic biological and physiological sex differences than feminists would have liked.

Wage discrimination against women has also been pervasive. It was not until 1972 that the Equal Pay Act of 1963 was extended to executive, administrative, and professional work, including those employed by private and public educational institutions. It was also not until the 1970s that the Executive Order 11246, which extended affirmative action and equal employment opportunity requirements to all federal contractors receiving $50,000 or more or employing more than fifty persons, was implemented on behalf of women with any frequency. (The importance of the Women's Movement is evident!) The implementation of this executive order by the Department of Labor's Office of Federal Contract Compliance and the actions of the Equal Employment Opportunity Commission facilitated progress for wage justice. For example, in the 1970s banks in Boston were forced to give cost of living increases to clerical workers and to post notices for administrative positions. In 1973 American Telephone and Telegraph was compelled to pay $15 million to women for previous discrimination. Though the reimbursement invariably fell short of actual earnings lost, the principle of recompense was established.

Pay equity requires fair and equitable payment for work performed. It is mandated by the 1963 Equal Pay Act, required by Title VII of the 1964 Civil Rights Act, and is supported by a 1980 Presidential Executive Order and a 1981 US Supreme Court ruling (Kelly and Bayes, 1988, p 239). Pay equity defends such sources of wage differences as merit, seniority, and quality or quantity of production while prohibiting pay disparities based on sex and race.

As of September 1986, at least ten states had a written pay equity or comparable worth policy, and twenty-seven states had completed studies to determine if sex-based wage differences and/or occupational segregation exists. Also in 1986 the Supreme Court decided that past practices in discrimination can be used to analyse current systems of pay and that statistical evidence of pay inequities are permissible in court. In 1987, pay equity actions were taking place in forty-five of the fifty states, and pressures were building to expand the comparable worth effort to encompass minority males as well as females (Kelly and Bayes, 1988, p 239).

By the 1980s gender wage justice had clearly become an important political issue. The role of federal law and legal reinterpretations of the Fourteenth Amendment and Women's rights under the Constitution in advancing the position of women in the economic system has been vital in facilitating and encouraging states to address these issues.

By the mid 1980s the US Supreme Court was addressing the very basic issue of the extent to which the First Amendment of the Bill of Rights protecting freedom of association could be used to discriminate against women. In *Hishon v King and Spaulding* (1984) the Court held that if a partnership is a privilege of employment, then firms may not discriminate on grounds of sex in hiring partners. In *Roberts v Jaycees* (1985) The Court upheld a Minnesota statute requiring women to be admitted to the Jaycees with full voting rights. The state's right to end discrimination overrode an individual's or a group's right to free association. In 1987 the Court reaffirmed this ruling in a California case involving the Rotary Club. In this case the Court asserted a two-pronged test to determine whether associational rights of private clubs exempt them from state anti-discrimination laws, i.e. whether they were an expressive or an intimate association. Essentially, the Court ruled that only close family-type relationships fell into the intimate category and that only those private groups whose purpose would be substantially impaired if forced to non-discriminate were exempt from anti-discrimination laws.

The impact of these decisions on women's careers was relatively quick. A 1986 survey of women partners in accounting firms (Hooks and Cheramy, 1988) following up on a 1983 survey, found that 'there were 157 women partners in 1986, more than a 125% increase from 69 in 1983.'

This brief overview of how the US Constitution and the US Supreme Court have reflected various sex-role ideologies reveals the great ideological change that has taken place in the United States among its populace at large and within its laws. The review also reveals several policy areas that need addressing in order to continue to improve the position of women.

Policy Areas Needing Attention in the 1990s

Three major areas will be highlighted: (1) strategies for empowerment; (2) gender difference in career patterns and career advancement within a segmented labour market; and (3) global economic and justice issues that intersect with women's empowerment.

1   Policy research on strategies for empowerment

In addition to focusing on substantive policy problems it is necessary to advance knowledge and policies on broader concerns such as the following:

how to *increase the accountability of decision-makers and decision-making systems* to women's organisations, leaders, and to women voters.

the *feasibility and advisability of establishing state-wide and local community group* that will facilitate (a) research and expansion of the knowledge-base on women and women's concerns; (b) build consensus on important policy problems and develop politically active and effective coalition/lobbying entities; and (c) provide a conduit for future leaders. Included in this set of concerns is identifying the most effective mechanisms for accomplishing these objectives.

clarification of mechanisms for moving American thought and policy-making from an assimilationist model to a multi-sociocultural model. All too often policy research has been done from a perspective that women are to be incorporated into the public realm of work, politics, and performance by changing women to fit a male model. Such absurd consequences of this paradigm are statements that 'women's bodies are too small for an artificial heart'! A more useful question is obviously how can we develop an artificial heart that will be effective for women. These absurdities arise because all too many of us accept the given social, economic, political and other structures of society as givens. From this assimilationist perspective the question all too often is, 'How can we change the talents, motivations, abilities, and bodies of women to fit existing societal structures and needs?' Policy on women needs to be embedded within the multi-sociocultural paradigm model, i.e. that societal structures and opportunities can and must be adapted to fit women's bodies and women's needs. Women do not need to become neuters or male clones to enter the labour force, rather the economy can accomodate itself to attract women.

2   Gender and career advancement within a segmented labour market

Much of the research on careers and attaining higher level managerial positions has been completed with little recognition that the US labour market is a segmented one. We need to explore in greater depth the implications of segmented labour markets for female career advancement, academic curricula, and job-related research and training programmes.

3   Global justice issues intersecting with institutionalisation of women's empowerment

In the 1990s due to the reduced number of younger white males both women and minorities will have a window of opportunity to penetrate previously foreclosed power bases. For these inroads to become significant *and permanent*, it is mandatory that we expand our understanding of how global policies and structural matters affect domestic policy for women. For example, we need to examine such topics as:

the design and content of international trade and immigration policies so that they will enhance rather than harm the domestic position of women;

the necessity of establishing a watchdog entity on international policies and global issues that will monitor developments from a feminist perspective;

the reconceptualisation of the notion of risk assessment so that it will be relevant to women's empowerment. Perhaps we need to develop criteria for assessing the impact of import/export policies on the status and well-being of women both in the US and without. For example, the salaries and status of American nurses will not improve if immigration policies continually allow the importation of nurses from Taiwan or elsewhere. Is such immigration affecting those segments of the labour market that women work in more than those in which men are clustered? In addition, can we defend fighting for justice for women in the US and not also fight for basic human rights abroad?

Conclusion

Social change typically stems from technological, economic, and other broad societal forces. Governmental policies are often reactive, attempting to control or channel these changes so as to impact existing societal structures and mores as little as possible. From a feminist perspective such reactive policy-making is not only insufficient and short-sighted, it is a barrier to the goal of women's liberation and full incorporation into society. A significant portion of the policy agenda for the 1990s must be the development of a proactive policy paradigm and the advancement of a multi-sociocultural policy paradigm.

BIBLIOGRAPHY

Board of Directors of Rotary International v Rotary Club of Duarte, 1987, 107 S. Ct. 1940.

Bradwell v Illinois, 1873, 83 US (16 Wall) 130.

Maxine N Eichner, 'Getting women work that isn't women's work: challenging gender biases in the workplace under Title VII', *Yale Law Journal*, 97 (June 1988), pp 1397–417.

N Glazer, 'The Affirmative Action Stalemate', *The Public Interest*, 90 (Winter, 1988), pp 99–114.

Goesaert v Cleary, 1948, 335 US 464–66.

Griggs v Duke Power Co, 1971, 401 US 424.

Hishon v King and Spaulding, 1984, 467 US 69.

Karen L Hooks and Shirley J Cheramy, 'Women accountants—current status and future prospects', *CPA Journal*, 58 (May 1988), pp 18–27.

Hoyt v Florida, 1961, 368 US 57, 61–2.

Johnson v Transportation Agency, Santa Clara County, 1987, 107 S Ct 1442.

Rita Mae Kelly and Jane Bayes, 'Conclusion', in *Comparable Worth, Pay Equity, and Public Policy*, Rita Mae Kelly and Jane Bayes, eds (Westport, CT, Greenwood Press, 1988), pp 239–46.

Rita Mae Kelly and Mary Boutilier, *The Making of Political Women* (Chicago, Nelson-Hall, 1978),

T H Marshall, *Class, Citizenship, and Social Development* (Garden City, NY, Double-day and Co, 1964).

Martha Minow, 'The Supreme Court 1986 Term leading cases: affirmative action—gender preferences', *Harvard Business Review*, 101 (November 1987), pp 300–10.

Karen O'Connor and Jeffrey A Siegal, 'Justice Sandra Day O'Connor and the Supreme Court's reaction to its first female member', *Women & Politics*, 10 (Summer, 1990).

Sandra Day O'Connor, 'Women and the Constitution: a bicentennial perspective', *Women & Politics*, 10 (Summer 1990).

G N Powell, *Women and men in management*. (Newbury park, CA, Sage, 1988).

Reed v Reed, 1971, 404 US 71.

Gunther Schmid, 'Equal Opportunity Policy: a comparative perspective', *International Journal of Manpower*, 5 (3) (1984), pp 15–25.

S Wermiel, 'Workers hurt by affirmative action suit', *Wall Street Journal*, June 13, 1989, A3, A-12.

Robin West, 'Jurisprudence and gender', *The University of Chicago Law Review 55* (Winter 1988), pp 1–72.

Williams, 'The Equality Crisis: Some Reflections on Culture, Courts, and Feminism', *Women's Rights L Rep* 175, 1982.

Wygant v Jackson Board of Education, 1986, 54 LW 4480.

CHAPTER 9

Gendering Rights

Elizabeth Kingdom

Abstract

In 1791, Olympe de Gouges published *Déclaration des Droits de la Femme et de la Citoyenne*. Her purpose was to draw the attention of her co-revolutionaries, of women in general, and of Marie Antoinette in particular, to the rights which she saw women as having lost in society. She adopted the same formal structure as the *Déclaration des Droits de l'Homme et du Citoyen* of 1789.

This paper begins with an analysis of the two texts, marking the articles in which de Gouges could not be content with the simple insertion of phrases such as 'and the rights of women', 'female and' and 'to both sexes', but which required radical revision. It becomes clear that, whatever the general critique of the 1789 Declaration as a social document, its formal constitution of the rights of the citizen could not reliably incorporate the 'lost rights' of pre- and post-revolutionary women.

De Gouges' exploit was a political failure, but it is valuable to contemporary feminists as an example both of the complexity of the claim that formal declarations of rights are gendered to the disadvantage of women and of the range of legal-political strategies which might be adopted to remedy that gendering of rights.

In the disputes surrounding the periodic resurgence of proposals for a Bill of Rights in the UK, references to women's rights are scarce. It may be that disputants take it for granted that, although it is typically in terms of the claimed rights of man or men that bills of rights are expressed, this time-

99

honoured legal terminology also refers to the rights of women. On the other hand, contemporary feminist writers on law and jurisprudence have seldom been persuaded of the innocence of the generic use of the singular or plural masculine pronouns. It may be, then, that the absence of a discernible feminist politics of a UK Bill of Rights is better explained by a different feminist critique. This is the critique of the discrepancy between, on the one hand, formal and ostensibly gender-neutral rights and, on the other hand, the adverse substantive or material social conditions experienced by women. With this critique translated into a heuristic applied to the Bill of Rights debate, feminists might well expect the formal rights of a Bill of Rights to be gendered, to the disadvantage of women.

Feminists could hardly want better support for this heuristic than a text which is most pertinent to the commemorative spirit of this Congress. In 1791, Olympe de Gouges published *Déclaration des Droits de la Femme et de la Citoyenne*. It was addressed to Marie-Antoinette. Her purpose was to draw the attention of her co-revolutionaries and of women in general, to what she saw as the 'lost rights' of women in pre- and revolutionary France.

Gouges' document follows the formal structure of the *Déclaration des Droits de l'Homme et du Citoyen* of 1789. The historical curiosity of the juxtaposition of the two declarations is the starting-point of this paper. But there is more to that juxtaposition than antiquarian interest. It repays attention for two reasons.

First, it is true that the narrow focus of the juxtaposition produces an idiosyncratic picture of the economic, social and political position of women in revolutionary France. But, for feminists, the juxtaposition captures a critical moment in women's history, the lacuna between the rhetoric and the reality of enlightenment philosophy and politics.

Secondly, charting the significant differences between the two Declarations exhibits the variety of Gouges' legal-political strategies. These strategies in turn reveal the complexity of the claim that formal rights are gendered to the disadvantage of women. The recognition of this complexity is an essential preliminary task in the development of a feminist politics in relation to a proposed Bill of Rights in the UK.

Olympe de Gouges

Gouges was by all accounts an extraordinary woman who surved an inauspicious youth to flout the conventional apolitical role of women and to become one of the most outspoken and hence notorious women publicists of the French Revolution (Groult, 1986; Kelly, 1989). Her literary and political writings were passionate and fearless, if not always stylish or sensible. They drew a predictable range of reactions from men and women: indifference, derision, and hostility.

The 1791 Declaration met with little interest. Indeed, of the various categories of people excluded from the vote, only the category of women was not the subject of debate among the constitution makers of the Constitution Assembly; a woman was not deemed politically competent (Hufton, 1989, p 26). Even so, it is useful today to observe the discrepancies between the two Declarations, juxtaposed at the end of the chapter,[1] as an early illustration of the problems facing any attempt to incorporate women's rights into a formal declaration of citizens' rights.

The two Declarations

One word in Gouges' 1791 Declaration is the clue to understanding the politics of the document. It is 'especially' in the phrase 'especially resistance to oppression' in Article 2. With it, Gouges gave a new twist to the natural and imprescriptible rights which appeared in Article II of the 1789 Declaration: life, liberty, property and resistance to oppression. Gouges was referring not merely to the oppression of all people under the *ancien régime* but, as the Preamble makes clear, primarily to the oppression of women by men, before and in the early years of the Revolution. This theme is developed through a number of critical departures from the 1789 document.

There are three main ways in which Gouges' document departs from the earlier Declaration. First, there are places where she was happy with the simple addition of phrases such as 'woman and', 'female and', or 'to both sexes'. Examples are in Articles 1, 14, and 17. These additions were neither cosmetic nor purely formal. Only a few women had or could hope to have property rights, and women had no liability to public functions (Hufton, 1975, *passim*; Kelly, 1989, pp 33 ff; Levy, Applewhite, and Johnson, 1979, p 6). Similarly, when Gouges proposed a voluntary tax to ease the national debt, a tax to which women would be subject, she was proposing a measure which would introduce women into public life as never before (Gouges, *Lettre*, 1788, in Groult, 1986, pp 69–72). The proposals in Articles 14 and 15 would be seen as similarly provocative. One might say that, with these additions, Gouges identifies the covert gendering of the formally declared rights and makes these rights explicitly gendered so as to achieve exactly equal rights.

Secondly, there are places where Gouges replaces references to the domination and tyranny of the *ancien régime* with references to the domination and tyranny of women by all men, whether of the *ancien régime* or of the Revolution. The most prominent example is her Preamble and Article 4. What is curious about these examples is the tension they create between, on the one hand, the attempt to raise women's social position to the level of men's and, on the other hand, the terminology which hints at a picture of a society in which women had rights over men—as if to shock men into envisaging what life would be like if women were in positions of power over them. Here it might be said that, whilst Gouges is usually content to note the gendered nature of formal rights to the disadvantage of women, and then to gender rights so as to achieve equal rights, with these examples she adopts the strategy of re-gendering rights, to women's advantage.

Thirdly, there are examples where Gouges introduces elements for which there is no parallel in the 1789 document. One example is, again, the Preamble. Her last paragraph audaciously removes the reference to the National Assembly as the author of the 1789 Declaration. Instead, it is women who are the authors of the 1791 Declaration; they are its authors because they are superior both in beauty and by virtue of their courage in maternal suffering. Another example is Article 11. Here she makes a special case of the general right of free communication and thought by drawing attention to a particular injustice of her day. As she notes in the Postamble:

> A married woman can, with impunity, give her husband bastards and give the bastards the fortune that does not belong to them. The woman who is not married has only the weakest of rights: ancient and inhuman laws have refused her the married woman's right right to the name and property of the father of her children. There have been no new laws on this matter (Gouges, Postamble, from Groult, 1986, p 109).

With these two examples, Gouges is content neither to note the gendering of a right to the disadvantage of women, nor to gender such a right in order to achieve equal rights, nor to re-gender such a right in such a way that women would have that right over men. Her strategy here is to introduce special right, to be claimed only by women.[2]

Gouges' exploit was, of course, in vain. Jane Abray has chronicled the various reasons for the failure of French feminism in this period. In her estimate, it was a 'minority interest', the feminists made a number of strategic and tactical errors, and their demands were, if anything, even more radical than those of their male revolutionary counterparts (Abray, 1975, p 56f). As Norman Hampson remarks drily, '... feminism was equally suspect to Jacobins and sans-culottes' (Hampson, 1979, p 114). Indeed, the position of women deteriorated rapidly after 1791. For example, Article XIII of the Police Code, proposed to the National Assembly in 1791, accorded only men the right to file a formal complaint against an unfaithful spouse. Susan Bell and Karen Offen note that, 'It also stipulated a two-year prison term for the wife, as well as giving husbands the opportunity to dispossess their wives of dowries or other property brought into the marriage' (Bell and Offen, 1983, p 98). And from October 1793, the women's clubs which had been one of the main vehicles for women's political involvement were prohibited by the Jacobins, forcing women back into an apolitical private existence (Groult, 1986, p 44; Kelly, 1987, p 127; Levy et al. 1979, p 5). A few specially chosen women were offered a symbolic public role as goddesses of reason to preside over religious festivals (Kelly, 1987, p 128).

Endnote

It is debatable whether the post-1791 reactionary gender politics was provoked by the political activities of women such as Olympe de Gouges or whether it represented merely the continuation of forms of oppression in practice before 1789. What is certain is that Gouges' 1791 Declaration provides the most concise and chilling illustration of the conservative nature of the 1789 Declaration with respect to gender politics. It is an object lesson in legal-political intervention and failure.

It is this intervention and failure that is so instructive for contemporary UK feminists, as they assess the debate over a draft Bill of Rights. The range of strategies which Gouges adopted in her attempt to remedy the hidden gendering of the 1789 Declaration provide two useful pointers. The first is that draft formal declarations of rights do indeed have to be scanned for hidden gendering. The second, however, is that the variety of ways in which formal declarations of rights may be gendered means that there is no simple formula for the redrafting of these rights. It follows that, for feminists, there is no substitute for piecemeal scanning of a draft Bill of Rights for hidden gendering of its proposed rights. A prior condition of that scanning is the analysis the real economic, social and political conditions on which the draft rights impinge. Indeed, Gouges' experience suggests that it is only when these analyses have been done that feminists can form a judgement not only about the content of a draft Bill of Rights but also about whether they should lend support to the general political case for such a Bill.

Declaration of the Rights of Man and Citizen

Preamble

The representatives of the French people, organised as a national assembly, considering that ignorance and neglect of, and contempt for, the rights of man are the sole causes of public misfortunes and of corruption of governments, have resolved to display a solemn declaration the natural, inalienable, and sacred rights of man, to the end that this declaration, constantly in the presence of all members of society, will continually remind them of their rights and duties, to the end that the acts of the legislative power and those of the executive power, being constantly measurable against the goal of all political institutions, will be better respected, so that the demands of citizens, based henceforth on simple and incontestable principles, will always contribute to the maintenance of the constitution and the happiness of all.

Consequently, the National Assembly recognizes and declares, in the presence and under the auspices of the Supreme Being, the following rights of man and citizen.

Article One. Men are born and remain free and equal in rights; social distinctions can be established only for the common benefit.

II. The goal of every political association is the conservation of the natural and imprescriptible rights of man; these rights are liberty, security, and resistance to oppression.

III. The source of all sovereignty is located in essence in the Nation; no body, no individual can exercise authority which does not emanate from it expressly.

IV. Liberty consists in being able to do anything that does not harm another person. Thus the exercise of the natural rights of each man has no limits except those which assure to the other members of society the enjoyment of these same rights; these limits can be determined only by law.

V. The law prohibits all acts harmful to society. There can be no hindrance to what is not forbidden, and no one can be forced to do what it does not order.

VI. The law is the expression of the general will; all citizens must participate in its expression personally or through their representatives; it should be the same for all, whether it protects or punishes. All citizens being equal in its eyes are equally admissable to all public honours, positions, and employments, according to their capacities and with no distinctions other than those of their virtues and talents.

Declaration of the Rights of Woman and Citizen

To be decreed by the National Assembly in its last meetings or at the last meeting of the next legislature.

Preamble

The mothers, daughters, and sisters, representatives of the nation, demand to be constituted a national assembly. Considering that ignorance, disregard of or contempt for the rights of women are the only causes of public misfortune and of corruption of governments, women have resolved to display in a solemn declaration, the natural, inalienable and sacred rights of woman, to the end that this declaration, constantly in the presence of all members of society, will continually remind them of their rights and duties, to the end that the acts based on women's power and those based on men's power, being constantly measurable against the goal of all political institutions, will be better respected, so that the demands of female citizens, based henceforth on simple and incontestable principles, will always contribute to the maintenance of the constitution and of good morals, and may contribute to the happiness of all.

Consequently, the sex that is superior in beauty as well as in courage of maternal suffering, recognizes and declares, in the presence and under the auspices of the Supreme Being, the following rights of women and citizen.

Article One. Woman is born free and remains equal in rights to man; social distinctions can be established only for the common benefit.

2. The goal of every political association is the preservation of the irrevocable rights of Woman and Man; these rights are liberty, property, security, and especially resistance to oppression.

3. The principle of all sovereignty is located in essence in the Nation, which is none other than the union of Woman and Man; no group, no individual can exercise any authority which does not emanate from it expressly.

4. Liberty and Justice consist of rendering to persons those things that belong to them; thus, the exercise of women's natural rights is limited only by the perpetual tyranny with which man opposes her; these limits must be changed according to the laws of nature and reason.

5. The laws of nature and of reason prohibit all acts harmful to society; there can be no hindrance to what is not forbidden by these wise and divine laws, and no one can be forced to do what the law does not command.

6. The law should be the expression of the general will; all female and male citizens must participate in its expression personally or through their representatives. It should be the same for all; female and male citizens, being equal in the eyes of the law, should be equally admissible to all public honours, positions, and employments, according to their capacities and with no distinctions other than those of their virtues and talents.

VII. No man can be accused, arrested, or detained except in cases determined by the law, and according to the forms which it has prescribed. Those who solicit, draw up, execute, or have executed arbitrary orders must be punished; but any citizen summoned or seized by virtue of the law must obey instantly; through resistance, the citizen renders himself culpable.

VIII. The law should establish only punishments that are strictly and clearly necessary, and no one can be punished except under a law established and promulgated prior to the offence and legally applied.

IX. Every man is presumed innocent until he has been declared guilty, if it is judged indispensable to arrest him, all severity that is not necessary for making sure of his person must be severely repressèd by law.

X. No one should be threatened for their opinions, even religious opinions, provided that their public demonstration does not disturb the public order established by the law.

XI. The free communication of thoughts and opinions is one of the most precious rights of man: every citizen can therefore freely speak, write and print; he is answerable for abuses of this liberty in cases determined by the law.

XII. The guarantee of the rights of man and citizen necessitates a public utility; this guarantee should be established for the advantage of eveyone, and not for the personal benefit of those entrusted with this utility.

XIII. For the maintenance of the public utility and for administrative expenses, a tax, supported in common is indispensable; it must be assessed on all citizens in proportion to their capacities to pay.

XIV. Citizens have the right to determine the need for public taxes, either by themselves or through their representatives, to consent to it freely, to investigate its use, and to determine its rate, basis, collection, and duration.

XV. Society has the right to demand an accounting of their administration from every public agent.

XVI. Any society in which the guarantee of rights is not assured, or the separation of powers not determined, has no constitution.

XVII. The right of property is inviolable and sacred; no one may be deprived of it except when public necessity, certified by law, clearly requires it, subject to just and prior compensation.

7. No woman is exempt; she can be accused, arrested, and detained in such cases as determined by law. Women, like men, must obey these rigorous laws.

8. The laws should establish only punishments that are strictly and obviously necessary. No one may be punished except under a law established and promulgated prior to the offence, and which is legally applicable to women.

9. Since it is possible for a woman to be declared guilty, then, in that event, the law must be enforced rigorously.

10. No one should be threatened for their opinions, however fundamental. Woman has the right to mount the scaffold; she should likewise have the right to speak in public, provided that her demonstrations do not disrupt public order as established by law.

11. The free communication of thoughts and opinions is one of the most precious rights of woman, since this liberty assures the legitimate paternity of fathers with regard to their children. Every female citizen can therefore freely say: 'I am the mother of a child that belongs to you,' without a barbaric prejudice forcing her to conceal the truth; she is also answerable for abuses of this liberty in cases determined by law.

12. The guarantee of the rights of woman and female citizen necessitates a public utility. This guarantee should be established for the advantage of everyone, not for the personal benefit of those entrusted with this utility.

13. For the maintenance of the public utility and administrative expenses, the contributions of women and men shall be equal; the woman shares in all forced labour and all painful tasks, therefore she should have the same share in the distribution of positions, tasks, assignments, honours, and industry.

14. Female and male citizens have the right to determine the need for public taxes, either by themselves or through their representatives. Female citizens can consent to this only if they are admitted to an equal share not only in wealth but also in public administration, and in their right to determine the proportion and extent of tax collection.

15. The mass of women, allied for tax purposes to the mass of men, has the right to hold every public official accountable for their administration.

16. Any society in which the guarantee of rights is not assured, or the separation of powers not determined, has no constitution; the constitution is nullified if the majority of individuals who compose the Nation have not co-operated in writing it.

17. The right of property is inviolable and sacred to both sexes, jointly or separately; no one can be deprived of it, since it is a true inheritance of nature, except when public necessity, certified by law, clearly requires it, subject to just and prior compensation.

NOTES

1 I have produced my own translations both of Gouges' political writings and of the two Declarations. I have used Gouges' texts as they are reproduced in Groult, 1986. To preserve the greatest symmetry between the two Declarations, so that the differences between them are more visible, I have omitted the first two paragraphs of the Preamble of the 1791 document. I use the standard reproduction of the 1789 *Declaration*.
2 For a discussion of the relation between equal rights and special rights in contemporary feminist politics, see Kingdom, 1989.

BIBLIOGRAPHY

Jane Abray, 'Feminism in the French Revolution', *American History Review*, 80 (1975).

Susan Groag Bell and Karen M Offen, *Women, the Family, and Freedom: the debate in documents* Volume One 1750–1880 (Stanford, 1983).

Olympe de Gouges (aka Marie Gouze), *Déclaration des droits de la femme et de la citoyenne* (1791), in Groult (1986).

—— 'Lettre au peuple ou projet d'une caisse patriotique par une citoyenne' (1788), in Groult (1986).

Benoîte Groulte, *Oeuvres d'Olympe de Gouges*, with an introduction (Mercure de France, 1986).

Norman Hampson, *The First European Revolution 1776–1815* (Thames and Hudson, 1979).

Olwen H Hufton, 'Women and the family economy in eighteenth century France', *French Historical Studies*, Vol 9 (1975).

—— 'Voilà la citoyenne', *History Today*, Vol 39 (1989).

Linda Kelly, *Women of the French Revolution* (Hamish Hamilton, 1989).

Elizabeth Kingdom, 'Birthrights: equal or special?', in *Birthrights*, Robert Lee and Derek Morgan eds (Routledge, 1989).

Darlene Gay Levy, Harriet Branson Applewhite, and Mary Durham Johnson, *Women in Revolutionary France*, selected documents translated with notes and commentary, University of Illinois (Chicago, 1979).

CHAPTER 10

Rethinking the Grounds for Reproductive Freedom

J Ralph Lindgren

Abstract

During the past two decades restrictions on access to contraceptive and abortion information, procedures and measures have been increasingly rolled back in the United States. The main impetus for this has come from the courts relying mainly on the newly discovered constitutional right of privacy. Public and court opposition to this linkage is one reason for seeking a new basis for defending reproductive freedom. In this paper I present yet another reason. Although privacy has thus far secured important protections of reproductive freedom, it has also exacted significant costs. The judiciary's commitment to upholding the right of privacy has resulted in undermining the integrity of the marital union and in reinforcing traditional patterns of sex segregation in the workplace. On balance, the right of privacy is an unattractive compromise. These costs are developed in the first two sections of the paper. The paper ends by proposing an alternative basis for defending reproductive freedom, equal opportunity.

Over the past two decades the right of privacy has assumed overwhelming importance in American law because of its strategic role in securing reproductive freedom. Before that this role had increasingly been filled by equality of opportunity. In recent years public support has softened for both privacy and reproductive freedom. This paper proposes disconnecting the two and renewing the drive toward grounding reproductive freedom on equality of opportunity.

Contraception and abortion information, procedures and measures began to come under increasing restrictions about a hundred years ago. First adopted at the instigation of the American Medical Association, the anti-obscenity campaign led by Anthony Comstock, and the eugenics movement, they were only later endorsed by some of the churches (Mohr, 1978).

The first major break with this pattern of restriction came in 1942 when the Supreme Court, in *Skinner v Oklahoma*, invalidated on equal protection grounds a statute authorising compulsory sterilisation of persons convicted two or more times of felonies involving moral turpitude. There the Court rejected the eugenics rationale proffered in support of the statute and asserted for the first time that the right to reproduce was 'one of the basic civil rights of man'.

After two decades of excruciatingly slow progress in rolling back accumulated restrictions on reproductive choice under an equality of opportunity analysis, the movement toward greater reproductive freedom was diverted by the Supreme Court. In a 1965 decision, the Court struck down a statute that made criminal the provision of contraceptives to and their use by married couples (*Griswold v Connecticut*). The statute, however, was invalidated not because it violated equal protection guarantees, but because reproductive decisions of married persons were seen to fall within one of the zones of privacy purportedly guaranteed by the Bill of Rights. Within a decade the Court extended the protection of the newly discovered right of privacy to include choices by unmarried people regarding the use of contraceptives (*Eisenstadt v Baird*) and by pregnant women regarding the termination of their pregnancies (*Roe v Wade*). By the early 1980s many of the restrictions on access to birth control and abortion information, procedures and materials had given way under the weight of the privacy analysis (Gordon, 1977 and Wildung, 1983). At the end of the decade, both reproductive freedom and privacy had fallen on hard times (*Webster v Reproductive Health Services*).

The increased protection of reproductive choice afforded by the privacy analysis virtually eclipsed the disadvantages experienced as a result of increased emphasis on privacy. Two of these disadvantages will be discussed. The first is that increased reliance upon the right of privacy has contributed to undermining the mutuality of the marital relationship. The second is the reinforcement that privacy has afforded to traditional patterns of sex segregation in the workplace.

When addressing the first of these disadvantages it will be useful to distinguish two models upon which marriage relationships might be patterned, viz. the familistic and the contractual models. I follow Sorokin's usage when referring to these patterns (Sorokin, 1947). The familistic model, best exemplified by the relation between a mother and her child, is characterised by an affective bond in which the separate identities of the parties merge. In marital units patterned after this model the parties are motivated by mutual love, devotion, care and self-sacrifice.[1] The contractual model, best exemplified by market relations among strangers, is characterised by co-operation for the purposes of advancing the advantage of each party considered as a separate individual. In marital units patterned after this model the parties are motivated by the desire to advance their own well-being.

When the Court first invoked privacy to protect reproductive freedom in 1965 it did so to protect marriages, seen as familistic unions, from intrusion by the state:

> Marriage is a coming together for better or for worse, hopefully enduring, and intimate to a degree of being sacred. It is an association that promotes a way of life, not causes; a harmony in living, not political faiths; a bilateral loyalty, not commercial or social projects. Yet it is an association for as noble a purpose as any involved in our prior decisions. (*Griswold*, p 486)

By 1972 the weight of the privacy argument drew the Court in a different direction. In *Eisenstadt* the Court struck down a Massachusetts statute that criminalised the distribution of contraceptive materials to unmarried people. Admitting that in *Griswold* the privacy right had been based upon the familistic character of the marital relationship, the Court abandoned that orientation and substituted a contractual model in its stead:

> Yet the marital couple is not an independent entity with a mind and heart of its own, but an association of two individuals each with a separate intellectual and emotional makeup. If the right of privacy means anything, it is the right of the *individual*, married or single, to be free from unwarranted governmental intrusion into matters so fundamentally affecting a person as the decision whether to bear or beget a child (*Eisenstadt*, p 453).

The Court's commitment to a contractual model of marriage began directly to undermine support for familistic marital practices in 1976. In *Planned Parenthood v Danforth* the Court struck down a Missouri statute that required spousal consent for first trimester abortions, a provision through which Missouri sought to secure the mutuality of important family decisions. In so doing the Court discounted the importance of mutuality within marriage as incompatible with the contractual model. Instead of regarding the abortion decision as one to be made jointly by the spouses, the Court saw it as a right of the woman considered as a separate individual.

The shift in the Court's preference from a familistic to a contractual model of marriage is regrettable for two reasons. First, as Aristotle (*Nicomachean Ethics* VIII, 3) observed, associations based on reciprocal advantage tend to be temporary both because the needs and abilities of the parties are continually changing and because alternative relationships become available from time to time. Second, parties in contractual relationships tend to be self-absorbed, intent upon advancing their own individual needs and securing their own individual rights. 'The egos of the parties', as Sorokin put it, 'remain unmerged in any real "we" ...' (Sorokin, 1947, p 103).

These qualities have come to be seen as disadvantageous for marriages.

The temporary quality of marriages has received considerable attention from social scientists in recent years. They have documented the damage it occasions for the lives of women and children (Garfinkel and McLanahan, 1986; Weitzman, 1985). The self-absorbed character of contractually structured marriages undermines the moral education of children. Spouses who are deliberately self-absorbed experience considerably greater difficulty in cultivating in their children respect for the unique worth of the individual, benevolent as opposed to egoistic dispositions, co-operative rather than free-riding attitudes and a capacity sensitively to empathise with others—all of which are necessary features of an adequate moral education.

A second disadvantage that has resulted from increased reliance on the right of privacy is reinforcement of traditional patterns of sex segregation in the workplace and the consequent denial of equal employment opportunities to deserving people. The linkage between privacy and sex segregation developed in two contexts. The earliest was the debate in the 1970s over the ratification of the Equal Rights Amendment. Opposition was based in part on the expectation that it would infringe upon personal privacy interests. Opponents charged that passage of the Equal Rights Amendment would effectively repeal existing laws requiring separate public restrooms for women and men and sex segregated prisons (Ervin, 1970; Mansbridge, 1986). Proponents countered that those results would not follow ratification because the courts would understand that the mandate of the Equal Rights Amendment is limited by the right of privacy as approved earlier in the *Griswold* decision. The argument supporting that claim was straightforward. The right of privacy established in *Griswold* protects individuals from being coerced by government officials into sexual relations; but 'under current mores' anyone required by a government official to disrobe in front of a person of the other sex is being subjected to officially coerced sexual relations; finally, failure to segregate public restrooms, sleeping quarters in prisons and similar practices, effectively requires people to disrobe in front of the other sex (Brown, Emerson, Falk and Freedman, 1972, pp 900–1).

The second context in which privacy and sex segregation became linked is Title VII of the Civil Rights Act of 1964. Since the mid 1970s about three dozen court decisions have addressed clashes between privacy and equal employment opportunity under Title VII. In the overwhelming majority of these cases privacy interests prevailed because privacy was seen as of more fundamental moral significance. Four job categories were involved: sales clerk, washroom attendant, nurse and prison guard. The reasoning in these decisions is best developed in the prison guard cases.

The job of prison guard has traditionally been seen as man's work. Correctional officers are expected to be men. This expectation parallels men's traditional role as protector and defender. The expectation is reinforced by the fact that the vast majority of prison guards are men. This *de facto* segregation of the profession has been challenged by women who aspire to careers in the field of correction. Their challenges have often been thwarted by male inmates who argue that the assignment of women to guard positions would violate their privacy because guards are required to watch inmates constantly, even while they shower, dress, sleep and use toilet facilities, and occasionally to conduct strip searches. Courts typically decide in favour of the inmates, declaring that the assignment of female guards to these duties 'clashes with a deeply held social, moral and emotional bias pervading Western Culture.' (*In Re: Long*)

In both The Equal Rights Amendment and Title VII contexts, privacy has been seen as requiring the maintenance of traditional patterns of sex segregation because privacy is rooted in what is represented as moral standards. Two central assumptions flaw this doctrine. On the one hand, it conflates sexual intimacy with the viewing and/or touching of certain body parts. On the other, it casts that combination as a plain and fundamental fact of morality.

Neither of these views can withstand critical scrutiny. Were the viewing and/or touching of certain body parts offensive because it constitutes coerced sexual relations, intimate care and observation would be equally offensive whether undertaken by a physician, a nurse or a prison guard of the other sex. Indeed, it would be even more offensive when undertaken by professionals of the same sex.

What is distinctive about those instances of viewing and/or touching that involve sexual intimacy is the assumed erotic motivation of the actors 'Why else', runs the rhetorical question, 'would a woman want to work in the men's wear department, washroom, or prison?' 'Why else would a man want to work as a nurse in an obstetrics department of a hospital?' Decisions invoking privacy to identify those job categories that *ought to be denied* to women and men rely, not on high moral principle, but on expectations prompted by stereotypes about the motivations of people who pursue non-traditional careers in traditionally sex segregated jobs that require personal contact. Those stereotypes in turn are but reflections of the types of opportunities that *have been withheld* from women and men in the past. In the employment context, then, privacy has served to rationalise the denial of important job opportunities to some people in order to avoid disturbing the ingrained expectations of some other people.[2]

Restrictions on the availability of and access to birth control information, procedures and measures, and more recently on research and development of relevant new technologies, impact upon the freedoms of everyone, but especially of women. The right of privacy, which for the past two decades has been the main instrument for rolling back such restrictions, has outlived its usefulness.

Even if the Court had not begun the process of reversing *Roe v Wade*, an alternative basis for defending reproductive freedom would still be warranted. Privacy simply is not as fundamental an interest as reproductive freedom.

Protection of the latter should no longer be secured at the expense of perpetuating costs associated with the former. A renewal of the equal opportunity analysis sidetracked by the *Griswold* decision two decades ago promises a more secure ground for reproductive freedom. That renewal, however, must begin with an examination of the feminist complaint that restrictions on reproductive choice oppresses women.[3]

The central importance of reproductive freedom is difficult to over-emphasise. Although restrictions on birth control affect both men and women, the overwhelming burden of such restrictions falls upon women. Three factors contribute to this disparate impact. First, under present technology, the biological consequences of conception are very different for women and men. Of course, sympathetic and supportive lovers and spouses can, to a significant extent, share the pregnancy experience. However, they do not experience pregnancy as an overwhelming physical intrusion as do women. Second, under the prevailing division of labour, the responsibility for caring for the resultant children falls overwhelmingly upon women. Of course, conscientious and generous lovers and spouses can, to a significant extent, share in the nurture of their children. Unresponsive employer expectations for 'seriously' aspiring professionals, however, combine with the male breadwinner stereotype to limit the extent of that involvement. Finally, under traditional standards of appropriate behaviour, the choices available to women regarding whether to engage in sexual relations at all and if so, when, with whom and under what circumstances, are considerably more restricted than are the choices allowed to men. Restrictions on birth control measures insulate this sexual double-standard from significant erosion.

It is sometimes difficult for men, especially intellectual men, the sort found in such abundance on the bench, to grasp the point here. Withholding RU 486 from the American market appears to have nothing to do with gender. Gender does not appear in the statement of the regulation or the description of the practice. It looks innocent. But, when one considers that restriction in the concrete context of the biological, sociological and moral differences sketched above, these restrictions look quite different. We then see, as with the Fable of the Fox and the Stork (*Griggs v Duke Power Co*), that the *procedure* is biased, i.e. the burdens and benefits allocated by the restrictions are not distributed randomly among women and men. The procedure disproportionately burdens women. We also see that these restrictions magnify the burdens already imposed by biology, social structure and mores on women, all to the relative advantage of men.

When viewed concretely, restrictions on reproductive choice are recognisable as the very bulwark of patriarchy, the central means traditionally deployed to contain women within the domestic sphere, there to be constantly occupied in child producing and tending. Seen in that light, the full irony of relying on the right of privacy to secure reproductive freedom is revealed. Privacy appeals serve to render women more, not less, susceptible to male domination (MacKinnon, 1983).

The drive for equality of opportunity for women as well as men has been under way for a long time (Lindgren and Taub, 1988). The enactment of Married Women's Property Acts by most states in the mid nineteenth century was among the first steps. The extension of suffrage in the early 1920s was another. The Civil Rights Act of 1964 protecting equal employment opportunity was a third. Then, in the early 1970s, came a flurry of initiatives. Among them were a series of constitutional decisions under the Equal Protection Clause and the passage by the Congress of the Equal Rights Amendment and of Title IX protecting equal educational opportunity. Not all of these initiatives were targeted sharply on equality of opportunity. One set of decisions that strayed from that goal related to reproductive freedom. They were inspired by a fascination with the newly discovered right of privacy. Having lived to regret that distraction, it is now time that the push for reproductive freedom, so central to the neutralisation of patriarchy, return to the goal of equality of opportunity. That is the source of the grievance, the source of our energy and the source of our hope for eventual triumph.

NOTES

1 Those familiar with recent feminist work in ethics will recognise a parallel with the distinction between the justice and care perspectives. (See, for example, Gilligan, 1982; Hanen and Nielsen, 1987; Kittay and Meyers, 1987; and Noddings, 1984.)
2 Nothing here implies that the alternative is callous indifference toward these expectations. Individuals may be afforded even greater protection against unwanted intimate viewing and/or touching in a number of ways provided only that those authorised to have such access are not screened on the basis of their race, colour, religion, national origin, handicap or sex.
3 The same point has been made in the context of a discussion of abortion.

> State restrictions on access to abortion plainly oppress women. *Roe v Wade* condemns such laws as a violation of the constitutional right to privacy. The rhetoric of privacy, as opposed to equality, blunts our ability to focus on the fact that it is *women* who are oppressed when abortion is denied. A privacy right that demands that 'the abortion decision ... be left to the medical judgment of the pregnant woman's attenting physician', gives doctors undue power by falsely casting the abortion decision as primarily a medical question. The rhetoric of privacy also reinforces a public/private dichotomy that is at the heart of the structures that perpetuate the powerlessness of women. (Law, 1984, p 1020. Also see Powers, 1979, p 78.)

BIBLIOGRAPHY

Aristotle, *Nicomachean Ethics*, in *Ethics* (London, Penguin, 1953).
B Brown, T Emerson, G Falk and A Freedman, 'The Equal Rights Amendment: a constitutional basis for equal rights for women', *Yale Law Journal*, 80, 871 (1972).

Eisenstadt v Baird, 405 US 438 (1972).

Sam Ervin, 'A Statement by Senator Sam Ervin', *Congressional Record*, 116, 29668, 29671 (1970).

Irwin Garfinkel and Sara McLanahan, *Single Mothers and Their Children* (Washington, DC, Urban Institute Press, 1986).

Carol Gilligan, *In A Different Voice* (Harvard University Press, 1982).

Linda Gordon, *Women's Body, Women's Rights* (Penguin Books, 1977).

Griggs v Duke Power Co. 41 US 424 (1971).

Griswold v Connecticut, 381 US 479 (1965).

Marsha Hanen and Kai Nielsen, eds, *Science, Morality and Feminist Theory* (University of Calgary Press, 1987).

In Re: Long, 127 Cal. Rptr. 732 (Ct.App.3d D. 1976).

Eva Kittay and Diana Meyers, eds, *Women and Moral Theory* (Rowman and Littlefield, 1987).

Sylvia A Law, 'Rethinking Sex and the Constitution', *Univ of Pennsylvania Law review*, 132, 955 (1984).

J Ralph Lindgren and Nadine Taub, *The Law of Sex Discrimination* (West Publishing Co, 1988).

Catherine MacKinnon, 'The male ideology of privacy: a feminist perspective on the right to abortion', *Radical America* 17, 23 (July/Aug, 1983).

Jane J Mansbridge, *Why We Lost the ERA* (University of Chicago Press, 1986).

James C Mohr, *Abortion in America* (Oxford University Press, 1978).

Nell Noddings, *Caring: A Feminine Approach to Ethics and Moral Education* (University of California Press, 1984).

Planned Parenthood v Danforth, 428 US 52 (1976).

Kathleen Powers, 'Sex segregation and the ambivalent directions of sex discrimination law', *Wisconsin Law review* 55 (1979).

Roe v Wade, 410 US 113 (1973).

Skinner v Oklahoma, 316 US 532 (1942).

Pitirim A Sorokin, *Society, Culture and Personality* (Haper & Bros, 1947).

Webster v Reproductive Health Services, US (1989).

Lenore J Weitzman, *The Divorce Revolution* (New York, Free Press, MacMillan, 1985).

Beverly H Wildung, *Our Right to Choose* (Beacon Press, 1983).

CHAPTER 11

The Rights of Man and the Goals of Women

Richard B Parker

Abstract

Modern liberalism, as exemplified by the work of the American philosophers John Rawls, Ronald Dworkin, and David A J Richards, rejects the use of race or religious caste as a basis for ordering a just society. The problem my paper addresses is: how should modern liberalism treat the difference between male and female? Are distinctions based on gender as patently unjust as those based on race or religious caste? I argue that the difference between male and female should be seen as similar to a profound difference in religious belief. Just as social institutions in a just society must not impose religious conformity and should protect and foster the freedom and capacity of individuals and groups to realise radically different visions of the religious life, so too a just society must not force persons, female or male, into roles which take no account of the deep differences between male and female, and should protect and foster the freedom and capacity of individuals and groups to realise plans of life which acknowledge those differences.

There is a rapidly growing body of American feminist literature which argues that modern liberalism, as exemplified by the work of the American philosophers John Rawls, Ronald Dworkin, and David A J Richards, is inadequate to deal with the problems of social injustice which women face in post-industrial societies.[1] This essay is an exploration of the question of whether the concepts and vocabulary of modern liberalism can adequately express the grievances and goals of these feminists. The issue is important because if modern liberalism is adequate to this task, then the moral authority and rhetorical power which the concepts and vocabulary of modern liberalism enjoy in American constitutional law and in American society generally can be enlisted in support of feminism. On the other hand, if feminists cannot use liberal theory to state their concerns, then, in order to succeed, they must create new theory, and the concepts and vocabulary of that new theory must become accepted usage in political and legal discourse in place of the currently prevailing vocabulary of liberalism. Before this extraordinarily difficult course is undertaken, liberal theory should be re-examined to see if it can be adapted to serve feminist purposes.

I argue in this essay that liberalism has been mistaken in treating the gender difference[2] in the same way that it has traditionally treated racial differences, that is, as irrelevant to any just distribution of liberties or social and economic goods. American feminists have been right to say that gender is so important that it should make a difference in determining what is a just distribution of liberties or social and economic goods. I argue that another part of liberal theory, namely liberalism's analysis of religious conflict and its compromise of that conflict by requiring separation of church and state and state protection of liberty of conscience and freedom of religious expression, can be used as a model for treatment of the gender difference. My argument will fail if differences between the genders are more difficult to compromise than differences in religious belief, but I argue that this is not so and thus liberal theory is adequate to the purposes of feminists.

The major reason for modern liberalism's hostility to discrimination based on race has been that such discrimination has historically been used to violate people's liberties. Another important reason is that racial discrimination seems to serve no useful general purpose. There is no general benefit to society in making the colour of a person's skin a fundamental basis for the distribution of social and economic goods. These two reasons correspond roughly to John Rawls' two principles of justice. (Rawls' full statement of his two principles of justice is reproduced in note 3 below.)

Liberalism recognises that, unlike racial differences, differences in ability or talent may be rational bases for unequal distribution of some social and economic goods. It may be to the advantage of every (representative) person in society if people of greater talent are given greater resources to develop that talent, so long as care is taken that such differential treatment really is to everyone's advantage. Talented elites naturally tend to over-estimate the benefit of the development of their talents to the rest of society or to over-estimate the amount of differential treatment necessary for that development. Still, if closely monitored, such differential treatment is not unjust treatment of those who receive less if they enjoy greater benefits than they would have if strict equality had been enforced. (Basic liberties cannot, however, be compromised in this way even to benefit the least advantaged class in society. This is the meaning of the 'lexical' priority which Rawls assigns to his first principle over his second principle.[3])

The received view among liberals has been that gender is similar to race; distinctions based on gender are dangerous to the liberties of women, and there is no general benefit in treating gender as similar to a difference in talent or ability so that unequal treatment of men and women might be justified by a benefit to all. This rejection by liberalism of gender as a basis for making important distinctions in a just society is the main reason why the authors of the feminist literature referred to above reject liberalism. How then should liberals respond?

It may seem on first inspection that the gender difference could be handled by Rawls' second principle as one of differential talent or ability. In the case of talent or ability, we can justify more resources going to mathematically or musically or entrepreneurially talented people on the grounds of greater benefit to society as a whole, the increase of mathematical knowledge, better musical performances, or greater economic prosperity. It is admittedly much harder to know in the case of the gender difference whom we should favour for what general benefit to society. Beyond the provision of special treatment for pregnant or nursing women to foster healthy babies, it is not clear who should be favoured. Should all women, or all men, receive an unequal share of some social good, or just those with some particular male or female trait? How much more should they receive and what are the justifying benefits to all likely to be? Difficult as these questions are, they can be asked, and answers can be attempted, within the structure of liberalism. For some feminists, this may be sufficient recognition of the gender difference. However, I think that many feminists would view as inadequate a suggestion to treat the gender difference as similar to a difference in talent or ability and therefore adequately handled by Rawls' second principle of justice. These feminists would, I think, judge this suggestion to be inadequate because it would leave untouched the nature of the basic liberties which are the subject of Rawls' first principle and which must, in a just society, be different for each sex. Can liberalism be adapted so that each sex can in principle have different liberties? I think that it can.

Rawls' first principle of justice is that 'each person is to have an equal right to the most extensive total system of equal basic liberties compatible with a similar system of liberty for all'. Liberalism has assumed that these liberties are the same for men and women, and that the problem of justice for women has been to insure that they too enjoy the Rights of Man.[4] Liberalism may have to adjust to the feminist position by saying that in a just society there are liberties peculiar to each gender. To put it in terms of Rawls' metaphor of the original position, people in the original position do not know if they are male or female, but they do know the general facts of human nature including, thanks to discoveries of feminists, the fact that men and women are so different that the total system of liberties in a just society will have to incorporate different liberties for men and for women. The liberal treatment of liberty of conscience provides a model.

In developing his conception of equal liberty, Rawls makes central use of the example of equal liberty of conscience. Because there is often no compromise possible between the absolute claims of different religions, a just society in which all enjoy equal liberty of conscience must, in the liberal view, put the principle of religious toleration above the claims of any single religion, and must separate church and state. In his focus on religious toleration as an essential characteristic of a just society, Rawls follows the American liberal tradition. Americans commonly view the First Amendment as the single most important provision of the United States Constitution. Commentators such as David A J Richards view religious toleration as the foundation of American constitutionalism. (See note 1, Richards (1986))

The phrase 'liberty of conscience' in fact refers to a list of liberties: liberty to be a Lutheran, liberty to be a Roman Catholic, liberty to be a Jew, liberty to be a Mormon, liberty to be an atheist, liberty to hold no position at all on religious issues, and so on. Each person is usually interested in exercising only one or very few of these liberties in his or her lifetime. Liberalism requires that we allow other persons to exercise liberties from this list which we ourselves have no interest in exercising. Indeed we may believe such exercise to be ridiculous or blasphenous or dangerous to society.

Rather than view gender as being like race or like talent, it my be useful to view the difference between male and female as similar to a profound difference in religious belief. Just as social institutions in a just society must not impose religious conformity and should protect and foster the freedom and capacity of individuals and groups to realise radically different visions of the religious life, so too a just society must not force persons, female or male, into roles which take no account of the deep differences between male and female, and should protect and foster the freedom and capacity of individuals and groups to realise plans of life which acknowledge those differences.

Liberalism can thus accomodate the feminist insight that men and women are radically different from one another by positing an equal liberty of gender similar to equal liberty of conscience. The liberty to realise one's feminine or masculine nature or some combination thereof can be viewed as equal in importance to the liberty to develop one's religious nature.

One objection to the analogy of religion and gender is that gender is biologically given and religion is a matter of free choice. Choosing and expressing one's religious beliefs is central to the ideal of personal autonomy which underlies liberalism, but people do not choose their gender.

An answer to this objection is that most people are born into their religion and exercise their religious freedom by practising the religion into which they were born. Furthermore, it is now technically possible to change one's gender by means of medical surgery.

A related objection is that if the analogy of freedom of religion with freedom of gender works because the distinction between biologically and non-biologically determined traits is minimised, then the analogy to freedom of religion will work with freedom of race as well.

I agree. Racial discrimination can be accepted by liberals so long as such distinctions foster expanded liberties for all (Rawls' first principle) or contribute to the welfare of all without restricting liberty (Rawls' second principle). Affirmative action programmes which allow for racial discrimination in favour of blacks to correct the effects of past discrimination are defended by liberals on this basis. (For example, see note 1 below, Dworkin (1977), pp 223–39.)

The main problem with the analogy of freedom of religion and freedom of gender is not that gender is more biologically based than religion. The main problem is that we have no clear idea of what a society which respected liberty of gender would be like. The difficulty we have in imagining what gender pluralism would be like is analogous to the problem that a fifteenth-century Spaniard might have in imagining a religiously plural society. The fifteenth-century Spaniard might view legitimate political authority as requiring a king to act as a shepherd to his people on behalf of a Christian God. The reality of a secular society in which a government founded on consent of the governed was required to place the principle of religious toleration above the claims of the Christian religion might be very difficult for her even to imagine.

In the same way that the fifteenth-century Spaniard has difficulty imagining a society which respects liberty of conscience, we have trouble imagining a society which respects liberty of gender because many of the necessary social institutions are not yet in being, or even conceived of.

Imagining social injustice is usually easier than imagining social justice. The fifteenth-century Spaniard who could not imagine how a Jew could be a full member of society could easily recognise religious persecution of Jews. In the same way, it may be difficult for us to imagine a society in which freedom of gender is practised, but we can point to contemporary examples of the violation of freedom of gender.

Every major post-industrial society contains millions of highly educated women who cannot combine rewarding careers in the workplace with a child-centred family life. Japan and the United States represent two different ways in which this problem manifests itself. In Japan, mothering and a full-time job are each defined as so time-consuming that, as a practical matter, women must choose between a job and children. In the United States, millions of women are encouraged to pursue both a career and have a family with children, yet the careers are often stunted and the children suffer. It is clear to millions of Japanese and American women that none of the patterns of life available to them is satisfactory.

Men are not much better off. Consider the feeling of many Japanese men that they are in thrall to their mothers and then to their wives, or the feeling of many American men that they are trapped in marriage and that their families and elaborate households are more of a burden than a pleasure. Social institutions often seem a series of awkward compromises between what each gender really wants, leaving neither gender fully satisfied. The continual battle of the sexes is analogous to religious conflict. It may not be as violent (although see the problem of battered women, especially in the United States), but the participants are just as dogmatic. In the same way that religious groups may simply refuse to credit the legitimacy or humanity of religious points of view radically different from their own, men and women often simply refuse to acknowledge the existence, much less the legitimacy and humanity, of the point of view of the other gender. 'Why can't a woman (man) be more like a man (woman)'? is the lament on both sides, assuming that the gender difference is even acknowledged.

Many of the ills of modern society which are blamed on dislocations caused by industrialisation or by a lack of community may be problems caused by an absence of freedom of gender. Members of both genders are forced into social roles which are nominally gender-neutral, but which in fact are awkward compromises, styles of work or living which neither gender would choose for itself. Recognition of freedom of gender will require that female parents, female lawyers, or female bankers will be free to act in different ways from male parents, male lawyers, or male bankers. In a society which is pluralistic in gender terms, neither gender would be able to define what was appropriate for the other gender. Females would not define parenting or homemaking for males and males would not define banking or politics for women. Neither gender would feel obligated to abandon patterns of behaviour because the other gender characterised them as ridiculous or immature or dangerous to society. The fundamental differences between the genders would not be dogmatically denied; they would be understood, tolerated, and accommodated as part of the liberal vision of a just society.

Liberalism can accommodate the gender difference so long as it is no greater than differences in religious belief, a fairly large gap to bridge. In terms of Rawls' metaphor of the original position, so long as the contractors in the original position do not have to know their religion in order to reach agreement on principles of freedom of religion satisfactory to all, then liberalism can bridge the gap of differences in religious belief. In the same way, if contractors in the original position can agree to principles of freedom of gender satisfactory to feminists without knowing whether they are male or female, then the powerful vocabulary of liberalism with its appeal to fair and impartial principles can be used by feminists to state their grievances and goals. Feminist theory then becomes the task of formulating liberal principles of justice which would incorporate the liberties and freedoms which women need and which could be agreed upon by contractors in the original position who did not know their gender.

In Rawls' theory, as Rawls himself would admit, contractors in the original position are not genuine bargainers at all since they all know only what all human beings share in common and so all come to the same conclusion regarding the principles of justice. Some critics of liberalism argue that differences of race or ethnicity or economic class are so deep and so definitive of the individual that the Rawlsian contractor in the original position is too abstract a conception of the person to be useful.[5] I think that these critics are wrong, but if they are right, it is likely to be the difference in gender rather than race, ethnicity, or economic class which is the gap too great to bridge with the liberal concept of the person. If the difference between the genders is so great that what they share as persons is not sufficient to generate principles of justice to which both men and women can commit themselves, then liberalism cannot accommodate feminism. But if, as seems more likely, men and women share enough to make agreement on common principles of justice possible, then liberalism and feminism are compatible.[6]

NOTES

1 See Warren, 1989 for a list of more than 150 books and articles, most published since 1980.

2 Throughout this essay I use the term 'gender difference' to mean the biological difference between the female and male sex. Other psychological or sociological definitions of the gender difference are possible and could be used without affecting my main line of argument.

3 *First Principle*
Each person is to have an equal right to the most extensive total system of equal basic liberties compatible with a similar system of liberty for all.

Second Principle
Social and ecnomic inequalities are to be arranged so that they are both:
    (a) to the greatest benefit of the least advantaged, consistent with the just savings principle, and
    (b) attached to offices and positions open to all under conditions of fair equality and opportunity.

First Priority Rule (The Priority of Liberty
The principles of justice are to ranked in lexical order and therefore liberty can be restricted only for the sake of liberty. There are two cases:
    (a) a less extensive liberty must strengthen the total system of liberty shared by all;
    (b) a less than equal liberty must be acceptable to those with the lesser liberty.

Second Priority Rule (The Priority of Justice over Efficiency and Welfare)
The second principle of justice is lexically prior to the principle of efficiency and to that of maximising the sum of advantages; and fair opportunity [Principle 2(b) above] is prior to the Difference Principle [Principle 2(a) above]. There are two cases:
    (a) an inequality of opportunity must enhance the opportunities of those with the lesser opportunity;
    (b) an excessive rate of saving must on balance mitigate the burden of those bearing this hardship. (Rawls, 1971, pp 302–3)

4 For most of its history, the women's movement has concentrated on insuring that women would be treated in the same way as men. For example, two years after the National Assembly in revolutionary France decreed the Declaration of the Rights of Man and the Citizen, Olympe de Gouges (1748–93) published the less well known Declaration of the Rights of Woman and the Female Citizen. The language tracks the language of the more famous declaration. For example, Article One of the Declaration of the Rights of Man reads, 'Men are born and remain free and equal in rights. Social Distinctions may be based only on the common

utility.' Article One of the Declaration of the Rights of Women reads, 'Woman is born free and lives equal to man in her rights. Social distinctions can be based only on the common utility.' (See Kingdom, Ch. 9) Such piggybacking of the rights of women on the rights of men was explicitly rejected by the men of the French Revolution. In October of 1793, the National Convention barred women from political activity on the grounds that 'a woman should not leave her family to meddle in the affairs of government.' (Anderson and Zinsser (1988) Volume II, p 351.)

American, British, and Japanese women fared little better until the twentieth century. What is most interesting about the feminists discussed in the text is that achieving the same rights as men is no longer their only goal. As I argue in the text, I think that liberalism can adjust to this change.

5   The best example is Sandel, 1982.
6   I am indebted to John Bruce Moore for his extensive comments on an earlier version of this essay.

BIBLIOGRAPHY

Bonnie S Anderson and Judith P Zinsser, *A History of Their Own* (Harper and Row, 1988).

Ronald Dworkin, *Taking Rights Seriously* (Harvard, 1977).

——*A Matter of Principle* (Harvard, 1985).

——*Law's Empire* (Harvard, 1986).

John Rawls, *A Theory of Justice* (Harvard, 1971).

David Richards, *A Theory of Reasons for Action* (Oxford, 1971).

——*The Moral Criticism of Law* (Dickenson Wadsworth, 1977).

——*Sex, Drugs, Death, and the Law: an essay on decriminalization and human rights* (Rowman and Littlefield, 1982).

——*Toleration and the Constitution* (Oxford, 1986).

Michael J Sandel, *Liberalism and the Limits of Justice* (Cambridge, 1982).

Karen J Warren, 'Selected bibliography on western philosophical conceptions of reason, rationality, and gender,' *American Philosophical Association Newsletter on Feminism and Philosophy*, 88, 2 (1989).

CHAPTER 12

Early Liberalism and Women's Liberty

Juhani Pietarinen

Abstract

Susan Moller Okin has argued that Hobbes's and Locke's reasonings about individualism are inconsistent, because on the one hand they accept the principle of equality but on the other hand assume the necessity for male dominance in both the family and society at large.

If Hobbe and Locke really argue both for the principle of equality and for the principle of patriarchalism, they should show how the latter could be made compatible with the former. My position is that Hobbes and Locke in fact do this, and that therefore their reasonings are not inconsistent in the way that Okin claims.

Early liberalism

The foundations of liberalism were laid by the seventeenth-century philosophers Thomas Hobbes (1588–1679), Benedict Spinoza (1632–1677) and John Locke (1632–1714). They rejected the Aristotelian conception of man and society, according to which society, as well as all reality, should be considered as a static hierarchy, in which each class or 'species' has a special place and function. This view regarded individuals as socially and morally significant only as representatives of their class or 'species'.

The liberal social thinking has been based on the idea that men are by nature independent and equal individuals, and that therefore everyone has exactly the same right to provide for their life, freedom and property to the best of their ability.

The idea of free and equal individuals is strongly opposed to the Aristotelian conception that there ought to be an essential difference between men and women, viz., that men would, by nature, be more capable leaders than women, and that the division of power in society should correspond to this difference. Therefore one could expect that the early liberals would have argued for equal political rights and equal liberty of men and women. However, this is not the case. On the contrary, each of our three philosophers clearly supports male power in family and in social life.

This has engendered astonishment and bitter criticism. Susan Moller Okin frankly accuses Hobbes and Locke of inconsistency (Okin, 1980, pp 198–201). Lorenne Clark writes that Locke's political theory is based on 'sexist assumptions' of the natural inequality of the sexes and of the natural superiority of men (Clark, 1977, p 700).[1]

I shall consider the criticism as far as Hobbes is concerned. My position is that Hobbes is not inconsistent: he argues quite logically for the reasonableness of male pre-eminence in domestic and political life. But as a defender of male pre-eminence Hobbes is definitely not a patriarchalist; he might merely be called a paternalist.

I shall also consider briefly what might be said about women's freedom from the Hobbesian viewpoint.

The criticism of Hobbes

Susan Moller Okin's criticism of Hobbes's argumentation is as follows (op. cit., pp 197–8):

Hobbes's political philosophy is founded on the idea of the natural equality of human beings in the sense that 'they are equally able to kill one another'. Hobbes also acknowledges that the mother is the original master of her children in the state of nature. But, on the other hand, Hobbes proceeds to present the family 'as a strictly and solely patriarchal institution', because he assumes 'the necesity of male dominance in both the family and society at large'. This, however, runs counter to the initial premises of human equality and egoism.

Let us write down the crucial principles here. The first one expresses the idea of the natural equality of individuals:

(E)   All human beings are equal by nature. (The principle of natural equality)

The second principle shows the foundation of authority:

(C)   Legitimate authority is always based on the free consent of subjects. (The principle of consent)

The third principle is concerned with pariarchalism:

(P)   The father is the natural authority in the family. (The principle of patriarchalism)

Now, according to Moller Okin, Hobbes accepts all three principles, and this leads him necessarily to an inconsistency.

Family in the state of nature

In the state of nature, Hobbes says, each person has the liberty

> to use his own power, as he will himself, for the preservation of his own nature; that is to say, of his own life; and consequently, of doing anything, which in his own judgment, and reason, he shall conceive to be the aptest means thereunto (*Leviathan*, 14 § 1, p 189).[2]

This kind of *ius naturale* does not make any difference between men and women.

The equality stated by principle (E) can therefore be interpreted as an equal natural liberty:

(E1)   All human beings have equal natural liberty to preserve their life. (The principle of natural liberty)

But although Hobbes takes (E1) as one of his initial premises, he does not think that all individuals are in fact equally able to preserve their life. He writes that we find 'one man sometimes manifestly stronger in body, or of quicker mind than another' (13 § 1, p 183). And presumably very small children, seriously ill persons and old people are quite helpless to protect themselves against attacks.

Thus Hobbes rejects the following reading of (E):

(E2)   All human beings are equally able to preserve their life. (The principle of equal ability of preservation)

Would men be more capable than women? In an interesting passage, quoted by Moller Okin, Hobbes says that 'there is not always that difference of strength or prudence between the man and the woman, as that the right can be determined without war' (20 § 4, p 253). By 'right' Hobbes means here the right of dominion over children. But what does this 'always' mean? Does the difference *usually* exist? It is easy to imagine that at least in certain situations a woman is in a much more unfavourable position than a man, for instance when she is pregnant or feeding a baby. Hobbes does not mention such reasons, but they might have loomed before him.[3] Anyway, Hobbes obviously thinks that usually, though not always, men are better at and more capable than women of protecting themselves against the other persons.[4]

There is still another important reading of (E), the one suggested by Moller Okin. Although acknowledging individual differences of physical and mental abilities among persons, Hobbes argues that the differences are not 'so considerable, as that one man can hereupon claim to himself any benefit, to which another may not pretend, as well as he', which means that 'the weakest has strength enough to kill the strongest' (13 § 1, p 183). The third reading of (E) would then be:

(E3)   All individuals are equally capable of endangering each other's life. (The principle of equal ability to kill)

Presumably this principle does not apply to certain marginal persons, but women, in general, do certainly not belong to such marginal groups.

Hobbes's reasoning about the establishment of families is straightforward. Families are set up for security, and it would be to the advantage of all parties if the less able persons submit to the power of a strong and prudent individual.[5] The submission is based on mutual agreements on two conditions: (i) the subjects refuse to use their natural liberty against the family authority and each other (non-interference); (ii) the authority promises to protect the family members against enemies. The power of the authority is therefore based on the *free consent* of all family members, i.e. the individuals entering into the family contract only make use of their natural liberty to which they are equally entitled. The Hobbesian families are in fact small-scale civil societies.[6]

Who then will be the head of the family, the family sovereign? Hobbes's answer is that the parties have to decide: the best one should be elected! As mentioned above, Hobbes admits the possibility that a woman may be superior and therefore become the family sovereign.

It is true that Hobbes does not pay very much attention to the special power relations between men and women. What he does emphasise is that (i) all power relations must be founded on the free consent of the parties, (ii) the power must be as absolute as possible, and (iii) the power must not be divided, but should remain strictly in the hands of one person.

Hobbes categorically rejects the possibility that the husband and his wife would govern the family as equal companions, because 'no man can obey two masters' (20 § 4, p 253).[7] In other words, two masters equally entitled to be leaders would seriously weaken the security of the whole family if they quarrel with each other and give conflicting orders to their subjects.

In sum, Hobbes admits the equality of men and women in the sense of (E1). He reasons further that since (E3) is true, family contracts are necessary for a reasonable life. In making these contracts, people use their natural liberty and submit by free consent to an authority, and this is reasonable in view of the fact that (E2) is *not* true. The argument implies that individual variations may exist between persons with respect to their physical and mental abilities, but all kinds of male and female essences are denied. In this respect Hobbes's thinking differs decisively from the Aristotelian and the Roman

patria potestas traditions. It is obvious that he does not argue for patriarchalism in the sense that fathers should have by some natural or divine law
the authority in the families.

On the other hand, it is true that Hobbes does not take very seriously the
possibility that women would be elected as family heads. He appeals here to
empirical evidence that usually men are elected as family sovereigns: '... for
the most part commonwealths have been erected by the fathers, not by the
mothers of the families' (20 § 5, p 254).[8] He concludes from this that the male
pre-eminence has been and will be in most cases the best choice. But he denies
clearly that it would be an absolute necessity, for the basic tenet in his
reasoning is that paternal power, whenever it occurs, is based on a deliberate
and common agreement between men and women.

This kind of reasoning does not contain any inconsistency of the kind
Susan Moller Okin refers to.

It is important to distinguish here between two different meanings of the
principle of patriarchalism (P). In the strict sense patriarchalism claims that
the fathers should have the authority in the family merely due to the fact that
they are fathers, i.e. because some divine or natural law, or tradition, so
requires. Hence the first meaning of (P):

(P1)   The father should necessarily be the authority in the family.

This is rejected by Hobbes. What his argument implies is that the father is a
'natural' authority in the sense of being in most cases the best guarantor of
protection. The other reading of (P) would therefore be:

(P2)   The father would in general be the most reasonable choice as the
       family authority.

In other words, the father's power derives from the free consent of the family
members. As a result, principle (P2) is perfectly compatible with principles
(E1), (E2) and (C), and Hobbes's reasoning is not therefore inconsistent in
the way Susan Moller Okin states.

What I have said above concerns 'families by institution' where the authority is established by contract.[9] However, the sovereign power may sometimes be acquired by force. When a physically superior person becomes the
master of another person's life and death, then the latter has only one
reasonable choice: to promise not to resist the master. From this kind of
consent stems the right of dominion of the superior over the inferior.

Hobbes seems to think that certain familial relation are based on this kind
of right. He explains that the mother has the right of dominion over her child
unless she does not alienate it to another person. In a family based on
contracts the right belongs to the head of the family, by virtue of the mutual
agreement between the mother and the father. Another type of dominion is
the master-servant relationship, where the right of dominion is based on the
consent of the servant.

Hobbes nowhere mentions the possibility that the husband-wife relationship would be based on the acquisition of dominion by force. It does not affect my argumentation, however, if we grant this as a real possibility.

The general conclusion is that it does not matter very much whether the family sovereigns receive their power by contract or by acquisition. In both cases the sovereign has absolute power over the other family members, and in both cases the most capable should get the sovereignty—regardless whether this person is a man or a woman.

Family in the commonwealth

In the state of nature the family sovereign has unlimited natural liberty with respect to individuals outside the family.[10] By *ius naturalis* he/she is entitled to use any means in protecting the family members against the attacks of other families and individuals. But the family leader must not do damage to his/her own subjects, for otherwise the covenants and other consensual arrangements would lose their significance.

But the state of nature is not beneficial for people. The next step is therefore that the family leaders submit by mutual covenants to one person who becomes the state sovereign. Through this kind of social contract the unlimited power of the family heads is transferred to the political sovereign who becomes obliged to protect the subjects. There is nothing in this construction which would exclude the possibility that a woman becomes elected as the state sovereign.

Hobbes emphasises again and again that the social contract is reasonable only when each family is compensated for the loss of unlimited natural power by something much more valuable, viz., by civil rights or liberties. In civil society, and only there, men have 'the liberty to buy, and sell, and otherwise contract with one another; to choose their own abode, their own diet, their own trade of life, and institute their children as they themselves think fit, and the like' (21 § 6, p 264). The civil liberties are genuine legal rights because the sovereign sees to it that the laws are obeyed. Such rights cannot exist in the Hobbesian state of nature.

The ultimate aim of such political liberties is of course the welfare of citizens. Hobbes's theory of civil society can be understood as a kind of justification for the new social order that step by step replaced feudalism and this is now called the market system.

But who are endowed with civil liberties or rights? My interpretation is that only family leaders can have such rights, because these rights are based on their mutual covenants and concern therefore only them. Of course it is in the interests of the heads of families that the state sovereign will protect all members of their families, and therefore the most important laws of the state, those which protect the lives of persons, concern all subjects equally. But this is the case because the family sovereigns wish it to be so.

One might ask here that if the state sovereign is absolutely free to enact any kind of laws whatever, why could the other members of the families not get civil liberties as well? This, however, would be incompatible with Hobbes's rationale. When the individuals in the state of nature give up their original power (or a substantial part of it) to the family sovereign, it means that this person becomes fully authorised to represent the family always and everywhere. The alienation of power is irrevocable as long as any party does not violate the covenant. When the family sovereigns further alienate part of their power to the state sovereign, they at the same time transfer part of the original natural power of the other family members. Because the transfer of power in this way is a transitive event, the state sovereign cannot give back to the family members any liberties and powers they have once relinquished.

Hobbes is quite explicit on this point. The life of all members of the family is protected by the common laws, but 'in all other actions, during the time they are under domestique government, they are subject to their fathers, and masters, as to their immediate sovereigns' (22 § 14, p 285).[11] The family sovereigns keep their authority except for the part that 'the law of the commonwealth takes from them'. Therefore only the heads of the families have full political rights, i.e. only they are authorised to make contracts in the name of the family.

Hobbes's reasoning seems quite odd. Why should the same kind of persons be qualified as the best leaders both in the state of nature and in civil society? It may be natural to think that in the state of nature one needs physical strength and skill in hunting and fighting. But in civil society the most important aims are, as Hobbes himself remarks, the increasing of one's property and the education of children. Because the responsibility for the protection of subjects has been transferred to the state sovereign, should not the head of the family now be chosen on entirely other grounds than in the state of nature?

Hobbes does not think so. His opinion is that strong authorities are needed in civil society as much as in the state of nature. Strength and prudence are the personal properties he seems to regard as most important. For instance, education cannot be successful if the children do not absolutely obey the family authority. The children 'are to be taught, that originally the father of every man was also his sovereign lord, with power over him of life and death; and that the fathers of families, when by instituting a commonwealth, they resigned that absolute power, yet it was never intended, they should lose the honour due unto them for their education' (30 § 11, p 382). The educator must remind the children of the fact that it is absolutely *reasonable* for them to obey and honour the head of the family, just as in the state of nature, i.e. remind the children of their free consent to submit to the authority of the family sovereign.

The education aims at producing loyal and industrious citizens, citizens who will promote the most important ends of the society: peace, productivity and welfare. Strength, courage and prudence are the properties most approved of by Hobbes; they will help best in hunting as well as in trading.

It is no wonder then that Hobbes took it as almost self-evident that the family sovereign with full political rights should be a man. In the state of nature a man is more capable, at least in general, to take care of the duty of protection, and when this very same reason is transferred as such to the political realm, then power will remain in men's hands.

Hobbes on freedom

By the *ius naturale*, all individuals in the state of nature are equal with respect to their natural liberty, as principle (E1) states. This kind of freedom may be defined as follows:

(L1)   A person X is naturally free $=$ X is entitled without restrictions to do anything for the subsistence. (Natural freedom)

But natural liberty, Hobbes says, is 'most fruitless' in the state of nature, because it allows the individuals to frustrate each other's endeavours.

Therefore another kind of freedom is needed: 'Liberty, or freedom, signifies (properly) the absence of opposition; (by opposition, I mean external impediments of motion)' (21 § 1, p 261). Call this freedom from intervention:

(L2)   A person X is free to do A $=$ there exist no external constraints which would render A impossible for X. (Freedom from intervention)

A person is free, says Hobbes, if he 'in those things, which by his strength and wit he is able to do, is not hindered to do what he has a will to' (21 § 2, p 262). Michael Taylor calls this conception the 'pure negative freedom'. He remarks that according to this conception, neither threats nor offers, however great the associated penalties or rewards, restrict a person's freedom for the simple reason that such things do not render their actions impossible (Taylor, 1982, pp 144–5). Hobbes makes the same point by saying that 'fear and liberty are consistent', so that for instance 'all actions which men do in commonwealths, for *fear* of the law', are free when the violations of law are not made impossible (21 § 3, pp 262–3).

If we want, *contra* Hobbes, to regard threats and offers as relevant restrictions of freedom of action, we have to define another notion of freedom:

(L3)   A person X is free to do A $=$ there exists no coercion upon X to do or not to do A. (Freedom from coercion)

The primary aim of the establishment of a state sovereign in Hobbes's theory is to guarantee to subjects certain important liberties of the type (L2), 'such as is the liberty to buy, and sell, and otherwise contract with one another; to choose their own aboad, their own diet, their own trade of life, and institute their children as they themselves think fit' (21 § 6, p 264). But are all subjects granted such liberties equally? We have concluded from

Hobbes's reasoning that only the sovereigns or masters of families can be invested with them, because they are authorised to decide for the whole family in civil matters. However, the main point of his reasoning is that all family members have after the establishment of the sovereign power more opportunities than previously for providing for their welfare, because their freedom from intervention increases.

Hobbes also argues that the submission by consent to the power of an authority is not inconsistent with the natural liberty of subjects, as the submission to a sovereign is a free decision of the subjects, i.e. the subjects only use their natural liberty, and, moreover, 'every subject has liberty in all those things, the right whereof cannot by covenant be transferred', for 'covenants not to defend a mans own body, are voyd' (21 § 1, p 268).

However, by consent the subjects deny themselves certain kinds of action: they are not morally free to violate their covenants. Hence the fourth type of freedom emerges:

(L4)   A person X is free to do A = X is permitted to do A. (Moral permission)

In this sense the subjects are not free to disobey the sovereign's orders (although in the sense of (L2) they are), except when the orders are against the end for which the covenants are made. Hobbes even says that when 'our refusal to obey, frustrates the end for which the Sovereignty was ordained; then there is no liberty to refuse: otherwise there is' (21 § 11, p 269). Thus the family members would always be permitted to disobey the orders and decisions of the family sovereign when the disobedience is not detrimental to the end of the covenants made.

But what kind of cases would they be? According to Hobbes, every subject is, by free convenant, the 'author of all the actions, and judgments of the Sovereign instituted', and therefore 'it follows, that whatsoever he doth, it can be no injury to any of his subjects; nor ought he to be by any of them accused of injustice' (18 § 2 mom 4, p 232). The sovereigns are thus the agents of their subjects. Moreover, the sovereign judges what doctrines are 'fit to be taught' to the subjects and what goods they may enjoy and what actions may be performed 'without being molested by any of his fellow subjects' (ibid. mom 6). The decision-making concerning socially important matters remains therefore tightly in the hands of the family sovereigns—they 'lose afterward no more of their authority, than the law of the common-wealth taketh from them' (22 § 14, p 285). In any case, where the sovereign has not prescribed any rule, 'there the subject has the liberty to do, or forbear, according to his own discretion' (21 § 13, p 271). As Hobbes remarks, this kind of liberty, i.e. freedom of type (L4), is in some cases more and in some less, 'according as they that have the Soveraignty shall think most convenient' (ibid.).

In sum, the Hobbesian model of freedom can be expressed in the following way: originally all individuals have equal and unlimited natural freedom (L1), but their actual freedom of action in the sense of (L2) is small. By establishing family and state sovereigns the freedom of type (L2) of people is essentially increased, and in a commonwealth new kinds of liberties of type (L2) are created (civil liberties). It also makes sense to speak in a commonwealth of freedom of type (L4) (moral permissions) and of restrictions on it.

The freedom from coercion (L3) does not play any role in this model, nor freedom in the sense of personal autonomy, i.e. the idea of authentic or self-governing persons.

Women's freedom

What kind of implications might the Hobbesian model have with respect to women's freedom? Because the nature and the relative amount of freedom depends on the social standing of a citizen, we have to consider four different cases: woman as a state sovereign, as a family sovereign, as a servant in the family, and as a solitary citizen.

The first two cases are quite marginal, because the Hobbesian model does not favour women as sovereigns, although it does not altogether exclude this kind of possibility. As state sovereigns men and women are equal with respect to their freedom, and the freedom is maximal in any sense of (L1)–(L4). But the opportunity for a woman to get this position is negligible.

As family sovereigns women would have full political liberties, and they would also have practically an absolute power of making decisions concerning such family affairs which fall into the scope of what Hobbes calls the 'silence of law'. In brief, they would be equal to men as family sovereigns. But, again, this remains a purely theoretical possibility, for Hobbes's argument implies that in general it would be unreasonable to elect women as sovereigns.

The most common situations are, according to Hobbes's reasoning, those where the women is either the wife or a servant of a male family sovereign. In both cases she has more freedom of intervention after the family contract than before it, and more of it in the commonwealth than in the state of nature. But as the wife she shares only partly in the civil liberties of her husband, and she has no moral or legal right (liberty in the sense of (L4)) to interfere with the regime of her husband. Perhaps Hobbes would remark here that the wife would in any case be free to disobey her husband, free in the sense of (L2), although she might be punished for such conduct. But this would not be an interesting remark. It is of course not very significant to have an open option between two alternatives, both of which are very negative. More importantly, the wife would not be free from coercion anyway (free in the sense of (L3)).

To what extent would the wife be morally permitted to act against her husband's will? One interpetation of Hobbes's reasoning (perhaps the correct one) is that only in cases in which her husband's rule endangers her security of life. But as remarked above, Hobbes also says that the subject always has the liberty to refuse to obey when the refusal does not frustrate the end for which the sovereignty had been established. Perhaps he thinks these two things will amount to one and the same? But more importantly, Hobbes cannot see any rational grounds for a subject to disobey the sovereign, because 'all that is done by him [the sovereign] in virtue of his power, is done by the authority of every subject, and consequently, he that brings an action against the sovereign, brings it against himself' (21 § 13, p 271). Because the family head is the rational agent of all family members, it would be irrational for them to disobey, and all irrational behaviour can easily be judged as detrimental to the rational ends of commonwealths!

The Hobbesian model presumes that men and women share common views on the ends of life as well as the reasonable means to achieve these ends. Then, together with the idea of free consent ('free' in the sense of (L1)), it follows that there is nothing in the thoery itself that would violate the basic liberty of women. This seems to be Hobbes's conclusion, and a similar type of argument prevails in the whole liberal tradition.

As servants women are in a similar position to housewives. Perhaps we are allowed to assume that the male family sovereign will use less coercion against his wife than against his servants, and less against servants 'by institution' than servants 'by acquisition'.

What about the liberties of a solitary woman? Hobbes is silent about such a case. Because the chances for the survival of a woman living on her own are very low in the state of nature, it would be irrational for anyone to refuse to make a family contract, and in a civil society such an individual would be outlawed. As an outlawed person she retains all of her natural liberty, but that would be the only liberty she would have.

I would like to make a few concluding remarks about the male bias in Hobbes's reasoning.

The idea of equal natural liberty of men and women was a revolutionary achievement. Without the rejection of the Aristotelian view of an essential difference between men and women as well as the Roman tradition of patriarchalism, the later liberal development of women's rights would not have been possible.[12]

On the other hand, Hobbes's argument for the reasonableness of male dominance in domestic and political life was apt to retard female emancipation. The most obvious sources of male biases are his presumption of the common rational ends of men and women and his appeal to empirical evidence concerning male and female abilities.

If we could take for granted that men and women would agree on the most important ends of social life and that both of them would have certain special abilities to pursue these ends, then Hobbesian reasoning would be quite appealing. Of course, it would then be reasonable to establish all power relations on the basis of free deliberation in such a way that everyone would be able to use their abilities to their best possible advantage and thereby promote the welfare of society. But can this kind of presumption of common rationality ever be justified?

And furthermore, how do we verify what the typical 'male' and 'female' qualities are? The early liberal thinkers appealed to the fact that throughout human history men have had leadership positions, and they explained this as a result of a difference between the abilities of men and women. But of course this kind of reasoning is open to severe criticism.

The idea of personal autonomy creates another serious problem. Does it have any place in Hobbes's model of liberty? I think Hobbes simply assumed that people in the state of nature are rational decision-makers with clear-cut desires and beliefs required for making 'autonomous' or free decisions. But this is a very simplified view of an autonomous person. Should a housewife who does not share her husbands values and beliefs still think that it is reasonable to obey him and educate herself to do so autonomously? To prevent such disagreements, the Hobbesian ideal of hierarchical power structures demands a strongly paternalistic socialisation of citizens to assume various family roles, which seems to be antithetical to the idea of personal autonomy.[13]

Perhaps Hobbes did not regard such a mode of socialisation as problematic at all, because, in his view, its aim was to educate rational persons who would then be able to pursue freely and eagerly common ends. Or perhaps he thought that only leaders need to be autonomous persons.

NOTES

1 Christine de Stefano (1983) has also argued carefully that Hobbes's social theory reflects a male bias.
2 The page numbers refer to MacPherson's (1968) edition.
3 John Locke refers to woman's lot to 'give birth to her children in pain and dolor', which makes her the 'weaker sex' (Locke, 1967, book I § 102).
4 Hobbes uses for instance the expression 'men of feminine courage' when he speaks of 'natural timorousness' (*Leviathan*, 21 § 12, p 270).
5 The Hobbesian family consists of a man, his spouse and children, and servants.
6 Hobbes remarks that family 'is itself, as to the rights of sovereignty, a little monarchy' (*Leviathan*, 20 § 9, p. 257). That he in fact regards families as small-scale commonwealths has been carefully documented by Richard Chapman (1975).
7 As to the right of dominion over children, Hobbes's argument is that originally the child is possessed by the mother, but she may transfer the dominion to the other parent by contract; see *Leviathan*, 20 § 5, p 254.
8 Similarly, Spinoza asks whether 'women are subordinate to men by nature or by institution', and argues as follows: if women were by nature equal to men, 'equally developed with respect to the strength of their character and their ability, on which properties the human power and also the rights first of all are based', then there would certainly have been states governed by both of the sexes as well as by women alone. But because such states exist nowhere, women are inferior to men by their nature and must therefore necessarily give way for them. (*Tractatus Politicus*, 11 § 4).

9   Hobbes makes the distinction between commonwealths by institution and com-
     monwealths by acquisition in *Leviathan*, 18 § 15, p 228. It applies to families
     regarded as small-scale commonwealths.
10   For an illuminating discussion of the status and significance of the family sov-
     ereigns, see Gordon Schochet (19670.
11   From this quotation we may notice that Hobbes writes as if it were self-evident
     that the family sovereign is the father. He often writes in this manner in *Leviathan*.
     But this fact does not disprove the argument that Hobbes's *theory* grants women
     a possibility to become family sovereigns.
12   Cf. Ginerva Conti Odorisio's (1983, p 71) conclusions of Hobbes's significance
     for female liberation.
13   For an interesting general discussion of personal autonomy and feminine social-
     isation, see, e.g. Diana Meyers (1987a,b).

BIBLIOGRAPHY

R Chapman, 'Leviathan writ small: Thomas Hobbes on the family,' *American Political Science Review*, 69 (1975), pp 76–90.

L Clark, 'Women and John Locke; or, who owns the apples in the Garden of Eden?' *Canadian Journal of Philosophy*, 7 (1977).

G Conti Odorisio, 'Matriarcat et patriarcalisme dans la pensée politique de Hobbes et de Locke', in Ida Magli & Ginerva Conti Odorisio, *Matriarcat et/ou pouvoir des femmes* (Des Femmes, Paris, 1983).

T Hobbes, *Leviathan*, ed C B MacPherson (Pelican Books, 1968).

J Locke, *Two Treatises of Government*, ed P Laslett (2nd ed, Cambridge, 1967).

D T Meyers, 'Personal autonomy and the paradox of feminine socialization', *The Journal of Philosophy*, 34 (1987a), pp 619–28.

D T Meyers, 'The socialized individual and individual autonomy: an intersection between philosophy and psychology', in *Women and Moral Theory*, E Feder Kitan and D Meyers, eds (Rowman & Littlefield, Totowa, NJ 1987b), pp 139–53.

S Moller Okin, *Women in Western Political Thought* (Virago, London, 1980).

G Scochet, 'Thomas Hobbes on the family and the state of nature', *Political Science Quarterly*, 82 (1967), pp 427–45.

B Spinoza, *Tractatus Politicus*, in C Gebhardt, ed, *Spinoza Opera*, 4 vols (Heidelberg, 1925), 3, pp 269–354.

C di Stefano, 'Ideology in political theory: Hobbesian man considered', *Women's Studies International Forum*, 6 (1983), pp 633–44.

CHAPTER 13

Women as Ends—Women as Means in the Enlightenment

Patricia Ward Scaltsas

Abstract

Throughout the eighteenth century, there were women philosophers and thinkers who argued on functionalist grounds for women's right to education. But there is evidence that there was a second, very different strand of argumentation developing within the same century, from women who were arguing from liberal/perfectionist principles (notably Mary Astell and Catharine Macaulay Graham). The result is a tension between the two camps: the functionalist arguments for the education of women in the eighteenth century were premised on the assumption that women have a functional role to play in man's life; this is incompatible with arguments that hold the self-fulfilment of women as the ultimate justification of women's rights to education and development. My thesis in this paper is that this tension in the eighteenth-century arguments for the emancipation of women is resolved by an integration of the liberal/perfectionist and functionalist positions in Mary Wollstonecraft's 1792 monograph, *A Vindication of the Rights of Woman*. Her defence is built on two different types of argument: the one type of argument rests on liberal/perfectionist principles, making reference to what is intrinsically valuable to the individual; while the other type of argument follows functionalist principles with reference to what promotes maximal benefit in society at large. The integration is achieved by making functionalist principles derivative from and conditioned by liberal/perfectionist principles. The culmination of this integration is in Harriet Taylor Mill's 1851 article, 'Enfranchisement of Women'. She extended the application of the combined use of liberal/perfectionist and functionalist arguments, from the defence of women's right to an equal education to a more vigorous justification of women's rights to vote and choice of employment. Her liberal/perfectionist argument is that increased social and intellectual responsibility will stimulate and exercise the moral and mental faculties of the individual woman, thus furthering her individual fulfilment. Her functionalist/utilitarian arguments rest on the beneficial results that the individual development of women will have on men and society in general. Denying women social and political equality demoralises and vulgarises the character of both women and men.

Throughout the eighteenth century, there were women writers and thinkers who argued on functionalist grounds for women's right to education. But there was a second, very different strand of argumentation developing within the same century, from women writers and philosophers who were arguing from liberal/perfectionist principles. There is a tension between these two ways of argumentation for the improvement of the condition of women in society. The tension is created by the fact that functionalist arguments for the education of women in the eighteenth century were premised on the assumption that women have a functional role to play in man's life. This is incompatible with arguments that hold the self-fulfilment of women as the ultimate justification of women's right to education and development. My thesis in this paper is that this tension in the eighteenth-century arguments for the emancipation of women is resolved by an integration of the liberal/perfectionist and functionalist positions in Mary Wollstonecraft's defence of women's rights in 1792. The culmination of this integration is in Harriet Taylor Mill's defence of women's right to vote in 1851.

Liberal/perfectionist principles

Let us first examine some of the liberal/perfectionist lines of argumentation that were developed. Perfectionism advocates a particular goal or end because it is intrinsically valuable. The fundamental goal in most perfectionist theories is to realise a person's potential as a human to its fullest degree because this is considered intrinsically valuable. Liberal theories advocate principles of freedom and fairness. The works of the seventeenth-century philosopher John Locke are commonly seen as the root of the eighteenth-century Enlightenment. Locke's arguments that 'Mankind' has Natural Rights as human beings to freedom and equality provided the conceptual and theoretical basis for social and political reform movements and revolutions of the eighteenth and nineteenth centuries. As early as 1700, just ten years after the publication of Locke's *Essay Concerning Human Understanding* and *Two Treatises of Government*, a woman writer, Mary Astell, argued in print for the freedom and equality of women, applying Lockean principles of natural rights to the case of women in a way that Locke himself did not.

Locke argues in the *Second Treatise*, ch ii, § 4, that 'all Men are naturally in ... a *State of Perfect Freedom* to order their Actions, and dispose of their Possessions, and Persons as they think fit, within the bounds of the Law of Nature, without asking leave, or depending upon the Will of any other Man.' In § 6 he goes on to argue:

> the *State of Nature* has a Law of Nature to govern it, which obliges every one: And Reason, which is that Law, teaches all Mankind, who will but consult it, that being all equal and independent, no one ought to harm another in his Life, Health, Liberty, or Possessions ... And being furnished with like Faculties, sharing all in one Community of Nature, there cannot be supposed any such *Subordination* among us ...

In ch vi, § 54, Locke explains that when he says 'That all Men by Nature are equal' he does not mean *all* sorts of equality. Inequalities may arise because of, for example, age, virtue, 'Excellency of Parts', merit, birth, or alliance. But Locke argues:

> yet all this consists with the *Equality*, which all Men are in, in respect of Jurisdiction or Dominion one over another, which was the *Equality* I there spoke of, as proper to the Business in hand, being that *equal Right* that every Man hath, *to his Natural Freedom*, without being subjected to the Will or Authority of any other Man.

However, Locke does not apply his principles of Natural Rights to liberty and equality in the same way to the case of women. One of his main concerns in the *First Treatise* is to argue against the view that divinely established conjugal power justifies monarchical power, as part of his attack on Sir Robert Filmer's (*Patriarcha*) attempt to justify autocracy on Biblical and 'natural' patriarchal grounds. Locke argues that the Bible does not give 'any Authority to Adam over Eve, or to Men over their Wives, but only foretels what should be the womans Lot, how by his Providence he would order it so' and, given that the laws and 'customs of Nations have ordered it so', he assents to this inequality and says 'there is ... a Foundation in Nature for it'. At most, Locke goes on to explain in the *First Treatise*, ch v, § 47–8, the words spoken to Eve

> can be no other Subjection than what every Wife owes her Husband, and ... if this be the *Original Grant of Government* and the *Foundation of Monarchical Power*, there will be as many Monarchs as there are Husbands. If therefore these words give any Power to Adam, it can only be a Conjugal Power, not Political, the Power that every Husband hath to order the things of private Concernment in his Family, as Proprietor of the Goods and Land there, and to have his Will take place before that of his Wife in all things of their common Concernment ...

Later in the *Second Treatise*, ch vii, § 82, Locke justifies the husband's power over the wife's when he argues that in cases of disagreement over common concerns, it is 'necessary, that the last Determination, i.e. the Rule, should be placed somewhere, it naturally falls to the Man's share, as the abler and the stronger'.[1]

Mary Astell turns Locke's argument around. As seen above, one of Locke's arguments is that absolute authority in the family cannot justify absolute sovereignty in the state. Mary Astell argues that if there is no justification for absolute sovereignty in the state, there can be no justification for absolute authority in the family. While Locke then goes on to argue that there is in fact no absolute authority in the family,[1] Astell argues that there *is* in fact absolute authority in the patriarchal family. In *Reflections Upon Marriage* (1700) Astell argues

> ... If Absolute Sovereignty be not necessary in a State how comes it to be so in a Family? or if in a Family why not in a State; since no reason can be alleg'd for the one that will not hold more strongly for the other ... If *all Men are born free*, how is it that all Women are born slaves? As they must be if the being subjected to the *inconstant, uncertain, unknown, arbitrary Will* of Men, be the perfect Condition of Slavery? (quoted in Mitchell, 1976, p 387)

Astell also argues in *An Essay in Defence of the Female Sex* (1694, p 2) that such conjugal power is based on force and *not* on the Law of Nature or 'natural' inequalities of capacities:

> ... I found 'Woman', by nature, formed no less capable of all that is good and great than 'Man'; and that the Authority which they have usurped over us, is from Force, rather than the Law of Nature.

Only a couple of years later, in 1702, Catherine Trotter Cockburn published *A Defence of Mr. Locke's Essay of Human Understanding*, attacking the doctrine of innate ideas and innate affections and arguing that experience and training create character. Although she does not explicitly argue for women's rights in her *Defence of Locke's Essay*, her support of empirical principles provides a justification for opening the way equally to men and women towards perfectionist goals of self development. Later, in a 'Letter of advice to her son', Catherine Trotter Cockburn argues from liberal principles for the fair, equal treatment of women:

> There is nothing more unjust, more base, and barbarous, than is often practiced towards [women], under the specious names of love and gallantry; as if they had not an equal right, with those of the other sex, to be treated with justice and honour. (Trotter Cockburn, 1751, vol 2, p 119)

By the end of the eighteenth century, Lockean principles were still being used to argue for women's equality. Catherine Macaulay Graham complains in a collection entitled *Letters on Education*, published in 1790, that despite acceptance of an empiricist psychology which maintains that character is formed by experience, the contradictory belief in innate characteristics of the female mind persists. She argues:

> the great difference that is observable in the characters of the sexes ... as they display themselves in the scenes of social life, has given rise to much false speculation on the natural qualities of the female mind. For though the doctrine of innate ideas, and innate affections, are in a great measure exploded by the learned, yet few persons reason so clearly and so accurately on abstract subjects as, through a long chain of deductions, to bring forth a conclusion which in no respect militates with their premises.
>
> It is a long time before the crowd give up opinions they have been taught to look upon with respect; and I know many persons who will follow you willingly through the course of your argument, till they perceive it tends to the overthrow of some fond prejudice ... (Macaulay Graham, 1790, p 203)

Functionalist principles

On the functionalist front, since the seventeenth century women had been arguing for the right to education on the grounds of social benefit in both the moral and the spiritual domains. By the end of the eighteenth century, the functionalist arguments for the education of women gained ground and influence. The focus of debate shifted from whether women should be educated to how women should be educated. But the utility value was cashed in in terms of the contribution that the educationally improved woman would make by being better wives and mothers. Since the goal, according to these arguments, is not self-fulfilment but utility to men, the question that became prominent was what should women study and how, in order to fulfil their role as wife and mother (Browne, 1987, p 2). This type of view was strongly supported by the widespread religious belief that Eve was created to serve Adam. Functionalist arguments abounded, and had both liberating and restrictive effects. Anything not necessary to women for fulfilling their role as wife and mother was considered superfluous and even harmful.

As Dale Spender has pointed out, the so-called 'bluestocking' women like Hannah More expanded the role respectable and wealthy women were permitted by developing their talents but justifying it 'as a direct means of counteracting card-playing for money, which they saw as barbarous' with evenings for intellectual 'co-ed' discussion (Spender, 1983, p 101). Hannah More in her 1799 book, *Strictures on the Modern System of Female Education*, argues for improved education for women to enable them to achieve 'purity of conduct' and the women of rank and fortune to then lead a revival of morality and religion in Britain. Her elitism is based on her belief that 'among the talents for the application of which women of the higher class will be peculiarly accountable, there is one, the importance of which they can scarcely rate too highly ... this talent is influence'. (More, 1799, vol 1, pp ix, 1) But her conventionalism restricts women's conduct in exercising this important social influence. She calls women of rank and wealth to their social and moral duty in the following way:

I would call on them to come forward, and contribute their full and fair proportion towards the saving of their country. But I would call on them to come
forward, without departing from the refinement of their character, without
derogating from the dignity of their rank, without blemishing the delicacy of
their sex. I would call them to the best and most appropriate exertion of their
power, to raise the depressed tone of public morals, to awaken the drowsy spirit
of religious principle, and to re-animate the dormant powers of active piety. (vol
1, p 4)

But despite her insistence of maintaining a 'female modesty', Hannah More
advocates a serious, rigorous intellectual training for women. As a physician
prescribes 'bracing medicines for a body of which delicacy is the disease, the
[educational instructor should] prohibit relaxing reading for a mind which is
already of too soft a texture, and should strengthen its feeble tone by invig-
orating reading' (vol 1, p 163). She goes on to make specific recommendations
and to justify them:

Let not a timid young lady start if I should venture to recommend to her, after
a proper course of preparation, to swallow and digest such strong meat, as Watt's
or Duncan's little book of Logic, some parts of Mr. Locke's Essay on the Human
Understanding, and Bishop Buter's Analogy. ... While ... enervating or absurd
books sadly disqualify the reader for solid pursuit or vigorous thinking, the
studies here recommended would act upon the constitution of the mind as a kind
of alternative, and, ... would help to brace the intellectual stamina. ... For what
is called dry, tough reading, independently of the knowledge it conveys, is useful
as an habit and wholesome as an exercise. Serious study serves to harden the
mind for more trying conflicts; it lifts the reader from sensation to intellect; it
abstracts her from the world and its vanities; ... it corrects that spirit of trifling
which she naturally contracts from the frivolous turn of female conversation,
and the petty nature of female employments ... Yes; I repeat it, there is to woman
a Christian use to be made of sober studies; while books of an opposite case ...
at best feed habits of improper indulgence, and nourish a vain and visionary
indolence, which lays the mind open to error and the heart to seduction. (vol 1,
pp 164–6)

On the one hand, despite using sexist vocabulary, More's recommendations
and arguments are progressive, promoting women's rights to serious intellectual eduction; but on the other hand, she is conventional with respect to
woman's role in society and denounces advocates of women's equality in
employment and politics:

... the enlargement of the female understanding being the most likely means to
put an end to those petty cavils and contentions for equality which female
smatterers so anxiously maintain ... The more a woman's understanding is
improved, the more obviously she will discern that there can be no happiness in
any society where there is perpetual struggle for power; and the more her judgment is rectified, the more accurate views will she take of the station she was
born to fill, and the more readily will she accommodate herself to it. (vol 2, pp
13–14)

Other women advocated more restrictive limits on women's intellectual education. Laetitia-Matilda Hawkins in her *Letters on the Female Mind, its powers and pursuits* (1793) argues that women 'are not formed for those deep investigations that tend to the bringing into light reluctant truth' but are superior to men in then giving truth 'spirit and decoration' once it 'appears'. She warns that women's countenance and features become 'unpleasant' if strained by intense thought. (Hawkins, 1793, vol I, p 7; quoted at length in Browne, 1987, p 160)

Mary Wollstonecraft

The tension in the arguments of these two traditions can be smoothed out by combining the principles into one position, along the lines of Mary Wollstonecraft's 1792 monograph: *A Vindication of the Rights of Women*. Her defence is built on two different types of argument: the one type of argument rests on liberal/perfectionist principles, making reference to what is intrinsically valuable to the individual; while the other type of argument follows functionalist principles with reference to what promotes maximal benefit in society at large. Wollstonecraft argues on liberal/perfectionist grounds that women are human beings and, *qua* human being, not only have the right to acquire human virtues or perfections by the cultivation and exercise of their own reason, but that this is the only way to attain virtue. She argues:

> ... whatever effect circumstances have on the abilities, every being may become virtuous by the exercise of its own reason; ... the most perfect education, in my opinion, is such an exercise of the understanding as ... to enable the individual to attain such habits of virtue as will render it independent. In fact, it is a farce to call any being virtuous whose virtues do not result from the exercise of its own reason. This was Rousseau's opinion respecting men: I extend it to women ... (Wollstonecraft, 1988, p 45)

Allowing women to be educated 'by the same means as men, instead of being educated [as Rousseau advocates] like a fanciful kind of half being' will make women rational, truly virtuous beings, which will also benefit the society at large (p 54). The functionalist argument which runs through Wollstonecraft's monograph is that rational, independent women make good wives, mothers and daughters. For example, she argues that 'women cannot be confined to merely domestic pursuits, for they will not fulfil family duties, unless their minds take a wider range ...' (p 81) and that if we 'make women rational creatures, and free citizens, ... they will quickly become good wives and mothers (pp 84–5). In Wollstonecraft's essay functionalist principles are derivative from and conditioned by liberal/perfectionist principles.

Harriet Taylor Mill

Harriet Taylor Mill developed this integration of these two traditions, and extended the application of the combined use of liberal/perfectionist and functionalist arguments, from the defence of women's right to an equal education to a more vigorous justification of women's rights to vote and choice of employment than Mary Wollstonecraft's. Wollstonecraft argues that if:

> [women are allowed] to share the advantages of education and government with man, [we would] see whether they will become better as they grow wiser and become free ... to render this practicable, day schools, for particular ages, should be established by government, in which boys and girls might be educated together. (Wollstonecraft, 1988, pp 77–8)

Harriet Taylor Mill, in her 1851 article 'Enfranchisement of Women' (*Westminster Review*, July), argues that women should be granted the right to vote on the grounds of the difference this would make to the development of their moral and intellectual character. Her liberal/perfectionist argument is that the increased social and intellectual responsibility resulting from participation in political activities will stimulate and exercise the moral and mental faculties of the individual woman, thus furthering her individual fulfilment. Here, individual fulfilment is presupposed to be of value to the agent and a person's capacities to be largely the result of opportunities for their exercise. Taylor Mill argues:

> The proper sphere for all human beings is the largest and highest which they are able to attain to. What this is, cannot be ascertained, without complete liberty of choice ... Let every occupation be open to all, without favour or discouragement to any, and employments will fall into the hands of those men or women who are found by experience to be the most capable of worthily exercising them ... Each individual will prove his or her capacities, in the only way in which capacities can be proved—by trial; and the world will have the benefit of the best faculties of all its inhabitants. But to interfere beforehand by an arbitrary limit, and declare that whatever be the genius, talent, energy, or force of mind of an individual of a certain sex or class, those faculties shall not be exerted, or shall be exerted only in some few of the many modes in which others are permitted to use theirs, is not only an injustice to the individual, and a detriment to society, which loses what it can ill spare, but is also the most effectual mode of providing that, in the sex or class so fettered, the qualities which are not permitted to be exercised shall not exist. (Taylor Mill, 1859, vol 2, pp 422–4)

Her functionalist/utilitarian arguments rest on the beneficial results that the individual development of women will have on men and society in general. Denying women social and political equality demoralises and vulgarises the character of both women and men. She argues that it 'produces vices of power' in men and vices of 'artifice' in women (p 440) and that 'all social or sympathetic influences which do not raise up, pull down; if they do not tend to stimulate and exalt the mind, they tend to vulgarise it' (p 444). According to Taylor Mill, it is 'in the interest not only of women but of men, and of human improvement in the widest sense' that the emancipation of women should be promoted (p 444).

Conclusion

In conclusion, the eighteenth-century division between the liberal/perfectionist and the functionalist defence of women's rights led to incompatible results concerning the subordination of women to men. Mary Wollstonecraft resolved this incompatibility at the end of the eighteenth century by the interaction of the two kinds of argument into a single system: functionalist principles were made derivative from and conditioned by liberal/perfectionist principles. This resolution of the fundamental theoretical predicament of the feminist struggle for complete emancipation was fully developed in Harriet Taylor Mill's work.

NOTES

I would like to thank the following people for their useful comments and criticisms of earlier drafts of this paper: Wade Robinson, Cheryl Hall, and Phyllis Furley. I am also grateful for the opportunity to have presented and discussed earlier versions of this paper at: the Society for Women in Philosophy Conference (University of Massachusetts at Amherst); and the Research Colloquium in Women's Studies, Princeton University.

1   It has been objected that Locke is here merely describing the contemporary state of affairs and is not condoning let alone justifying this prevalent practice. But how would this be read if Locke were discussing disagreement between two men over their common concerns? Would he say that the rule 'naturally' falls to the abler and stronger class of man? Where is the appeal to Natural Law which teaches that 'being furnished with like Faculties, sharing all in one Community of Nature, there cannot be supposed any such Subordination among us'? Where is the appeal to 'that equal Right that every Man hath, to his Natural Freedom, without being subjected to the Will or Authority of any other man'? Locke is arguing that a husband's power over his wife is not absolute (he does not have the right to take her life—*1st Treatise*, see § 48; *2nd Treatise*, § 82—and his power does not reach to 'what by contract is her *peculiar* right' (my emphasis), i.e. what is contracted *not* to be a shared interest and property but hers exclusively—*2nd Treatise*, § 82); hence, he concludes, conjugal power is not an appropriate analogue for absolute monarchy. Locke seems to use two criteria to justify authority: what is 'natural' and what is socially 'necessary'. He argues, *2nd Treatise*, § 83, 'If it were otherwise, and that absolute sovereignty and power of life and death naturally belonged to the husband and were necessary to the society between man and wife, there could

be no matrimony ... where the husband is allowed no such absolute authority. But the ends of matrimony ['viz., procreation and mutual support and assistance whilst ... together'] requiring no such power in the husband, the condition of conjugal society put it not in him, it being not at all necessary to that state.' So when Locke says that it is *'necessary*, that the last Determination, i.e. the Rule, should be placed somewhere, it *naturally* falls to the Man's share, as the abler and the stronger' (my emphases), I take him to be justifying this power of the husband over the wife in matters of shared interest and property. In this corner of matrimonial life (usually the whole of most women's married life unless she had an elightened father to arrange her marriage contract or an enlightened husband with whom to contract better terms), the husband is given complete authority; having the power to decide whenever there is a disagreement over an issue of 'common concernment' is complete authority over those issues. The right and freedom to disagree without the power to decide is hardly a genuine right or freedom. And this 'limited' dominion is based on an alleged inequality of ability between the sexes. Although Locke was more advanced than many of his contemporaries in arguing that wives have some rights that can be extended by 'condition' or contract, he does not extend natural rights arguments as far into the patriarchal family as Mary Astell does.

BIBLIOGRAPHY

Mary Astell, *An Essay in Defence of the Female Sex* (London, C Hitch and R Akenhead, 1694).

Mary Astell, *Reflections on Marriage* (London, 1700).

Alice Browne, *The Eighteenth-Century Feminist Mind* (Brighton, Harvester Press, 1987).

Robert Filmer, 'Patriarcha', in John Locke, *Two Treaties of Government*, Thomas I Cooke, ed (New York, Hafner Publishing Co, 1947).

Laetitia-Matilda Hawkins, *Letters on the Female Mind, its Powers and Pursuits* 2 Vols (London, 1793).

John Locke, *Two Treaties of Government*, Thomas I Cooke, ed (New York, Hafner Publishing Co, 1947).

Catharine Macaulay Graham, 'No characteristic difference in sex', Letter xxii, *Letters on Education with Observations on Religious and Metaphysical subjects* (London, C Dilly, 1790).

Juliet Mitchell, 'Women and equality', in J Mitchell and A Oakley, eds, *The Rights and Wrongs of Women* (New York, Penguin Books Ltd, 1976).

Hannah More, *Strictures on the Modern System of Female Education*, 2 vols (London, T Cadell Jun and W Davies, 1799).

Dale Spender, *Women of Ideas* (London, Ark Paperbacks, 1983).

Harriet Taylor Mill, 'Enfranchisement of women' in J S Mill, *Dissertations and Discussions* (London, John W Parker & Son, vol II, 1859).

Catherine Trotter Cockburn, *Works Theological, Moral, Dramatic, and Political*, 2 vols (Thomas Birch, ed, London, J & P Knapton, 1751).

Mary Wollstonecraft, 'A vindication of the rights of woman' in Alice Rossi, ed, *The Feminist Papers* (Boston, Northeastern University Press, 1988).

CHAPTER 14

Obstacles to Implementing Equal Rights in Third World Countries

Fanny Tabak

Abstract

UN efforts to eliminate sex-based discrimination have contributed to improving the status of women in Third World countries, as well as some social movements, especially the feminist movement.

But a series of obstacles still prevent or make it extremely difficult to implement equal rights for men and women in those countries, in spite of a general trend to democratisation that can be observed e.g. in many of the Latin American countries.

We could mention at least five different groups of such obstacles:
political—a 'formal' democracy, authoritarian regimes, political instability, armed conflicts and wars etc;
economic—crises, inflation, low salaries, high concentration of land property etc;
cultural—patriarchy, sexual stereotypes, traditional and obsolete values, illiteracy etc;
social—low rates of organisation and community action, lack of social institutions to help women to participate in society etc;
religious—strong influence of the Church (especially the Catholic, on women, in resisting to change traditional values on the role of women in society.

Women's rights legislation so far has had a narrow impact on improving the status of the large masses of poor women, who constitute the large majority of the population in Third World countries.

Besides, the specific needs women have are not taken into account when public policies are defined. Even in those countries where new progressive laws have been passed, there is still a hard way to go before they will be implemented.

Introduction

The 1970s and the 1980s registered important changes in the status of women, shortening the road to equal rights between men and women. The changes have occurred in many different countries and not only in the private sphere of daily life, but also in the public sphere of politics and business. In this respect, the contribution made by the United Nations has been critically important. The United Nations not only established the International Year of Women (1975) and the Plan of Action (1976/1985), but it also approved the Convention that prohibits sex-based discrimination. The attention paid by different bodies belonging to the UN structure and the insistence of the UN that governments sign that anti-discrimination Convention produced positive effects in many countries of the world.

Together with the UN, UNESCO also supported numerous studies and projects that increased knowledge about the *de facto* status of women all over the world. Thanks to that support we now have considerable documentation on the position of women in dozens of countries on all continents. In the particular case of Third World countries a great concern existed about expanding such knowledge, as official statistics in those countries and the data available are usually very incomplete.

Women's organisations in the Third World have been able to use the UN's Convention and the Plan of Action to support their demands for more favourable policies that would address women's basic needs and that would implement concrete measures to prevent discrimination. Feminist groups played a particularly important role in denouncing violence against women, sexual abuse, pay inequities and discrimination in hiring and promoting women and in attaining access to power. Most of these feminist groups were able to use the UN data in their battles on behalf of women.

The Situation on the Eve of the Twenty-First Century

Since we are rapidly approaching the beginning of a new century and entering the last decade of the twentieth century, it is wise to examine the present situation of the status of women in Third World countries; for it is in these countries that the majority of the world's population lives.

First, we should keep in mind that it would be a serious error to approach these countries as if they are equal and homogeneous. Of course they are not.

The level of development, economic growth, wealth, illiteracy, and level of public services that are available vary markedly from country to country. Hence, to complete a comprehensive analysis it would be necessary to consider these differences in analysing the main obstacles to the implementation of equal rights. Nonetheless, it is also important to emphasise that at present a certain number of common features can be found that point to an improvement in the implementation of equal rights for women and also other common features that pose obstacles to such implementation. It is these common features that I wish to highlight in this paper. Among these features are the following positive factors: (a) the greater democratisation of Third World political systems; (b) the rise of feminist movements in the Third World, and (c) the rise of other social movements emphasising women's values.

The greater democratisation of Third World political systems

In Latin America, for example, the 1990s will begin with new democratic regimes, democratically elected new governments, which will replace the military that dominated their nations for many years after replacing constitutional presidents by authoritarian and antidemocratic rule. Such military regimes lasted twenty-one years in Brazil (from 1964 to 1985), closed down the National Congress in Chile (1973), held elections based on fraud, imposed a strict censorship on mass media, adopted corruption as a normal instrument of power, increased the external debt enormously, and generally suppressed human rights. They kept power using violence, torture, and murder as the method of domination. Thousands of people 'disappeared' in Argentina, Brazil, Chile, and Paraguay. Among them were many women. Political amnesty permitting the return of thousands of political exiles, general elections, the abolishment of censorship, the approval of new democratic constitutions and their implementation, all will certainly contribute to creating real possibilities for improving the status of women more rapidly and for reducing existing inequalities.

The rise of feminist movements in the Third World

Active feminist movements spread all over the world during the 1970s and the 1980s, and in those countries where much still needs to be done to implement equality such movements have helped to denounce different sorts of sex discrimination and to put forward a political agenda demanding legal measures to improve the status of women.

The rise of other social movements emphasising women's values

In the latter quarter of the twentieth century other social movements inspired greater political involvement among women. In the Third World, as well as in Europe and the United States, the environmental movement and various peace movements struck responsive chords among women. These movements helped reinforce the need to re-evaluate female political participation and to insist on equality of participation.

In spite of the above three positive factors and some rather significant moves toward an improved status for women, the fact remains that women in most countries—and certainly women in the Third World—are not equal to men. They are not equal in work, in the family, or in the political arena. Salaries, access to the formal labour market, to promotion to top positions, to better qualifications and to improved working conditions still put women at a disadvantage relative to men. Motherhood is still regarded as something that has to do only with the mother, which makes things much more difficult if the mother is in the labour force, whether as a skilled professional or as an unskilled worker.

Very few women have access to power. They are still a very small percentage of national congresses, though in local parliamentary bodies they might sometimes reach larger proportions. They are certainly not typically visible at the higher levels of government. The few exceptions, such as the case of Indira Gandhi or presently Benazir Butto and Corazon Aquino, are indeed exceptions. These women hold power for reasons that have nothing to do with an effort to assure equal rights to women. Most of the Third World female prime ministers, just like Margaret Thatcher of Great Britain, have done little to improve the status of women in their own countries. Even when political parties do include female candidates to run for office, they rarely provide these women with real support, especially financial support, that will result in their being elected.

Studies and research conducted among women in Third World countries confirm that few changes have been implemented that are likely to reduce, much less eliminate, the burden of tradition, culture, and religion on the process of socialisation of girls in the Third World.

Factors Contributing to the maintenance of Unequal Rights

Five basic factors can be identified as posing major obstacles to implementing equal rights for women in the Third World. These five encompass political, economic, cultural, social, and religious reasons.

Political reasons or obstacles

In many Third World countries a formal political independence was achieved which did not simultaneously lead to effective political and economic control. In Africa, for example, numerous countries became formally independent of British rule in the 1960s. Nonetheless, the British or other First World countries retained control over the key positions in the economy and maintained their influence over the nation's political agenda. New forms of neo-colonialism precluded the newly independent nations from improving the living conditions of the majority of the population, from increasing economic growth and social development that would benefit the masses.

In some Third World countries a formal democracy existed while an authoritarian government remained in office for decades. In other words, Parliament was kept open, elections were held regularly, political parties and candidates could run for office, but all these trappings of democracy were a facade for prohibiting leftist and populist parties from existing legally.

The formal democratic institutions were lauded while thousands of activists engaged in political action to change the regime were forced to go into exile. Freedom of speech, of the press, and to organise were suppressed while the fake democratic institutions continued to function.

In many Third World countries political instability has been the rule, not the exception. Coups d'états (led usually by the military) have been commonplace, used as means of eliminating constitutional governments trying to establish and reinforce democratic rules. In the last few decades, coups d'états established military dictatorships in most of the Latin American countries, although some of the authoritarian regimes have ruled for over forty years (e.g. in Paraguay). In Bolivia, dozens of coups have taken place since the beginning of the century. Sometimes that instability is considered to be a result of—or at least closely related to—the weakness of the existing political parties. Strong political parties, such as the PRI in Mexico, or the Peronist party in Argentina, are rather exceptional. In Brazil, the presidential elections held on 15 November 1989, after twenty-nine years of being prohibited, had twenty-two candidates supported by thirty-eight political parties. Many of these parties were created a few months before the election day just to respond to a legal requirement. Such parties often disappear immediately after the elections.

In some regions of the Third World an effort to implement equal rights is delayed or is impossible because of military conflict or prolonged war. unsolved territorial conflicts, religious disputes, and the fight for leadership over regional organisations are political reasons that delay the implementation of concrete conditions capable of bringing women to the same level as men. The Israeli and Palestinian dispute, the long war between Iran and Iraq, the border disputes between other countries, such as India and Pakistan, cannot be considered favourable factors facilitating women's move toward equality.

Economic reasons or obstacles

Third World countries are exactly those countries where the economic crisis has reached its peak. Huge external debts are commonplace (e.g. over 100 billion US dollars in Brazil at the beginning of 1989), low rates of economic growth or no growth at all, high rates of inflation (Argentina and Brazil reached over 1,000 per cent a year in 1988/1989). These problems are, in turn, connected with extreme concentration of land ownership, property in the hands of a few individuals and families, low levels of productive investments, increasing rates of unemployment and a decrease in purchasing power.

Women are always much more affected by these factors than men. In most of the Third World countries women continue to be mainly engaged in domestic services, even when they are paid. They still have very low professional skills, which means that they receive lower salaries. The shortage of public financial resources, on the other hand, is used by governments to justify not meeting the demands for more social institutions, e.g. day care and recreational centres, schools, hospitals, and public transport.

Cultural reasons or obstacles

Maintaining the traditional definition of sex roles, according to which marriage and motherhood are the goals women should pursue, certainly does not contribute to changing the status of women. Both the traditional expectation and reality reinforce the notion that women ought to participate very little in public life and are to remain in a subordinate, marginal position in society.

The burden of patriarchy is evident in the field of education. 'Traditional' careers are still much more popular among girls than the so-called 'modern' ones of science and technology. Although in the 1980s computer sciences began to attract large groups of young women, most of them were occupied with the less sophisticated operations. Even if some of the courses in engineering and biologicl sciences are already chosen by more and more women, women still constitute a very small proportion of the professionals working in these areas. Moreover, many studies have shown that women occupy the lower ranks, even when they are equally qualified.

The explanation for the inequality is that sexism has not yet been eradicated from the mass media, from academic programmes, and from primary schools. Stereotypes are still very strong in some of those societies that resist changing their cultural values. Since many of these values are nothing more than traditional values that have been kept for ages, these stereotypes are difficult to eliminate.

In Third World countries women constitute the large majority of the illiterate, which means they are unable to read what is being published about the need for changing those values. But even when women are able to read, the criticism made by feminist groups or other women's organisations very often does not reach them. Millions of poor women live in the countryside, in small villages where they have to work hard just to survive. Most have children and live in ignorance and out of the reach of the mass media. We should not be surprised to see that they keep believing in non-scientific ideas about their bodies and their role in society.

Even skilled professional women in Third World countries—as many studies made by feminist-oriented research centres have shown—are affected by traditional cultural values: a strong feeling of guilt can be found among such women when they are unable to combine a career with family responsibilities, i.e. being simultaneously 'good' wives, 'good' mothers, and 'good' professionals.

Social reasons or obstacles

One of the main obstacles to overcoming underdevelopment and marginality more rapidly in Third World countries is certainly the low rates of organisation of the working people. Trade-unionism in most of the Third World organises only a very small percentage of the male workers; and women join the unions in even smaller proportions. Sometimes there is a large variety of different organisations among women: mother's clubs, housewives' or neighbourhood associations, co-operatives and production groups, but they are almost always small in numbers and the activists, those women who really engage in action, are even fewer in number. In other words, a strong cultural tradition of participating in the community, and in public life very often does not exist in Third World countries. On the contrary, the need to work hard to guarantee physical survival, to fight against inflation, combined with the shortage of public services and so forth stimulate much more the trend toward isolation and individualism than to solidarity and collaboration.

In addition, the absence or the shortage of social institutions (public and free), such as day care and recreation centres, elementary schools, medical assistance, healthy sanitary and dwelling conditions contributes to increasing the burden of poor mothers and housekeepers. It means that little or no time is left for social action and the struggle for equal rights.

Religious reasons or obstacles

One cannot underestimate the role and the influence of religion on the behaviour, the accepted values and the reaction of large groups of women in Third World countries. Religion strongly affects the nature of the criticism made on sexism and discrimination based on sex, whether by feminist groups, political activists, or by scholars and researchers in the academy. Not only surveys and studies made during the past two decades, but also the experience of different women's organisations have shown that thousands of women do agree with the traditional definition of sex roles, i.e. with women having the exclusive responsibility for domestic services and the raising of children, and men having responsibility for political and public life. Traditional sex roles discourage female political participation.

The Catholic Church in Latin American countries exerts considerable pressure presently on legislatures to prevent laws permitting abortion. It has found against divorce in Brazil for twenty years and still resists its passage in countries like Chile. Thousands of Catholic women resist family planning and contraception because it is forbidden by the Church. The expression 'children are sent by God' is still heard in many of the extremely poor areas of most of the Third World countries. And one should not forget that in propagating the belief in an extra-terrestrial life, the Catholic Church indoctrinates women to accept passively all the inequalities and injustices committed against them on earth.

Other religious influences exist in addition to those of the formal hierarchical churches. Economic crises and the deterioration of living conditions have contributed to increasing the influence of various sorts of mysticism and beliefs in extra-sensory powers over millions of people, not only of the poorest strata, but also of the urban middle class. In short, all such conjectures or explanations actually turn into real obstacles obstructing the implementation of equal rights between men and women.

The narrow impact of woman's rights legislation

No doubt women have conquered rights that were denied to them for decades and even centuries; for example, the right to vote, to go to a university, to practise a profession, to be a candidate and elected to the highest positions in public life, both at the national and international levels. But the idea of 'equal opportunities' for both sexes—even when and where it became a reality—did not bring as a consequence equal share in the results. In other words, if we remember that women start from a much lower level than men, even when women do advance at a reasonable rate, there is still a considerable gap between men and women. At present, equal opportunities to enter college, to get training, to enter the labour market, to have a profession, or to obtain a seat in the House of Representatives, do not necessarily coincide with equality in the results of economic growth, technological advancement, and social development.

The fact remains that the responsibility for the family, the children and the household is still considered to be that of the woman. Thus, if we want to assure equal rights we must take into consideration this fact.

In addition, women have specific needs that men do not have as a result of physiological differences. Studies have shown that pregnancy, puberty, menstruation and menopause do affect female behaviour and account for disruptions in women's professional careers.

All this means that when we speak of equal rights, such as to education, to professional training, to leisure, to power and to an improved quality of life, we need to demand simultaneously that men adopt equal levels of responsibility and duties as women traditionally have had in the private sphere of life. Men need to agree to free women from unpaid domestic service and to share equally in being responsible for child care and the family.

In many Third World countries the first step is passing new laws and changing specific legislation, abolishing the discrimination on the basis of sex that still exists in the civil and penal codes. Though difficult, the passage of such legislation will certainly be more easily achieved than changing the cultural values and diminishing the influence of religion on women.

Brazil's experience supports this view. Substantial changes were made in legislation in 1962—thanks to an active campaign conducted by different groups of activists and women's organisations. The status of married women became much better than it had been in the civil code even though that code remains unchanged up to the present. For example, in 1978 a law permitting divorce was passed after twenty years of debate and in spite of the resistance of the Catholic Church. A proposal to establish a new code was passed by the Brazilian House of Representatives in December 1985, but it was not passed in the Senate. In 1988, a new Constitution was adopted by the national Congress after the military regime had come to an end, and efforts began to adopt specific legislation to assist liberating women.

Even now Brazilian women are struggling for the decriminalisation of abortion. Numerous other suggestions and proposals have been put forward by women's organisations and feminist groups, in congresses, conferences, seminars, and meetings at international, national, regional, and local levels in an effort to launch initiatives that will contribute to improving women's rights. Among these proposals are such items as shortening the work day for mothers of small children, and establishing part-time jobs for women for a period of time after birth so they can remain active in the labour force. The idea underlying these proposals is to keep women linked to the labour force so as not to fall behind in their experience and potential for advancement. Most women, middle class as well as women of the poorer classes, need the money that they receive from their jobs. Such specific legislation will facilitate maintaining this income and help prevent more and more families from entering poverty or being even more impoverished.

Conclusion

Throughout the Third World many women who have fought for equal rights and who have been politically active for many years are experiencing frustration and pessimism. Year after year—even decade after decade—economic crises, inflation, starvation, illiteracy, authoritarianism, conflicts and wars are still present in their daily life. In spite of the rise of feminism and other social movements and the recent greater democratisation of Third World countries, equal rights between men and women is not an issue of the highest priority on the political agenda of Third World countries. We will be well into the twenty-first century before real progress for large numbers of Third World women, particularly the poorer of these women, will be made.

NOTES

Warm thanks to Rita Mae Kelly for her assistance in preparing the English version of this paper.

CHAPTER 15

'Husband and Wife are one Person: the Husband' (Nineteenth-century English aphorism)

Sybil Wolfram

Abstract

This paper suggests that there has been undue concentration on the second half of the title aphorism, possibly as a result of its use as a political slogan in nineteenth-century campaigns for women's rights, and that this has stood in the way of understanding the first half of it: the old English doctrine that 'husband and wife are one person'. Interpretation and aspects of this doctrine are discussed and some of its wide-ranging applications in legal and non-legal settings described. It is distinguished from suggested equivalences such as that the wife's legal existence is suspended during marriage, which (*contra* Blackstone) is argued not to have been the case, or that women/wives were disadvantaged, which it is held is less central and less well substantiated than it is often presented as being. The gradual decline of the doctrine of the unity of husband and wife in England is evident from examples, but the reasons for it are not obvious.

'By marriage', Blackstone wrote in 1765 in a much quoted passage of his *Commentaries on the Laws of England* 'the husband and wife are one person in law: that is, the very being or legal existence of the woman is suspended during marriage or at least is incorporated and consolidated into that of the husband' (Blackstone, 1765, I.15.III; cf. also 1766, II.29.VI). 'Husband and wife are one person, and that person is the husband' said a Parliamentary

Report of 1868.[1] It was at the time and continues to be widely accepted that such accounts, and especially the second half, the suspension of the wife's existence, summarise the state of marriage in England at least until the late nineteenth century. The wrongs of women or loss of their rights in marriage are commonly supposed to be *ipso facto* evident. 'The two [husband and wife] are called "one person in law" for the purpose', Mill complained in *The Subjection of Women* 1869 (chapter 2), 'of inferring that whatever is hers is his, but the parallel inference is never drawn that whatever is his is hers'. The 'doctrine of spousal unity', we are told from the United States in 1982, 'meant that a man assumed legal rights over his wife's property at marriage' (Shanley, 1982, p 360).

The emphasis on the wrongs of wives, readily derived from Blackstone's claim that the legal existence of the woman was suspended during marriage, has, in my opinion, stood in the way of understanding the doctrine of husband and wife being one person, as it operated in England in the past and still to some extent does today.

As it stands the doctrine that husband and wife are one person is of course extremely strange. If an anthropologist claimed to have discovered a society in which it was believed that a brief set ceremony, followed by a single act of sexual intercourse, transformed a man and woman into one person or suspended the woman's existence, we should either suppose the society to have a primitive pre-rational mentality or suspect the anthropologist of some absurd misunderstanding. It is so palpably impossible for two people to be or become one person that it is inconceivable that anyone moderately rational should believe that they were. It seems equally improbable that not very long ago people in England believed that women did not exist while married.

The addition of 'in law' to the claims that in England husband and wife were considered one person and/or that the existence of the wife was regarded as suspended makes them much more plausible. For it does seem on the cards that there could be a special *legal* sense of 'one person' whereby a husband and wife rate as such along with single people. Or it could be understood that one man is always one person but a woman is only one person if she is not married, married women not counting as persons in this special sense of 'person'. This is not impossible, but only some kind of denial of or addition to rights to married people as against those not married. In the latter case, it would be a removal of rights and obligations from married women. From here it is only a short step to supposing that the society which was purported to hold the apparently absurd belief that husband and wife are one person really just had perfectly intelligible, although very unfair, laws whereby a woman's property became her husband's at marriage.

While it is easy to see how the claim that husband and wife were one person and that person the husband *could* just have been a way of stating the brute fact that by English law a husband had control over his wife's property, it seems to turn on the facts whether this is actually what it amounted to. And it is my contention that this now rather common suggestion seriously misconstrues a doctrine which, while no doubt leading to inequities (it is difficult to think of many doctrines that do not) was very much more complex and, moreover, not in fact guilty of the particular inequity attributed to it in this simplified version.

The account probably derives from taking too seriously what was said by Mill and others in their campaigning for the Married Women's Property Acts in the 1860s. They were apt to talk as if a husband acquired legal rights over his wife's property at marriage, to indict the law as unfair, and often to hammer the point home with the aphorism I have employed as my title. The position was not in fact quite like this. It was rather that the husband gained some rights over certain of his wife's property *unless* certain procedures, known as making marriage settlements, were followed.[2] These procedures were open to anyone and widely employed, certainly in the middle and upper classes; they were a routine accompaniment to marriage where there was any property at all.[3] Marriage settlements were not a new institution in the nineteenth century but some three centuries old. They consisted of settling property on the wife for what was known as 'her own use'. The property so settled might have been her own or her father's or her husband's; once settled on her it was hers, even if with some restrictions on disposal of capital. We do not normally say of a machine that it does X if X is just what it defaults to and it can easily be got to do Y instead, even though the default may have tiresome features and/or be something we should like to alter. However, in the political arena it is quite common for someone wishing to effect a change to exaggerate, and one way of exaggerating is to speak as if a default were the only possibility: and so it was with Mill and others. The rich, they said, escape from the rigours of the law, and so on. It is rather as if someone had thumped a drum to have married women's earnings taxed separately in say 1980 when they already could be by request, and a hundred years after this the position was portrayed as if (as had indeed been the case before 1971) there was no such option.

If one turns back to Blackstone (1765) for illumination of the doctrine that husband and wife are one person in law, one gets a fuller, less distorted but I think also rather confused picture. There are two principal difficulties in Blackstone's exegesis. One is that he tells us in I.15 that husband and wife were one person in law but proceeds to cite respects or branches of the law in which husband and wife were treated as two separate persons. The other is that he speaks of husband and wife being one person in law as tantamount to, or brought about by, suspension of the wife's legal existence. However, he gives examples which do not bear this equation out and cites instances where the law seems to treat husband and wife as one person but not to treat the husband rather than the wife as that person since what went for the one also went for the other.

It is indeed quite clear from Blackstone's own examples, and many others that can be adduced, that although husband and wife counted as one person for *some* legal purposes, they were not so considered for *all* legal purposes. The criminal law for instance treated them like two separate people in a number of ways. Each could be convicted for and only for his or her own crimes. Neither could be convicted for those of the other. There were crimes, such as theft or rape, which could not be committed by one spouse against the other. But there were other crimes where husband and wife were no different from any other two people. Killing a spouse, for example, was like killing anyone else and not, as it would be if husband and wife were altogether as one person, like killing oneself; that is, it might be murder (if deliberate, and so on); it was never suicide. It is also abundantly plain that in *some* instances where husband and wife were treated as one person in law, there was an asymmetry whereby the person was in fact the husband. In other instances, however this was not so. A wife could not be a witness for or against her husband, but a husband could not be a witness for or against his wife either. A husband could not steal from his wife but nor could a wife from her husband, and so on. It is not therefore correct to say that husband and wife were always one person in some special legal sense of person, much less that the wife was not a legal person at all. The most that can be claimed is that there were laws in which they were treated as if they were one and the same person and not as if they were two different people and in some of these as if the husband was a person in a way that the wife was not.

I suggested earlier that a method of avoiding the absurdities of supposing that it was believed that husband and wife were one person is to construe the doctrine as it was often expressed, viz that they were one person 'in law'. However, this limitation is not entirely satisfactory. For one thing, the treatment of husband and wife as if they were one person was not confined to law but extended to a variety of customs, conventions and sentiments. For another the relevant laws, customs, etc seem to have been in some sense a *result* of the belief or sentiment that husband and wife really were, or ought to be, in some sense one person. And this brings us back to the question of how anyone could believe such an apparent absurdity, or, to frame it better, what it was exactly that was believed which was expressed as 'husband and wife are one person' or 'as one' or sometimes 'of one flesh' or as there being a 'mystical union' between husband and wife. Their treatment in law supplies a clue. What the doctrine as held amounted to was that there was a special relation between husband and wife which was closer than that between any other two people, and so close that they were, at least ideally, *more* like one person than like two.

'More like' is a fairly fluid notion. That husband and wife were more like one person than like two is not contradicted by the fact that each walked and talked like any single person or that they were not treated like one person in every respect. It was enough that, unlike any other two people, they were classed for *some* purposes as if they were one person.

When we turn to ways in which husband and wife used to be treated 'as one', possibly the most striking feature is the extent to which these have now disappeared. But it is also noteworthy that the inequity to the wife of which we hear so much today is not by any means the most prominent feature.

Both points are evident when we consider the place of husband and wife in the English kinship system. Some features of this system are set out

FIGURE 1   HUSBAND AND WIFE IN THE ENGLISH KINSHIP SYSTEM

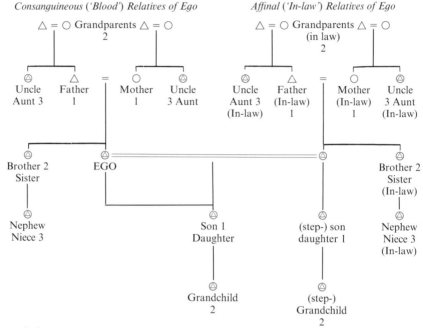

⊕   indicates men or women
△   indicates men
○   indicates women
=   indicates marriage
Numbers indicate degrees from Ego.

Prohibited Degrees: 16 C-1907 Named relatives, i.e. those in or within the third degree of consanguinity and affinity, may not be married by Ego, being in the Prohibited Degrees:
—1835   Marriages within the Prohibited Degrees voidable
1835—   Marriages within the Prohibited Degrees void *ab initio*
—1857   Sexual relations within Prohibited degrees—incestuous—punishable by ecclesiastical courts
—1923   Adultery within Prohibited Degrees (as shown) incestuous (incl. those affines permitted to marry 1907-)—grounds for woman to get divorce
1908—   Incest (sexual relations between close blood relatives (1st & 2nd degree)) a crime
1907—1921—1931—1960—1986—Affinal relatives become marriageable at death/divorce of spouse (1907: dec. wife's sister;—1986 (completion of process) affines in direct line)
Mourning at death of spouse and relatives shown in diagram required by custom, longer the closer degree—declining 1880s onward

diagrammatically in Figure 1 with respect to post-Reformation England. The general layout of this system is not confined to England or to the post-Reformation period: it is of Christian origin and found in one form or another throughout the Christian and ex-Christian world, and so far as I know nowhere else. However because even Scotland or pre-Reformation England differed in details that there are no time to discuss here, I am largely confining what I say to England after the Reformation.

The first point to which I want to draw attention is that husband and wife are not and never were *relatives*. One sense in which they constituted a unity was that they counted like one for the purpose of computing relationship. Among the effects of a marriage was that a wife was assimilated to the husband with respect to his relations, and similarly a husband was as one with his wife with respect to her relations. The relations of either spouse were and are the *same* relations of the other. A difference was retained, now more important than it used to be: a spouse's relatives are affinal or in-law relations while one's own are what were called 'consanguineous' or 'blood' relatives, now sometimes 'genetic' ones. (The marriage made the husband and wife 'one flesh' but not of one blood nor affines.) In the past, relatives by blood and in-law were treated as the same for a variety of, although again not *all*, purposes. For instance, marriage was forbidden by law with both types of relatives in exactly the same way, to the same degree of relationship and with the same stringency (or at some periods laxity).[4] Sexual relations with either of the types of non-marriageable relatives were equally incestuous and subject to the same penalties. The nomenclature, and various customs, such as going into mourning at their death, were identical. A married couple was supposed to have its own separate household but to keep up social relations with the kin of both, a propriety often adduced as a reason for preferring marriages to take place between equals. By marriage, as it used to be summarised, a husband and wife took on each other's relations.

The nomenclature is still with us but much of the rest has fallen away. In some cases this is because a custom, like that of going into mourning, or a legal category, like that of incestuous adultery, has altogether disappeared. It used to be imperative to wear black and so on at the death of relatives according to their degree (two years for a spouse, a year for blood and in-law relatives in the first degree, six months for those in the second, etc) and likewise, if often more briefly, at certain other deaths such as that of the Sovereign and Sovereign's relatives. But none of this is so any longer. Incestuous adultery, a specific ground for which a woman could procure a divorce, ceased to be a category in 1923 when adultery as such became sufficient (13 & 14 Geo c19[5]).

In other instances something rather different has taken place. This is that affinal relatives, often just called 'in-laws', have become much less like blood relatives or what would now be considered 'real' relations. Sexual intercourse between in-laws is no longer incest although it is between certain 'real' relatives,[6] and in-laws are now allowed to marry, if the last of them only very lately. The change to allowing marriage between affinal relatives was hotly contested in a dispute notorious in its day which focused on permitting marriage with a deceased wife's sister. This was debated almost annually in Parliament for nearly seventy years, from 1840 to 1907, the Deceased Wife's Sister Bill passing its second reading in the House of Commons eighteen times before finally becoming law in 1907 (7 Edw 7 c47). As forecast during the controversy, once the principle of allowing in-laws to marry was established by permitting it with one such relative, it was progressively extended

to the rest. The process was completed when the last of them, those in the
direct line, were allowed to marry in 1986. A great many arguments were of
course used in seventy years of debate about the deceased wife's sister, but
among the most potent opposition claims were that allowing marriage only
with a deceased wife's sister was illogical and destroyed the symmetry between
spouses' relations to each other's kin. If all in-laws could marry, something
it was always denied was proposed, this was contrary to 'the principle ... that
when a man and a woman married they became as one' (Churchill, 1903, col
1111) and it would no longer be the case that 'when a man marries a woman
her mother becomes his mother, her aunt his aunt, her sister his sister'
(Anonymous [C G Brown], 1883, p17). While in the much briefer contemporary debate about married women's property, the unity of husband
and wife represented as if it consisted of rights to property, in this controversy
it was as if the unity of husband and wife consisted of the non-marriageability
of each with the other's relatives.

Another way different from either of these in which husband and wife were
as one was that their union was usually for life. In particular, neither could
remarry during the lifetime of the other. This rule was absolute until the
relatively late date of 1700 and England was the only protestant country not
to allow what for brevity I shall call 'proper' divorce,[7] that is, the dissolving
of a valid marriage to allow remarriage, until eventually it was introduced by
means of private Acts of Parliament. Blackstone in 1765 spoke, as did everyone forever after, of *frequent* divorces (Blackstone, 1765, I.15.II). By 1765
the total of divorces to have been granted in England was thirty, the rate
about 1.5 divorces a year. However that already represented an increased
rate, and, as shown in Figure 2, the rate of divorce has continued to rise ever
since, usually by about three to six per cent each year. In 1857, with a fair
amount of opposition, a divorce court was set up (20 and 21 Vic 85, 1857),
and there was (as forecast) a jump in the rate, from a then average of 3.5 a
year to 150 a year. By 1900 there were 500 divorces a year, by 1980 150,000.

Ecclesiastical 'divorces', which did not permit remarriage and which were
what in 1857 became judicial separations, were open to both men and women
on equal terms—for adultery or cruelty. Until 1937, proper divorces were
granted to a husband on one ground only: the adultery of his wife, and this
only if certain conditions were met, such as that he had not committed
adultery himself. Until 1923 a wife was not able to get a proper divorce on
the same grounds, that is, if her husband committed adultery. Until 1857 she
could do so only if the adultery was incestuous or accompanied by bigamy,
after 1857 also if it was accompanied by desertion. Before 1857 only four
wives (the first in 1801) obtained proper divorces as against 321 husbands.
After 1857, when adultery plus desertion became grounds for a wife to divorce
her husband, 40 per cent of proper divorces were procured by women. When
the grounds were equalised in 1923, and women as well as men could get
proper divorces for simple adultery, the proportion obtained by wives rose

FIGURE 2 DIVORCE IN ENGLAND

Divorces enacted and decrees absolute, England (1730–1980)

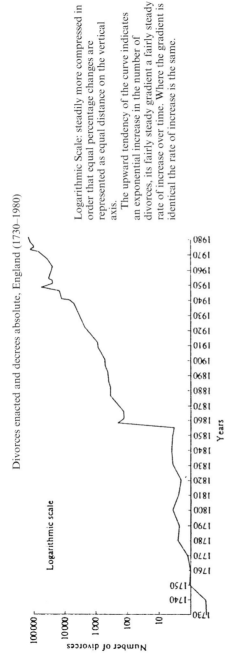

Logarithmic Scale: steadily more compressed in order that equal percentage changes are represented as equal distance on the vertical axis.

The upward tendency of the curve indicates an exponential increase in the number of divorces, its fairly steady gradient a fairly steady rate of increase over time. Where the gradient is identical the rate of increase is the same.

Figures are given in ten-yearly averages until 1857, then in five-yearly averages.

Compiled from a count of divorce Acts until 1857 (see Wolfram 1985 and 1987) and from 1858 onwards from data in Royal Commissions 1912–13 and 1956, and HMSO *Social Trends* (1981).

Sources do not quite tally, and all figures after 1857 should be treated as approximate *passim*.

'Proper' divorce: dissolves marriage to permit remarriage.
(Divorce *a mensa et thoro* (—1857, ecclesiastical courts, open to men and women; grounds: adultery or cruelty) does not permit remarriage; Divorce *a vinculo matrimonii* (—1857, ecclesiastical courts) annul 'marriage'.)

'Proper' divorce obtainable:

1700–1857 by private Act of Parliament; grounds: adultery (for husband), incestuous/bigamous adultery (for wife)
1857– in secular courts (ecclesiastical courts lose jurisdiction over matrimonial cases); adultery with desertion added ground for wife to get divorce
1923– by wife for simple adultery of husband
1937– for cruelty or desertion, as well as for adultery
1969– for 'irretrievable breakdown' of marriage

to 60 per cent. At this stage (as forecast more than a century before) husbands took to playing the gentleman and supplying evidence of adultery (the so-called hotel divorces). In 1937 (1 Ed 8 & Geo 6 c57) adultery ceased to be the only grounds for divorce. Desertion and cruelty were added as independent grounds; in 1969 it could be obtained by consent of the spouses (Eliz II 1969 c55).

One could make some play of the unequal rights of men and women to obtain proper divorces before 1923 but I am not sure how much. It was generally agreed to be unfair, a matter, it was said, of expediency, of somewhat restraining the lamentable growth of divorce.[8] What however is much more striking is the progressive change in the theoretical idea that a marriage is for life. Of course there have been increases in population and in the average age at death, but not at a rate comparable to that of divorce, which increased a thousandfold between 1858 and 1980.

So far I have mentioned mainly practices where the doctrine that husband and wife are or should be one operated more or less symmetrically and I have denied that the wife's legal existence was 'suspended' during marriage on the grounds that for some legal purposes she was regarded as a person separate from her husband and for other legal purposes on a par with him. I have also suggested that in the case of property where there was an asymmetry, the wife commonly had far greater rights than is often recognised.

I want now to turn to other asymmetries between husband and wife, with the caveat that asymmetry is not necessarily inequity. It need not even be tantamount to a difference of rights as between husband and wife.

It was often said in non-political settings as well as in literature of causes that when a woman married she became *part* of her husband, 'bone of his bone'. There were straightforward respects in which this was so. Thus, at marriage a wife took, and in many cases still takes, her husband's name, rank and status, whereas the husband does not normally take his wife's name and could not by virtue of the marriage take her rank and status. The wife of the King of England is Queen of England; a man who becomes husband of a Queen of England does not thereby become King of England. If a man XY is knighted, his wife is *ipso facto* Lady Y but if a woman is made, say, a Baroness, her husband gains no new title. In the past, the wife also generally took her husband's rank and status when this was lower than her own. This was never so in the case of the Sovereign, and, with differences in the way status is acquired, it has probably become increasingly common for women to retain their status when marrying a man of lower status.

The situation in the past was often used to help explain why in England a man marrying down, that is, marrying a woman of lower rank or status than himself, was more acceptable than a woman marrying down, i.e. marrying a man of lower status than herself. 'Where', the hero's sister enquires in Richardson's *Pamela* 1741–2, when the hero has married his mother's serving maid, 'can the difference be between a beggar's son married to a lady, or a beggar's daughter made a gentleman's wife?' Part of the reply is that:

a man ennobles the women he takes, be she *who* she will; and adopts her into his *own* rank, be it *what* it will: but a woman, though ever so nobly born, debases herself by a mean marriage, and descends from her own rank to his she stoops to. [Richardson, 1741–2; Everyman ed vol I, p 375; Tuesday morning, the sixth of my happiness]

That the wife took her husband's rank and status by marriage is by no means the *whole* explanation of the preference that in marriage between unequals, the husband and not the wife should be the superior. There are other attributes in which the husband should not be inferior which nobody supposed he passed on to the wife at marriage: a husband should be (or should in the past have been) at least as tall as his wife, at least as old, at least as clever.

However, it is worth noting the asymmetry that a wife takes her husband's rank and status, becomes in this sense *part* of her husband, because it is a case where husband and wife are made like one person through the wife being assimilated to the husband where it would be difficult to suggest that it is exactly *inequitable* to wives or women. It was also the case that a wife's domicile was wherever her husband was living, irrespective of whether she too was living there. Ideally and usually, of course, husband and wife would be living together, and their domicile was where both were living. That the domicile of a married couple, like their rank and status, was determined by the position of the husband is another asymmetry which is not, at least obviously, an inequality between them.

I do not of course wish to dispute the existence of inequalities, but, as I have already suggested, marriage as it used to be in England does not seem best understood in terms of inequities suffered by the wife. Even concentrating on inequities, this is simplistic, as we can readily see by considering taxation. It might well be said to be inequitable that a husband and wife should have been treated as one person for the purposes of taxation. In a system of progressive taxation this results in two people who both have incomes incurring much higher taxation if they are married than if they are not. The rule until 1971 that the wife's earnings were taxed, with some slight concessions, as if additional to the husband's and, until 1990, that unearned income was taxed at the husband's rate resembled earlier rules about status, domicile and so on, in that the *husband's* position was used as the determinant of the married couple's position. For this reason it might look clearly inequitable to the wife. In fact the inequities here are less clear. By the practice of PAYE, where tax is subtracted before earnings are received, this did until 1971 result in a wife's earnings being taxed at a higher rate than her husband's. On the other hand, the fact that the husband was liable for all the tax payable by a married couple has meant that the husband has to pay tax on unearned income or capital gains received by the wife.

It might be said that I have avoided mentioning the *real* inequity between husband and wife, namely that the husband is or was the superior of the wife with an authority over her which she did not have over him. That this was so, at least in theory, is evidenced by the Church of England marriage service, which was until recently almost, but not quite, symmetrical between husband

and wife. The most conspicuous asymmetry was that where the husband promised to comfort the wife, the wife promised to obey and serve the husband.

I cannot do other than concede the point, but with the proviso that it was very commonly thought in the past that the wife might do quite well out of the arrangement. There are, I think, several reasons why we do not hear a great deal about this at the present time. One reason why this alleged advantage is rarely discussed can be found in political contexts in England where legislation is proposed for equalising the position of woman. It has been objected that this approach in fact produces greater injustice and unfairness to women.[9] This is one of a group of arguments that appears to be particularly effective in the legislative field. Another effective argument which is often produced in favour of a measure is that it is not really a change, but merely the logical consequence of a change already made. Another such argument is that it opens to the poor what is open to the rich and that it brings England into line with Scotland. Those who oppose the measure will argue the contraries, namely that it is a change, that it favours the rich, etc. If the legislation occurs, it is often subsequently described in history books as having been due to one or another of these considerations. Whether the history books are always right to give this kind of account seems somewhat doubtful, and certainly requires more critical attention than it often receives, and this is so I think also with respect to at least some of the measures apparently passed primarily to equalise the position of women, like the Married Women's Property Acts.

I have of course no intention of disputing that the position of women, married and unmarried, has changed in the past hundred years. Two changes are particularly relevant. The first is that, as is frequently pointed out, in the past women rarely had any viable alternative to marriage, since they were effectively unable to earn or enter professions, and also often suffered in status from remaining unmarried.[10] So whatever the disadvantages of wives, a woman was generally better off as a wife than not. Of the evils between which she had to choose this was the lesser. Now, on the other hand, women, like men, can enter professions, and earn in many occupations, or marry, or both earn and marry. The second change often pointed out is in the nature of marriage, husband and wife now being treated as one in far fewer legal and other respects than they used to be and in those that are left with a reduced incidence of asymmetry and inequity between husband and wife. It is commonly taken for granted that women and wives must have benefited both by the addition of alternatives to marriage and by changes in the nature of the marriage.

Clearly, things are different. It does not seem to me absolutely obvious that it is all gain. We have to take into account other changes. Among these is the concomitant disappearance (or diminution) of a high status, moneyed, influential, leisured class, with a much prized social life. Leisure, or at least not having to earn a livelihood, was an aspiration, and a good more readily available to women than men, and it was women who largely controlled the elite's prized social life. When, in Trollope's novel *Phineas Redux* 1874 (chapter 6), his unmoneyed hero, Phineas Finn, risks his all on a career in politics, half its attraction is the social life and here the question is not acceptance by men but whether countesses and ministers' wives will open their drawing rooms to him. Domination of this kind in the social sphere must be accounted some kind of asset, and its loss therefore a loss.

However, more relevant to this paper than wrongs or privileges of the sexes over the centuries is the question of why it is that ancient doctrine of the unity of husband and wife has dwindled as it has. If, as I have tried to suggest, we do not know to what the change is really due, our grounds for supposing that the process will continue are comparatively weak. Our basis for this forecast at present is similar to the one we have for supposing that the divorce rate will continue to rise by about 3 to 6 per cent a year: that because this has been happening, it is likely to go on happening. And arguably this is not the most instructive form of inductive inference.

NOTES

I should like to thank Dr B M Levick and Professor H Oberdiek for helpful criticisms of an earlier draft of this paper.

1   'On Married Women's Property Bill', Special Report 17 July 1968 para 2, repr in *British Parliamentary Papers: Marriage and Divorce*, vol 2 1970, p ix.
2   See Blackstone 1766 II.29.VI for some detail; he does not appear to mention marriage settlements.
3   See for instance MacQueen 1849 for legal details of marriage settlements in the nineteenth century.
4   Before 1835 marriage in the Prohibited Degrees of consanguinity and affinity were only voidable and not as they became in 1835 (5&6 Wm4 c54) void *ab initio*. It is said that many stood. See Wolfram, 1987 for detail on this and other facts mentioned here.
5   Repealed and re-enacted 1925.
6   The ecclesiastical courts until then responsible for penalties for incest lost their jurisdiction in 1857, and although the category of incestuous adultery persisted as grounds for divorce, there appears to have been no penalties until 'incest' became a crime in 1908 (8 Edw7 c45). It was then limited to sexual relations between blood relatives in the second degree. See Wolfram, 1983 and 1987 for detail.
7   The term 'divorce' had other applications: a divorce *a mensa et thoro* did not allow remarriage, a divorce *a vinculo matrimonii* nullified as opposed to dissolving a marriage. See Wolfram, 1985 and 1987 for detail of this and other facts mentioned here.
8   Divorced women were virtually outcasts. Since men were not, it was thought that a couple wishing to divorce would arrange for the husband to be the guilty party. See for instance Lord Brougham in *The Times*, 3 August 1850, p 6 col f (Mrs Hall's case). That the belief was correct is shown by events after the legislation of 1923. See for instance as the *Encyclopaedia Britannica* of 1929

noted: 'one result ... was the marked increase in the number of wives' suits in which the charge was based on a solitary instance in a hotel' (*Encyclopaedia Britannica* (14th edition) 1929, p 457.

9   A good example is supplied in the opposition to the Matrimonial Causes Act of 1857. Its promoters had most of the group, urging that there was already divorce, that Scotland had allowed it since 1560, and (falsely) that in England it was open only to the rich. Gladstone, a prominent opponent of the whole measure, making some one hundred speeches against it, made much of its unfairness to women (see e.g. Gladstone 1857 col 393).

10   While upper class men who were not heirs to property were expected to earn their bread, upper class women were not. They were normally supported by their relatives unless or until they married, whereafter the duty fell to their husband.

BIBLIOGRAPHY

Anonymous [C G Brown] 'What the Presbyterians say of the relationships which bar marriage scripturally and socially' (sent to non-conformist ministers in 1871) (1883) in *Tracts issued by the Marriage Law Defence Union* 2 vols (London, 1889), vol 1, Tract 8.

British Parliamentary Papers (Dublin, 1970).

W Blackstone, *Commentaries on the Laws of England* 4 vols (Oxford, 1765–9; course of lectures at University of Oxford 1753).

Lord Brougham, 'Mrs Hall's Case', *The Times* (London, 1850).

W Churchill, *Parliamentary Debates* 4th series, Commons 1903, vol 121.

Encyclopaedia Britannica 14th ed 24 vols (London & New York, 1929), vol 7.

W Gladstone, *Parliamentary Debates*, 3rd series, Commons 1857, vol 147 col 393.

J F MacQueen, *Rights of Husband and Wife* (London, 1849).

J S Mill, *The Subjection of Women* (London, 1869).

S Richardson, *Pamela or Virtue Rewarded. In a Series of Familiar Letters from a Beautiful Young Damsel to her Parents* 4 vols (London, 1741, 2).

Royal Commission on Divorce and Matrimonial Causes, Cmd 6478 (London HMSO, 1912–13).

M L Shanley, '"One must ride behind". Married women's rights and the Divorce Act of 1857', *Victorian Studies*, 25 (1982).

Social Trends (London HMSO, 1981).

A Trollope, *Phineas Redux* (London, 1874).

S Wolfram, 'Eugenics and the Punishment of Incest Act 1908', *Criminal Law Review* (May, 1983), pp 308–16.

—— 'Divorce in England 1700–1857', *Oxford Journal of Legal Studies*, 5 (1985), pp 155–86.

—— 1987 *In-laws and Outlaws. Kinship and Marriage in England* (London & New York, 1987).

Acts of Parliament cited

The Marriage Act, 5 & 6 Wm4 c54 (known as Lord Lyndhurst's Act), 1835

The Matrimonial Causes Act, 20 & 21 Vic c85, 1857

The Deceased Wife's Sister Marriage Act, 7 Edw7 c47, 1907
The Punishment of Incest Act, 8 Edw7 c45, 1908
The Matrimonial Causes Act, 13 & 14 Geo5 c19, 1923
Matrimonial Causes Act, 1 Ed8 & Geo6 c57, 1937
Divorce Reform Act, Eliz II 1969 c55, 1969

Index of Names